D1008948

About Island Press

Island Press is the only nonprofit organization in the United States whose principal purpose is the publication of books on environmental issues and natural resource management. We provide solutions-oriented information to professionals, public officials, business and community leaders, and concerned citizens who are shaping responses to environmental problems.

In 1994, Island Press celebrates its tenth anniversary as the leading provider of timely and practical books that take a multidisciplinary approach to critical environmental concerns. Our growing list of titles reflects our commitment to bringing the best of an expanding body of literature to the environmental community throughout North America and the world.

Support for Island Press is provided by The Geraldine R. Dodge Foundation, The Energy Foundation, The Ford Foundation, The George Gund Foundation, William and Flora Hewlett Foundation, The James Irvine Foundation, The John D. and Catherine T. MacArthur Foundation, The Andrew W. Mellon Foundation, The Joyce Mertz-Gilmore Foundation, The New-Land Foundation, The Pew Charitable Trusts, The Rockefeller Brothers Fund, The Tides Foundation, Turner Foundation, Inc., The Rockefeller Philanthropic Collaborative, Inc., and individual donors.

About River Network

River Network was founded in 1988 as a national nonprofit organization whose mission is to help people save rivers. River Network believes America needs a broadly based citizen movement to protect rivers and their watersheds. We work to build that movement by supporting river conservationists at the grassroots, state, and regional levels, helping them build effective organizations. We are bringing these river guardians together into a national River Network Partnership. River Network Partners gain increased and personalized access to our programs, as well as the opportunity to share with other river guardians the materials and strategies they have developed for protecting streams and watersheds.

River Network is headquartered in Portland, Oregon. We maintain four programs to assist river guardians: The River Clearinghouse provides information on river conservation through an 800 "hot line," a database of volunteer experts, a quarterly journal, and special publications. The River Leadership Program works to establish and support state river councils, and provides a link for local and state groups on national legislation and policy. The River Wealth Program builds the capacity of river organizations to support themselves financially through access to information, one-on-one assistance for Partners, workshops, funding alerts, and networking. The Riverlands Conservancy works with local people to purchase and conserve threatened riverlands and riparian areas.

HOW TO
SAVE A RIVER

3-12-20

HOW TO
SAVE A RIVER
A Handbook for Citizen Action

River Network
David M. Bolling

ISLAND PRESS

Washington, D.C.   Covelo, California

ISLAND PRESS is a trademark of The Center for Resource Economics.

Library of Congress Cataloging-in-Publication Data

Bolling, David M.
How to save a river : a handbook for citizen action / David M. Bolling, River Network.
p. cm.
Includes bibliographical references and index.
ISBN 1-55963-249-6.—ISBN 1-55963-250-X (pbk.)
1. Stream conservation—United States—Citizen participation.
I. River Network. II. Title.
QH76.B65 1994
333.91'6216'0973—dc20   93-50690
CIP

Printed on recycled, acid-free paper

Manufactured in the United States of America
10 9 8 7 6 5 4 3 2 1

This book is dedicated to everyone who has taken a stand for the life of a river or stream, and to everyone who will soon do so. Your efforts and your spirits are joined by the flow of the rivers you seek to save. You will prevail.

———————————

Contents

Acknowledgments

In 1988 I took on the job of executive director of Friends of the River, the West's largest river conservation organization, not knowing a fraction of the information in this book. I finished writing *How to Save a River* in 1993, somewhat bemused by the chronology of these two activities and wishing I had known then what I know now. Life would have been easier. It is my hope that this book will make life easier for anyone trying to save a river, and that it will inspire others who haven't yet done so to make that fateful commitment.

It should be acknowledged at the outset that the inspiration and much of the organization for this book came from Phil Wallin, the visionary founder of River Network. In his inimitable, offhand way, Phil asked if I'd be interested in a modest writing project. Phil proposed and I disposed, although neither of us fully grasped the scope of the job I was undertaking. That job wouldn't have gotten done without the patience, support, and expertise of River Network staff members Rita Haberman and Pete Lavigne. In their respective jobs directing River Network's River Clearinghouse and River Leadership programs, Rita and Pete provided rare insights and perspectives on the amazingly rich variety of river activists and conservation groups scattered around the country. Pete's guided tour of New England river issues broadened my California-based horizons immensely, and his introduction to the ice-choked Westport River added a new dimension to my kayaking experience.

I have learned much about river conservation from the staff of Friends of the River, and particularly want to acknowledge the advice and counsel of Steve Evans, Ron Stork, and former staff member Bea Cooley, as well as the technical support and editorial advice of my friend and former colleague Mandy Weltman.

Portions of this book were reviewed for factual accuracy by environmental veterans with expertise far surpassing mine. Particularly valuable were the comments of Suzanne Jones at the National Wildlife Federation; Pat Parenteau at the Vermont Law School; Dan Tarlock at the Chicago–Kent College of Law; Karen Russell at Water Watch of Oregon; Mathew Huntington at American Rivers; Andrew Jones at the Rocky Mountain Institute; and Phil Wallin, Pete Lavigne, and Rita Haberman at River Network. Their comments clarified numerous technical points and any remaining errors of interpretation are mine alone.

I am also compelled to acknowledge the inspiration of hundreds of people who have made it their life's work to save rivers. There is not room here for all their names, but I feel the need to identify at least a few. Rita Barron on the Charles River and Marion Stoddart on the Nashua were true pioneers. My time at Marion's kitchen table was one of the highlights of the research for this book. Don Elder is a river-loving trumpet player who has proved with the Cahaba River Society that conservation success depends less on where you come from than on the strength of your commitment. Alasdair Coyne learned to organize, wear a tie, and speak in public—all for the love of Sespe Creek. Lewis MacAdams looked at the Los Angeles River and somehow saw something more than a cement sewer. Wendy Wilson took on the cause of the Payette River and then the entire state of Idaho. Marty Griffin got mad at the gravel miners and decided to save the whole Russian River. These people, and thousands like them, are living this book.

Mark Dubois deserves a special line of credit because he has been an inspiration and a friend for almost 20 years, because he showed me on the Stanislaus what it really means to make a commitment to a river, and because I've never met anyone whose beliefs are so aligned with his life.

Finally, it's true that books aren't written in a vacuum. My wife Ellen, who has her own career, endured much as I pursued mine. She and our two daughters deserve part of the credit for this book.

Introduction

The Tuolumne River is born from the ice of a glacier, 13,000 feet up in Yosemite National Park, and it grows rapidly as it descends through an exquisite canyon of sculpted granite before encountering its first dam. That obstruction, which now floods the Hetch Hetchy Valley, became the focus of the nation's first river conservation fight and it still symbolizes the danger facing wild rivers. John Muir lost the struggle to save Hetch Hetchy and some say the sorrow from that defeat killed him. But had he known how far the movement to save rivers would grow in the years ahead, he might have found some solace in the knowledge that his efforts weren't in vain.

Twenty-seven miles below Hetch Hetchy, the Tuolumne is captured again by a dam, merging into the mud-ringed waters of a massive reservoir. But in between the two dams, the river runs wild, plunging and pooling through one of the most scenic canyons in the Sierra, hosting mountain lions, eagles, bear, and an abundance of rainbow trout. Rafters and kayakers come from all over the world to play in its challenging rapids.

In the early 1980s, in that 27-mile corridor of wilderness, in the only remaining stretch of wild Tuolumne outside Yosemite, the city of San Francisco and two Central Valley irrigation districts decided to build a multi-dam project to generate hydropower and store a small pool of water.

The result would have alternately flooded and dewatered the river, threatening one of the finest wild trout fisheries in the Sierra, eliminating a world-class whitewater run, and ultimately destroying what was left of the Tuolumne's free-flowing soul.

It didn't happen.

In the San Juan Mountains along the Colorado–New Mexico border, the Rio Chama gathers runoff from the Continental Divide and funnels it down a spectacular canyon, past multihued sandstone cliffs and ponderosa pine before merging with the Rio Grande.

The Chama's blue-green waters flow through a high desert landscape straight out of the genre of artist Georgia O'Keefe—a palette of browns and tans and whites and pinks drenched by the sun. The image is especially fitting: O'Keefe spent most of her career in the town of Abiquiu alongside the Chama. It is in part the magic of light and color, which she so

Tuolumne River below Clavey Falls, California. (Photo courtesy of Tim Palmer.)

effectively captured on canvas, that makes the Rio Chama such a magical river.

But that magic was apparently lost on the U. S. Army Corps of Engineers which, in 1985, unveiled plans to radically enlarge a reservoir at Abiquiu Dam that would flood several miles of the Chama, including its best whitewater rapids. Despite evidence of earthquake faults running through the dam site, and despite questionable economic assumptions, the Corps was determined to drown the Chama.

It didn't happen.

In 1962, the Nashua River, as it flowed past Groton, Massachusetts, was one of the most polluted waterways in America. The river's stench, a product of raw sewage, industrial wastes, and pulp from numerous paper mills, could be smelled two miles away. Some days the Nashua flowed blue, green, red, or white, depending on the color of paper dye being dumped by the mills.

So much abuse had been heaped on the Nashua that, with the exception of a few resilient carp, there was no life left in it. A 1965 survey by the U. S. Army Corps of Engineers even pronounced the river dead, incapable of hosting fish or wildlife. The Nashua could have stayed that way, a stinking reminder of human abuse, a perpetual open sewer.

It didn't happen.

The Tuolumne and the Chama and the Nashua are very different rivers, thousands of miles apart, separated by mountains and deserts and plains. But in one important respect they are very much alike: All three rivers were threatened by human development and all three rivers were rescued through the efforts of citizen activists who organized campaigns to protect them.

This book explains how those rivers—along with many others like them—were protected, and how ordinary citizens can build the organizational strength, the political power, and the campaign strategy to save the rivers they love. This is a practical, step-by-step guide with real-world examples culled from dozens of river-saving efforts that worked. It is also, perhaps, the blueprint for a growing movement that is beginning to make a paradigm shift in how the world looks at rivers.

Like the Tuolumne and the Chama and the Nashua, rivers all across America have been put at risk, not just from dams and reservoirs and industrial pollution, but from clearcutting and overgrazing, from agricultural run-off, from mining, channelizing, irrigation diversions, and urban growth. The Tuolumne, Chama, and Nashua Rivers are, after all, just three examples from a catalog of countless rivers dammed, diverted, dewatered, despoiled, and destroyed by human development. There are more than 60,000 large dams in the United States and, while many of them serve useful social and economic purposes, many more are products of bad judgment, bad planning, bad engineering, bad economics, and an indifference to the integrity of living rivers.

Twenty years ago the Tuolumne and the Chama would likely have been lost and the Nashua would have been left to rot. The power and politics behind big dams, and the influence of industry would have prevailed over the impassioned objections of conservationists. To the developers, rivers like the Tuolumne, the Chama, and the Nashua have traditionally been valued more for their hydropower potential, their water storage capacity, or their sewage utility, than for their natural beauty or the complex and vulnerable ecosystems they sustain. There are cement monuments and degraded rivers all over the country bearing testimony to this myopic view.

- Lake Powell buried the sandstone amphitheaters, the intricate grottos, and chapels of sculpted rock that was Glen Canyon.
- Garrison Dam, in betrayal of three Native American tribes, buried an Indian reservation, destroyed a way of life, and wiped out wildfowl habitat on the Missouri River.
- New Melones Dam flooded the upper Stanislaus River, inundating the most significant limestone canyon in California, drowning ancient caves, Gold Rush ruins, and the West's most popular whitewater run.
- Tellico Dam on the Little Tennessee River flooded one of the most scenic, unspoiled river valleys in the Southeast.
- The Tennessee–Tombigbee Waterway destroyed 100,000 acres of farmland and wildlife habitat to create a redundant $4 billion barge route to the Gulf of Mexico.
- The Kissimmee River Project straightened and shortened one of Florida's most important rivers, cutting its length in half, causing the eutrophication of Lake Okeechobee, and endangering the delicate health of the Everglades.

But now the tide of protection has begun to turn in favor of rivers. That's partly because boondoggle economics has lost favor in Washington and big dams are no longer guaranteed federal funding. But it's also because—in watershed after watershed—people are taking a stand to protect what hasn't yet been destroyed. The growing list of rivers saved includes not just the Tuolumne and the Chama, but the Gauley and the New, the Upper Mississippi, the Little Miami and the Obed, the Penobscott and the Hackensack, to name only a few.

Most of these rivers would not have been preserved without citizen action, and most of those citizens weren't career environmentalists—they were ordinary people with more passion and commitment than professional expertise. Consider these examples.

In 1962, when the environmental movement still didn't have a name, one woman—Marion Stoddart—had a vision of the Nashua River as a restored waterway, clear of pollution and full of fish. Stoddart's vision has been gradually transformed into reality over the past 30 years, thanks largely to citizen action.

In the Ventura Wilderness of Southern California, a grassroots group led by an organic gardener forged a successful campaign to protect Sespe Creek, which flows through the heart of a sanctuary where endangered condors are being coaxed back from the edge of extinction.

In Montana, the Clark Fork was a blighted and abused Superfund site, poisoned by mine tailings and paper mill waste, until a coalition of citizens, businesses, and sporting groups decided to make a stand for the river. They created a movement which is restoring the river and changing the habits of industry.

In Massachusetts, activists rescued the Charles River from decades of pollution and actually worked *with* the Army Corps of Engineers to develop a nonengineering approach to flood control which spared the river from a destructive dam.

There are countless other examples of successful river protection, outlined in the pages that follow, which prove ordinary citizens have the power to create change when they know how to organize themselves. Those successes demonstrate the strength of a growing movement which is reforming the way we treat rivers and streams in America. It is a movement at the interface of a conflict that is becoming the defining issue for life in the 21st century. The conflict is between development and preservation, and the issue is simply this: How much more damage can we do to the earth before we have done too much? What is an acceptable level of loss?

Asked in the context of rivers, that question produces some compelling answers. It has become a poetic cliche of the environmental movement to say that rivers are the arteries of the earth, but in this case poetry is also biological truth. Rivers sustain the ecosystems which support the creatures which make up the diversity of planetary life. When we reduce rivers to reservoirs, when we rip rap their banks, divert and pollute their flow, or wreck their watersheds, we are destroying the arterial system of the planet. And when we do that, we begin to threaten the multitudes of living things dependent on rivers for survival.

Ninety percent of the West Coast's anadromous fishery—salmon and steelhead—has been destroyed, largely through the loss of river habitat. What's left is in radical decline. The Atlantic salmon fishery was virtually wiped out and is only now beginning a slow recovery. The two most important estuaries in North America—Chesapeake Bay and the Sacramento–San Joaquin Delta—are in biological peril because the rivers feeding them are polluted and too much fresh water is being diverted for human use.

Cast in this light, saving rivers becomes one of the central environmental missions of our time and the need for river activists, empowered by both passion and practical organizing tools, will only grow. More often than not government will not be there to help because it does not yet own a vision of the value of rivers. Most of the destruction visited upon rivers, in fact, is either created, or sanctioned and licensed, by government. "We are governed," says Norwegian ecophilosopher Sigmund Kvaloy, "by persons who don't know where we are headed." In this country government has not yet shown enough initiative in tackling the issues which put rivers at risk. We squander water and power as though rivers had limitless life while resisting the logic of energy and water policies which could painlessly reduce our use of both.

What all this means to you is this: If you know of a river or stream in danger, you have an exciting opportunity to make a major difference with your life. Armed with the tools outlined in this book, you can begin a campaign to protect your river, to win for it a measure of freedom it will not have without your effort. If you don't, it's quite possible that no one else will.

In this book you will learn how to take action, how to get committed and how to commit others, how to form an organization and raise money, what tools to use and what tools not to use, how to develop coalitions with other groups, how to plan a campaign and build public support, how to cultivate the media and political allies, how to develop credible alternatives to damaging projects, how to negotiate, lobby, and win.

At first it may seem that the prospect of stopping a dam, ending pollution, or reversing abuse to a watershed, is impossible. Often the abusers are rich and powerful corporations or giant agencies of government. But the record of river-saving achievement detailed in this book proves that David really can slay Goliath, that giant corporations and government bureaucracies can be stopped and, in some cases, turned into effective allies.

A remarkable number of river-saving citizen campaigns have succeeded. This book is inspired by numerous such efforts from every corner of the country. They encompass the work of thousands of people who have fought to preserve what is left of America's free flowing river heritage. And they form the foundation of a movement which holds the promise and the power to redefine our relationship to rivers and the life our rivers sustain.

———————

Part One
Techniques

Like any activity devoted to social change, saving a river involves a host of separate techniques and specialized processes which have proven effective for organizing and planning a campaign, building public support, and getting the work done. The techniques outlined below could clearly be adapted to any activist effort—on behalf of rivers or forests, wolves or whales, or the homeless and the helpless in human society. The rules of organizing are universal, but they are arrayed and explained here from the unique perspective of rivers, and they are illustrated from examples of river campaigns that worked.

Chapter 1
Getting Organized

Until one is committed, there is hesitancy, the chance to draw back, always ineffectiveness. Concerning all acts of initiative (and creation) there is one elementary truth . . . that the moment one definitely commits oneself, then providence moves too. All sorts of things occur to help one that would never otherwise have occurred. A whole stream of events issues from the decision, raising in one's favor all manner of unforeseen incidents and meetings and material assistance, which no man could have dreamt would come his way.

W. H. MURRAY

Get Committed

On a summer afternoon in 1988, Wendy Wilson and Tom Watts were sitting in their kayaks in an eddy on the North Fork of the Payette River in Idaho. Wendy was upset. A wealthy Idaho potato farmer had announced plans to finance a hydropower project that would drain the river. The water would go through pipes to an underground generating plant, the power would go to California, and the river would, in a manner of speaking, go to hell.

As Wendy complained about this disturbing turn of events, her paddling partner posed a provocative challenge. "If you were a real environmentalist," he said, "you'd form a group and stop this thing." Wendy thought for a moment and then said, "I'll do it if you'll do it." Watts responded, "I'll do it." Wendy stared at him: "Are you serious?" Watts stared at her, "Are you serious?"

They explored that question further over a subsequent beer and by November they had an organization. As W. H. Murray predicted, a whole stream of events issued from that decision, and three and a half years later, following one of the most intense and well-organized lobbying campaigns in state history, the Idaho legislature passed a bill protecting the Payette from development.

Wendy Wilson is the first person to point out that the Payette River was saved through the efforts of thousands of people. "I didn't do it by myself,"

North Fork of the Payette River above Banks, Idaho. (Photo courtesy of Tim Palmer.)

she says. "I was smarter than that. It takes a group of people." But what Wendy Wilson and Tom Watts did do themselves was make the commitment that gathered the people who started the organization which saved the river. And that's where river protection begins: Someone has to make the commitment.

Falling in Love

Choosing to save a river is more often an act of passion than of careful calculation. You make the choice because the river has touched your life in an intimate and irreversible way, because you are unwilling to accept its loss.

Mark Dubois, a pioneering river conservationist who dedicated a decade to the Stanislaus River in California, recalls a conversation he once had with a Russian activist. "I asked him the question, how do you get people involved," Dubois, who has himself gotten thousands of people involved, remembers. "He said, 'First I think it is necessary to fall in love.'"

If you've fallen in love with a river, if you feel your life linked somehow to its flow, then at least half the commitment has already been made. But before you wed yourself to a river campaign, consider the experiences of Mark Dubois, Wendy Wilson, and others who took the plunge. As with marriage—an experience not entirely unrelated to river saving—it pays to have some idea of what you're getting into.

When the fight to save the Payette began, Wendy Wilson was working for the Idaho Trial Lawyers Association and during the first year of the campaign she was an unpaid volunteer. But by the second year she was working full time on the Payette, scraping by on donations, and the river began to rule her life. It has now become her career.

When Marion Stoddart moved to Groton, Massachusetts more than 30 years ago, she asked herself the question, "What am I going to do with my life?" Looking out across the polluted Nashua River she found the answer. "I wanted to devote my life to some good purpose," she recalls. "I was looking for a significant challenge." The Nashua became that challenge and consumed her for 25 years.

Mark Dubois, who was then a guide for an organization taking disabled people down rivers, had no idea what he was committing to when he agreed to help coordinate a statewide initiative drive to save the Stanislaus. "Sometimes ignorance is bliss," he confesses. "Had we known what we were getting into, I'm not sure any of us would have gotten involved." What Dubois got into was a battle royale waged up and down the length of California—in the state legislature, in Congress, and in the U. S. Supreme Court. It lasted a decade and it lost. But Dubois' life was changed forever,

Stanislaus River below Camp Nine, California. (Photo courtesy of Tim Palmer.)

transformed by his relationship with one river into a relationship with all rivers. And out of the defeat of the Stanislaus came an organization called Friends of the River and a movement that has helped save numerous rivers in the West.

So when you make the commitment to save a river it is by definition a big one, and a long one. Ignorance may sometimes be bliss but, when attached to a river-saving campaign, it can also wreak havoc with marriages and careers. Perhaps the most important things to understand about any commitment you make to a river are these: Your life will be challenged and enriched beyond your understanding, nothing else you do in life—short of raising a child—will seem as important, and your relationship to the planet will take on an intimacy and richness that will color your vision for the rest of your days.

Find Partners

As Wendy Wilson, and every other successful river saver makes clear, you can't save a river by yourself—you need partners. There may be a few organizational geniuses capable of launching a river campaign single-handedly, but most people don't get very far alone.

Take Jerry Meral. By any standard, Jerry Meral is a formidable organizer. He has placed so many successful initiative measures on the California ballot that the organization he heads has been dubbed "Initiatives R Us". But when Meral launched one of the nation's earliest river campaigns in 1969, he didn't do it alone. He found a partner in David Kay, who ran a nonprofit river company, and together they found partners in Rob Caughlan and David Oke, owners of a young public relations firm committed only to causes they believed in and people they liked. This team gave birth to Friends of the River, the oldest and largest river conservation organization in the West, and it launched the biggest grassroots campaign in California history.

To anyone standing alone at the put-in of a river-saving campaign, Caughlan offers this adamant advice: "You don't have an organization by yourself. You don't have an organization until you have someone else."

Finding someone else isn't usually a problem; indignation over the abuse and development of rivers and streams runs deep. But if you discover yourself ahead of the crowd, on the leading edge of a river issue with no one around to join you, there are a lot of proven ways to recruit some partners. If your river supports whitewater recreation, you have an automatic constituency and a pool of easily recruited volunteers. Paddling clubs are great places to find campaign partners. Wendy Wilson virtually created

Friends of the Payette in one night at a meeting of the Idaho Whitewater Association. Commercial river outfitters usually (but not always) have an urgent interest in protecting the resource that produces their revenue.

Many endangered rivers aren't runnable but most are fishable, and angling organizations are excellent sources of support since fishery degradation is one of the most common and inevitable consequences of river and stream development. Fly fishing clubs often have stream enhancement projects and are usually eager to support river conservation campaigns.

Many communities have environmental organizations; if yours does, they should be among the first places you look for interested partners. Then there are the Sierra Club and the Audubon Society whose local chapters attract the kind of people who become activists. Progressive church groups like the Quakers and Unitarians have politically active memberships and often welcome presentations on important public issues.

More often than not you won't be starting a river campaign by yourself; you'll be part of a small group of people working as an informal team. But if you're living in an environmental vacuum, stuck in some political backwater without any obvious sources of organizing support, there are still a lot of simple ways to find sympathetic souls. One way is to organize a meeting in your living room or at the local library, advertised through notices in the local newspaper and in posters placed around town.

Another way is to contact interested teachers in local colleges or high schools and ask them if you can present a lecture in their classrooms or lead a field trip to the river. Still another is to badger the local newspaper into doing a story about your river issue, listing a telephone number for readers to contact you. This combination of efforts will almost certainly arouse enough attention to bring some interested partners your way.

Clarify Your Role

A few other pointers about finding partners: Be as clear as you can about the role you intend to play in this river-saving effort, which will in turn allow you to be clear about the roles you will be comfortable having other people play. This is going to be an intimate and profound experience for the people leading the campaign. Egos and agendas will clash, disagreements over strategy and tactics will flourish, and dissimilar personalities will grate. All of that is, to some degree, inevitable and grassroots organizations have an organic life that you will be unable to control.

But you will improve the odds of success by choosing your partners carefully, both to establish the highest possible degree of compatibility, and to bring to the effort an appropriate blend of skills and abilities. You need to launch your campaign with a balanced team, the members of which share as much as possible a similar vision and values.

Establish an Organization

Here we're getting down to the nitty gritty. You've made the fateful decision to commit yourself to a river or stream, and you've found some kindred souls to share the grief and the glory. Now you need to build an organization capable of translating your commitment into successful action. How well you do that will determine the fate of your campaign.

Entire libraries of books have been written on building a successful organization, and some of them are worth reading. But before we discuss how to build one, let's review the mostly obvious reasons why you need an organization to begin with—why a loose-knit amalgam of activists can't just leap into the fray ad hoc.

First, of course, an organization, with a name, address, and telephone number lends instant credibility to your cause. It means you are, in fact, organized. Politicians and powers-that-be relate better to organizations than to people. Organizations tend to be taken seriously, people sometimes are not. Organizations also give the public something to join, a name to identify with. When you create an organization, you also create the accoutrements of doing business—letterhead, business cards, and a listing in the phone book. An organization with an office also provides a place for drop-in traffic to drop in, a place where volunteers can volunteer, and where the media can meet you.

Perhaps most importantly, an organization provides continuity to your campaign. People come and go, the players change, but if you have an organization, the cause can always continue. Don't even consider starting a river-saving campaign without creating an organization to support it.

Missions and Goals

Organizations are born many different ways—some casually over beer and pizza, some formally following prescribed steps and rules of order. But how you form your organization is a lot less important than what you decide to do with it. Which is why it's wise to be very clear at the beginning what your mission and goals are.

The creation of mission and goal statements is both a fundamental step in organizational development and a frequent *bête noire* for those who have to do it. Mission statements have become a cottage industry for management consultants partly because too many organizations aren't clear what their real mission is. Long tedious discussions about an organization's mission usually reflect serious disagreement or confusion about what the organization should fundamentally be about.

If you haven't done this before, you're likely to think, "How difficult can this be? Our mission is to save a river." But it's seldom that simple. Does saving the river mean stopping pollution being discharged into it or campaigning for stricter water quality standards? Does it mean killing a dam project or changing your state's water policies? Does it mean a Wild and Scenic campaign or a river corridor plan? Does it mean protecting a flood plain from development or attacking the growth policies which allow that development to occur? And does saving a river or stream also mean maintaining a permanent presence to watchdog the waterway so that future threats can be thwarted?

Some mission statements are, in fact, very simple. The Committee to Save the Kings River in California, which waged a successful campaign to stop a destructive dam, states succinctly that its goal is " . . . to protect the Kings River by having Congress designate a national Wild and Scenic River above Pine Flat Reservoir." The somewhat more complex mission of the Westport River Watershed Alliance in Massachusetts is "to protect and restore the environment and improve the economic, aesthetic and recreational value of the Westport River Watershed and its coastal environs on Buzzards Bay."

Friends of the River has a far less specific, more sweeping mission statement: "Friends of the River preserves, protects and restores rivers, streams and their watersheds. We accomplish these goals through public education, citizen activist training and organizing, and expert advocacy to influence public policy." For some groups, a mission statement that broad runs the risk of spreading organizational energies and resources too thin.

Your mission may evolve and change as your campaign moves along, and organizations constantly (sometimes obsessively) revise their mission statements in response to new realities. But when you're starting out on this river protection path, it pays to be clear about where you are going and how you intend to get there. In the words of Peter Nielsen, former executive director of the Clark Fork–Pend Oreille Coalition, "The mission is the common ground you're asking people to stand on."

Having a clear mission statement also allows you to test various campaign strategies and tactics against your central reason for being, thereby making it easier to weed out extraneous or tangential activities. It helps to ask from time to time, "Does what we're doing right now mesh with our mission?"

Before we leave the topic, let's be clear about what are occasionally confusing terms. In the hierarchy of organizational planning, a mission defines the overall purpose of the organization, goals define the specific outcomes you expect to achieve, and objectives describe how you intend to achieve your goals. So unless you define your mission, you're going to have a hard time stating your goals. Objectives are, at this point, still somewhere downstream, waiting to be discovered as you develop a campaign plan.

What's in a Name?

Once you're clear on your mission, you'll need to translate it into a name, an image, and an organizational identity. These are extremely important steps and require either serendipitous bursts of creative inspiration or careful and thorough analysis. Large corporations spend millions of dollars developing images to communicate messages they hope the public will embrace. You can only dream about that kind of money, but your efforts to market your message should be no less ambitious. Because that's what you're going to be doing during a river-saving campaign—marketing a message to the public, to decisionmakers, and to the media on behalf of a river or stream.

So the name you attach to your organization is important. Ideally, it should be positive, descriptive, and simple. It should be *for* something, not *against* something. It should communicate implicitly what you are about.

A small grassroots organization in Ventura County, California which successfully sought federal protection for wild and rugged Sespe Creek, has a name which perfectly describes its mission: Keep the Sespe Wild. Tatshenshini Wild instantly conveys an image of both the organization and the river it fought to save. American Rivers and River Network have names which clearly reflect their work. When Rob Caughlan and David Oke began plotting a campaign to save the Stanislaus they knew they wanted a name that was positive and proactive; they didn't just want to be against a dam, they wanted to be for the river. So that's what they came up with: F.O.R.—Friends of the River.

One example of how not to name your organization: A California group fighting an Army Corps dam near the San Andreas fault named itself the Warm Springs Dam Task Force. The name had no proactive message, it embraced the name of the dam instead of a river, and it was boring. The campaign eventually lost.

Let the name of your organization gestate a little, give it some thought, talk it around. Be sure the name you decide on captures the spirit and intention of your campaign. It helps if the name is also catchy and quotable.

As soon as you have a name you feel comfortable with, it's important to develop a symbol or logo which reflects that name and some compelling image of the river. If an important fishery is threatened on your river, consider including a fish in the logo. If your river has a spectacular waterfall or some other well known topographical feature, try working that into a graphic design. Sespe Creek flows through the heart of a wilderness area where the nearly extinct California Condor is being released back into the wild. Keep the Sespe Wild wisely includes the condor in its logo. Whatever image you choose to communicate the message of your organization, it should be simple, positive, and friendly. It should invoke the impression that you are protecting the public trust.

After you've chosen a graphic image, don't squander a good idea with sloppy execution. Hire or recruit a graphic artist to produce a professionally rendered logo. Many a good logo has been designed by a volunteer artist, but don't trade quality for price. In the end, a sloppy, unprofessional logo will do more harm than good for your image and credibility. This may seem like a superficial issue, like putting on a tie to go to a public hearing, but anything you can do to appear credible and professional will be worth the price as your campaign unfolds. Remember that the graphic images you create at the beginning of your campaign will be repeated endlessly in brochures, press releases, posters, and other promotional pieces.

Finding a Place to Be

If you've worked up a name and an image, next you'll need a place to keep it. Do you open an office, share space with another organization, or make do with the kitchen table and an extra phone line? This decision will probably be driven more by the state of start-up finances than by campaign strategy, but it represents one of the first important decision points for your organization.

Some very successful campaigns have needed nothing more than a telephone and a corner in someone's house. At least one organization worked out of the back of a van. The advantage of this minimalist approach is obvious—it's cheap. Saving money on overhead allows more to be spent on the campaign. For years, the headquarters for Friends of the River was a residential house which doubled as a dormitory for staff and volunteers. It came complete with an organic garden and enough floor space to accommodate an endless stream of sleeping bodies.

An alternative to the home office/dormitory is the marsupial strategy of sharing office space with an established and sympathetic organization. This can often be done for minimal rent and a share of the office overhead. Two immediate advantages are the more professional image that comes with having a real office and the access you'll get to high-cost equipment like copiers and FAX machines without having to make the initial investment. Then there's the synergistic advantage of working in proximity to like-minded professionals who share your goals.

When and if you can afford to open your own office, it helps to remember the three cardinal rules of retailing: location, location, and location. Remember that you are marketing a message and, notwithstanding the boundaries of your budget, the more visible and accessible you are, the more quickly and completely you'll get public attention.

So you should always position an office in the best strategic location you can afford. Some river campaigns embrace entire watersheds, including several cities, towns, and even states. The best spot for your office will usually be in the population center of the area affected by your campaign. That could range from the county seat to the state capitol. Sometimes it's wise to have an office near the threatened river itself. California's highly successful Mono Lake Committee has the best of both worlds. Because Mono Lake's declining water table is the victim of Los Angeles water policies which have drained the lake's tributary streams, the Committee has headquarters in L. A. But because the lake itself lies alongside a busily traveled highway at the edge of Yosemite National Park, the Committee also has an impressive visitor center there, offering environmental displays, books, and T-shirts—along with a 20-minute slide show—which pulls in a steady stream of walk-in and drive-by traffic.

Any retailer will tell you never to underestimate the value of walk-in traffic. The closer you can put your office to high-volume pedestrian flow, the more attention and interest you'll get. Try to find an office with enough space to create a display of photographs which dramatize the issue and with room for a literature rack and T-shirt sales. A storefront, if you can get one, is ideal because a good window display in a high-volume location is excellent free advertising.

For a start-up organization, one of the biggest deterrents to opening an office is finding people to staff it. Assuming you don't start your organization with enough money to hire an office manager or receptionist, the best way to cover this need is with volunteers and interns recruited from local campuses and from the constituencies outlined earlier. It doesn't make much sense to have a telephone if you don't have someone available to answer it. An answering machine works in a pinch, but it's far more effective to have a live human on hand to field questions and hand out literature.

Finally, opening an office is an excellent opportunity for free media coverage. Never open a campaign office quietly; make a lot of noise, announce yourself to the world. Always plan a press conference with an office opening, have experts on hand to discuss the river threat, provide press kits with fact sheets and photos and, if possible, present a brief slide show. Make this a gala event and be sure to create a crowd by insisting that all your supporters come. The media will be impressed if 100 people show up at the office opening of a river campaign.

Building a Board

While you've been busy developing a name, an image, and an office, there's one other crucial activity you should be immersed in—creating a board of directors. The very thought will make some hard-core activists groan. For some people a board of directors means just one thing: bureaucracy, a glacial decisionmaking process, endless meetings, mindless discussions, and control from above. A board of directors can mean all those things, but it doesn't have to and it shouldn't. And without a board of directors you don't have an organization. The best way to avoid board problems is to view board members as essential assets, not as burdens. If you structure a board intelligently, it will become your organization's greatest strength.

As you go about building a board, especially if this campaign is the product of your personal vision and initiative, it's important that you understand the inevitable need to share control and direction. When you create an organization, you have an immediate personal investment in its structure, its personality, its style, its vision. Organizations often become reflections, even extensions, of their founders, who are typically strong leaders unaccustomed to or uncomfortable with sharing control. This is often an asset for a young organization needing focused leadership, but it can become a real trap unless you recognize the problem and deal with it openly. Your organization won't succeed unless it has a strong and effective board of directors who share in decisionmaking. If it is strong and effective, that board may not always agree with you, the founder, and that is a reality you will have to accept.

Before you begin to build a board, it helps to inventory the human assets the organization needs. That will almost always include one or more members who can do the following.

1. *Raise money.* It's always nice if you have a wealthy, philanthropic board member, but most new organizations don't. At the very least you should try to find a few candidates who know and have access to wealthy people and who are comfortable asking for money. One California organization struggled for years to survive until a dynamic board member was recruited who loved fund raising. He brought along two wealthy directors and within 18 months the organization had more than doubled its budget.

2. *Represent an important constituency.* If bald eagles or willow flycatchers nest in your threatened watershed, look for a high-ranking Audubon Club member. If an important fishery is threatened, find a board member close to the fishing community.

3. *Provide credibility and prominence.* Big names are valuable, especially at the beginning of your campaign when they add instant credibility to your effort. But make sure that the image of your prominent person is compatible with the mission and message of your campaign.

4. *Provide expertise.* If you're fighting a hydro project it helps to have an attorney or an energy expert. If pollution is your problem find a board

member with biology and chemistry credentials. Hydrologists, geologists, fishery biologists, and agricultural economists have all made crucial contributions as board members of river-saving campaigns.

5. *Be a workhorse.*   Every good board has some key members lacking any special skill but who are willing to work like dogs. The workload on most boards is not evenly distributed and it is essential to have enough workhorses to execute the board's tasks.

It usually isn't hard to find enough people to form a board of directors—if your issue is compelling, a lot of people will want to get involved. But it is often very difficult to find the right blend of people to construct a successful board. At the beginning you will be wise to choose board members very carefully—keep the number small and leave some seats open until you can recruit people with the needed skills to fill them. Avoid corrosive egos and process junkies. The purpose of your board is to empower your campaign.

Choosing Your Tax Status

Some degree of bureaucracy is inevitable in any organization and one of the most bureaucratic tasks for any new board to deal with is the creation of bylaws. Bylaws are the legally required operating rules of your incorporated organization which cover everything from the selection and terms of board members to legal structure and tax status. Most bylaws consist of standard boilerplate adapted to the specifics of a given situation. They are most easily and painlessly assembled by an attorney with expertise in nonprofit law.

When you deal with your bylaws you will confront a couple of fundamental organizational issues which need to be decided up front: the tax status of your organization and its accountability. Accountability is basically an issue of public access, which means membership. Membership suggests grassroots, citizen involvement—people joining and having a say. A grassroots membership often, although not always and not necessarily, elects the board after start-up members serve a beginning term. Organizations with voting membership hold elections and are accountable to their members who can, if they so choose, reverse or reform board policy by replacing board members. In reality, most boards are self-perpetuating either by virtue of election slates with only enough candidates to fit the available openings, or because the bylaws specifically allow it.

You can, if you want, avoid the time and energy required to service a voting membership by vesting ultimate authority in the board of directors. A nonvoting membership is common in environmental groups, although this model may diminish grassroots involvement. If you don't like the way it's working, your board can change whatever model you choose by amending the bylaws.

A more urgent start-up decision involves the question of tax status, an issue rooted in the arcane codes of the Internal Revenue Service but vital for your financial future. Your group will almost certainly qualify as a state nonprofit organization, but don't make the mistake of believing that nonprofit means you can't be taxed. Unless you have one of two applicable tax-exempt classifications bestowed by the IRS, any surplus revenue you have at the end of the year, not derived from donations, is taxable. Which means, among other things, that Uncle Sam could underwrite a slice of the budget deficit with part of your membership income.

Almost nothing in the life of a river-saving campaign is more painful than surrendering hard-earned dollars to the IRS.

To avoid the tax-bite, it's necessary to become a tax-exempt nonprofit organization, a step which requires application to the IRS and a wait of anywhere from three months to a year. Two provisions of the Internal Revenue Code address this status—Sections 501(c)(3) and 501(c)(4). Reference to c–3 or c–4 organizations is simple shorthand for these code provisions. A c–4 organization has been granted tax exempt status by the IRS, which allows surplus income to be sheltered from taxation, allowing for the creation of a cushion of revenues for the campaign ahead.

A 501(c)(3) organization takes tax exemption a key step further by allowing contributors to deduct donations on their income tax returns. Every river conservation organization would obviously be a tax-deductible c–3 if it weren't for restrictions which accompany the status. The most important c–3 restriction imposes a strict limit on "direct" political lobbying, requiring that no more than 20 percent cent of the organization's budget be spent on that activity, and limiting "grassroots" lobbying to five percent of the budget. The definitions of direct and grassroots lobbying were defined recently with new precision, although there will always be some room for interpretation. Organizations that are confident "no substantial part" of their activities will involve lobbying can so declare and avoid the lobbying expenditures test.

If you're sure the majority of your campaign efforts will be focused on public education, grassroots organizing, and litigation, and that your overall lobbying expenses won't exceed 20 percent of your budget, you will probably want to pursue 501(c)(3) status. Volunteers, if they don't take direction from your organization, can lobby your cause without violating the conditions of your tax status.

Besides offering large donors a major incentive to give you money, c–3 status opens the door to foundation grants, which traditionally make up

15 percent or more of a nonprofit's budget. With few exceptions, foundations—themselves the beneficiaries of IRS tax exemptions—will not make grants to organizations without c–3 status. On the other hand, if you don't think you can live with the lobbying limits imposed by c–3 status, the c–4 option will at least protect you from paying taxes on surplus revenue.

Small groups with annual budgets not exceeding $5000 can claim c(3) status without applying to the IRS, but without a letter of certification from the agency, it may not be possible to qualify for foundation grants. Applying for c(3) or c(4) status is not overwhelmingly complicated but you'd be wise to leave it in the hands of an attorney.

Poised on the edge of this decision, some river activists will ask about the necessity of incorporating their new organization to begin with. The advantages are simple: if you incorporate, you shelter yourself and your staff from personal liability. If you apply for either of the IRS tax-exempt categories, you will have to adopt bylaws and articles similar to those required by incorporation. Unless your organization is tiny and expects to be short-lived, incorporation makes compelling sense.

There are excellent resource books available to guide you through the incorporation and tax code jungle, and one of the best is published by Nolo Press and titled, "How To Form a Nonprofit Corporation." It comes complete with tear out forms for all 50 states. And River Network has published a brief, crystal-clear analysis of the c–3 vs. c–4 question, called "C(3) Or C(4)? Choosing a Tax-Exempt Status."

The Obligatory Budget

Once you've got these crucial details nailed to the barn door, there's still one more pony to saddle before you're ready to ride off down the campaign trail. You will, if you're smart, prepare a budget. Teeth gnash and eyes roll at the mere whisper of the word. Financial management in many new nonprofits often consists of a process that goes something like this: "How much money do we have? Okay, let's spend it." This is a formula for trouble and a good board will head it off by imposing a process of budgeting and accounting which will keep the organization operating within its means, while preparing for upcoming expenses. (Besides, if you apply for 501(c)(3) status, or if you put together any foundation proposals, you'll *have* to create a budget.)

There are at least two key elements in the budgeting process. The first involves projecting income and expenses and establishing a method for keeping them in balance. The second involves a plan for raising future income. When you're starting an organization it's easy to project expenses but hard to project income, unless you're starting with a grant or large donation. Most river campaigns grow incrementally, gathering momentum and money as they become more visible. At the beginning, you may have nothing more than projections and income targets, but those figures are themselves valuable markers for measuring your progress and for knowing where you need to be financially at any given point in time.

The worst thing to do to your organization and your river-saving campaign is to treat income and expense with *laissez-faire*, go-with-the-flow complacency. If you do, you'll end up with a hole in the campaign boat.

Start-up costs for a river campaign can range from a few hundred dollars to several thousand. It's really important to have a target figure to work with, both to know what you can afford to do at the beginning and to provide donors a giving goal. It's hard to launch any kind of campaign without some clear income objectives.

Raise Money and Hire a Campaign Director

On at least one point, Margaret Thatcher had it right. "No one would remember the Good Samaritan," she is quoted as saying, "if he only had good intentions. He had money as well." Commitment, passion, outrage, and expertise are essential components of a river campaign, but so is money. When you create an organization to save a river, you're also creating an organization to raise money. For many people, that is an entirely new, and a sometimes frightening, experience.

While some campaigns can survive, and even succeed, on a shoestring budget, almost no river-saving effort has enough money. And there is probably nothing most people enjoy less than trying to raise it. The good news is that raising money for rivers can actually be a lot of fun, particularly if you raise it *on* the river. While this is not intended as a treatise on fund-raising, some basic points on the subject require attention.

Lots of organizations begin life with no money. When Jerry Meral kicked Friends of the River into gear, the only money he had was his own, and he used it. You may find it necessary to self-finance the first few expenses of your fledgling organization, but unless there's a Getty or a Perot in the family tree you'll soon be asking others for support. Before you begin looking for OPM (other people's money) you should spend a little time preparing a basic case statement, the most fundamental tool of fund-raising.

Making Your Case

A case statement is just what the name implies—a statement making the case for your organization and your cause. A case statement should be brief—three to four pages at most—and all good case statements contain at least these basic points:

1. A description of your organization and the problem it was created to address—in other words, the threat to your river or stream. This is a good place to introduce your mission statement.
2. A description of what your organization can do to solve the problem, meaning whatever specific goals you have for protecting the river.
3. A list of the people and groups already supporting your organization and cause.
4. A listing of your organization's needs—how much money you need to raise the first year, the staff support you need, the equipment and volunteer resources you need in order to do business, the expertise you need to recruit for the campaign.
5. The benefits a donor can expect to accrue from a donation. Here you can paint a glowing picture of what a healthy, free-flowing river will mean to those who use and enjoy it.

A good case statement is the foundation for all your promotional efforts. On it you can build brochures, press releases, foundation proposals, fund-raising appeals, action alerts and fact sheets. It also helps create a degree of consistency in the content of written materials that will flow from your office.

Putting People on the River

Environmental fund-raising has clearly gotten competitive. An ever-growing number of organizations are competing for a finite pool of money, and some who do the competing have compared the experience to watching a school of piranha feed on a leg of lamb. But river savers have a unique fund-raising asset which can set them apart from the piranha pack—the rivers themselves. Rivers play a leading role in the cultural, mystical, and environmental drama of our lives. They are places of recreation and renewal and they are accessible to most of us, all of which means that only the most indifferent people won't be touched and turned on by their magic. The trick, when you're trying to save a river, is learning how to translate that magic into money. The best way to do that is to get donors on the river. Do that and you've got a captive audience that is more often than not eager to support you.

Every river or stream has a natural constituency with a vested interest in its survival and health. Once you've created a case statement, the next step is to aim it at that constituency. It helps to make a list of every individual and group with a known or potential interest in seeing your river or stream protected. Among the likely candidates on your list: commercial river outfitters and whitewater liveries, paddling clubs, angling organizations and fishing shops, bird watchers, and landowners with property on or near the river.

If the river you're fighting for has a whitewater industry, the fundraising potential is high. In California, where Friends of the River pioneered the outfitter pass-through program, outfitters have raised hundreds of thousands of dollars for river campaigns by collecting a nominal daily donation from each commercial passenger. The program requires a lot of outreach and networking, but it has created a powerful river protection tool. At the peak of the successful fight to protect the Tuolumne River, outfitters were collecting five dollars per passenger to support the campaign. River groups in other states, including Amigos Bravos in New Mexico, have created similar programs. Detailed plans for an outfitter pass-through program have been prepared by one of its architects, Kevin Wolf, and are available from River Network.

Private boaters are also a source of significant revenue. One of the best examples of what private boaters can do for river conservation is the Friends of the River Rafting Chapter, a co-op which leads private river trips in California. Each year they take up to 2000 people down rivers, collecting voluntary donations for Friends of the River memberships and donating as much as $30,000 to the organization. Smaller river co-ops have been organized all over the country to support river campaigns.

Whitewater outfitters and river running co-ops are excellent but limited fund-raising resources, relevant on only a small percentage of rivers. Another source of recreational fund-raising is river festivals, which have been employed by several river campaigns. The most successful of these may be the Ocoee and Gauley River Festivals which, at their peaks, raised about $10,000 annually for each river. The Ocoee festival attracted up to 4000 participants.

The American River Land Trust holds a three-day festival each year on the American River in California, combining a whitewater rodeo with slalom and downriver races, a dance, barbecue, and raffle. That festival raises thousands of dollars to support the purchase of land and conservation easements along the river.

Finally, among the more obvious but often overlooked allies in funding a river campaign, are private landowners with property along the river. Landowners, as we will explain in greater detail later on, may or may not support you, depending on the issues you're confronting. But if private property is negatively impacted by the threat to your river, landowners could be your most committed supporters.

Keeping your river campaign financially afloat will require a variety of fund-raising activities beyond those mentioned here. You may in time find yourself resorting to direct mail and telemarketing appeals, you may try to build a sizable dues-paying membership, and you may sponsor annual auctions, dinners, raffles, and concerts to make your budget balance. As Gertrude Stein once said, "Money is always there, but the pockets change." Which ever pockets you explore for money, your efforts will be enhanced by your ability to be visible, quoted, in the public eye. It is axiomatic, therefore, that if you want to raise money you also have to raise your profile as high as possible. Everything you do to publicly promote your cause also promotes your fund-raising potential.

Having said all this, it is important to recognize the exceptions to the rule. Not every river campaign needs a big budget, not every river fight needs to pour energy into fund-raising. The Rio Chama Preservation Trust orchestrated a successful campaign to protect a 27-mile stretch of the river without raising a dime or hiring a single staff member. Of course the campaign was orchestrated from the offices of a major environmental organization and the Trust's membership was a roster of prominent recreational and environmental groups with significant independent resources. Ultimately, there is no single model for a river campaign—every one is unique.

Who to Hire

The decision to raise money begets the decision to spend it, which brings us to another river campaign crossroads. The biggest expense in most nonprofit budgets is staff salaries. Whether to have staff, and how many, is one of the crucial early decisions you will make. It is the nature of some campaigns that staff is unnecessary because the founder or founders provide the necessary leadership and expertise and other needs are met by high caliber volunteers. The Rio Chama is a good example. Numerous, usually small, river campaigns share the Chama experience, relying on volunteers and the professional resources of allied organizations. But a river campaign won't achieve much without someone working more or less full-time to make things happen.

If you decide you can't run the organization without staff, your next decision is what staff to hire. For the founder or founders of an organization, that decision can be an important moment of truth. You began this campaign because you wanted to save your river. Now it's time to decide whether leading this campaign is an appropriate job for you or one of your founding partners, or whether greater professional skills and experience are required.

When Wendy Wilson started Friends of the Payette, she knew virtually nothing about running a river campaign. But she surrounded herself with the necessary expertise; she made up in intelligence, determination, and commitment what she lacked in experience; and she learned the skills needed to make the campaign a success.

On the other hand, when a group of outfitters and private boaters organized into Citizens for the Gauley River, they realized they were unprepared to take on the Corps of Engineers, which wanted to divert the Gauley through a pipe to generate hydropower. So they hired David Brown, an experienced river saver who had just won a three-year battle to secure unprecedented water releases for boating on the Ocoee. Brown's salary was paid with proceeds from the Gauley River Festival, which he helped organize, and his expertise paid off with a successful campaign which won protection for the river.

Whether you bring in a hired gun or develop one of your own, the consensus from countless campaigns is that someone with the appropriate skills and temperament has to drive the process. This is not a judgment against the values and virtues of consensus decisionmaking; it is simply recognition of the fact that a river campaign is a little like a war and someone has to be in charge. How that person's authority is integrated into the campaign can vary radically from one case to the next and there is no rule that leadership has to come from one person. But the campaign has to be guided and pushed by a person or persons focused completely on that task. Anything less severely limits success.

David Brown is particularly persuasive on this point. "Remember," he says, "volunteers burn out within two years. The group needs one spokesperson who presents an image that the body politic (and ultimately politicians) will identify with. Just because you are committed doesn't make you the best spokesperson. I had to shave my prized beard because I had to appeal to conservative Congressmen from East Tennessee. If it's important enough to save, it's important enough to staff properly and professionally."

Get Going: Time Is of the Essence

When Jerry Meral first saw the Stanislaus River in 1967, the Army Corps of Engineers already had Congressional authorization to build the dam that would destroy it. That didn't stop Meral from launching a campaign, but it sure lowered the odds of success. By the time a statewide initiative on the river reached voters in 1974, New Melones Dam was well under construction. Eventually, despite an epic battle, the dam was finished, the reservoir was filled and the river was flooded. The effort, heroic though it was, came too late. Once the money has been appropriated and the bulldozers are in place, it is perilously late in the game to save a river. That's true whether the threat is a dam, a diversion, or a bedroom development.

The same alliance of river savers who suffered defeat on the Stanislaus rode the momentum of their experience, and the far more favorable circumstances of a project not yet approved, to save the Tuolumne River and win it permanent federal protection. On the Tuolumne, no money had been appropriated, no permits had been approved, no jobs had been created, and no mechanical monsters had begun to dig up the earth.

In 1980, almost no one outside the Tennessee Valley Authority knew of TVA plans to redivert most of the Ocoee River, drying up one of the most popular whitewater runs in the South. David Brown sniffed out the information before the plans were locked in cement and launched a three-year campaign to guarantee flows in the river. Timing was critical and so was the response of Brown and his allies who acted immediately once they knew of the danger.

Phil Wallin and the Rio Chama Preservation Trust swung into action to oppose the radical expansion of a water storage reservoir as soon as they heard about the Army Corps' plans. The reservoir proposal was stopped in part because of timely opposition. Whether you're dealing with pollution, development, dams, or destruction of watershed timber, the time to act is as soon as you know a waterway is at risk and even before you have mastered all the steps above.

This is no small commitment you've made to save a river and the road ahead may be long. But you are also about to embark on the most exciting and challenging work of your life and the result could make a difference in the fate of an important part of the planet. Besides, if you don't do it, who will?

Chapter 2
Planning a Campaign

You need a plan for everything, whether it's building a cathedral or a chicken coop.

JOHN GODDARD

A river campaign, like a life, needs direction, structure, and focus. It needs to be planned. And while every river campaign is necessarily unique, the elements of planning aren't. There are several fundamental steps required for any successful effort.

Survey the River

Any river campaign—whatever the source of the threat—should start with a thorough survey. You can't save what you don't know, and if you aren't better informed about your waterway than the people who want to degrade or destroy it you aren't very likely to succeed. Knowledge about the river will become your most important campaign tool.

The Committee to Save the Kings River understood this point when they produced a report on their river in 1987. The 124-page book they published, with the help of noted author Tim Palmer, is a river survey taken to the limit. It describes the Kings in exhaustive detail, covering recreation, wildlife, fisheries, archaeology and history, scenery, plantlife, hydrology, geology, botany, and the economy of the river. Twenty-four pages of photographs chronicle the Kings' stunning beauty.

The report was the outgrowth of a campaign to protect the Kings from a dam that would have flooded 10 miles of river for the primary benefit of a few members of the local water district. The Kings is the deepest river canyon in the United States and in its upper reaches it bisects some of the West's most beautiful wilderness. The Kings report devotes considerable space to an authoritative analysis of the proposed dam and reviews a list of water supply alternatives based on conservation and groundwater recharge. In 1987, Congress voted to include the Kings in the federal Wild and Scenic Rivers System.

Kings River above Garnet Dike, California. (Photo courtesy of Tim Palmer.)

While the Kings report is a definitive work, a river survey need not, and in many cases should not, produce a massive document. But it should provide enough information to give you a credible and comprehensive understanding of your river and the issues confronting it. And it should be translated into some kind of public report, written for easy consumption.

In Massachusetts in 1975 the Charles River Watershed Association got a $15,000 grant to conduct a comprehensive mapping of the river corridor, which included an inventory of properties, owners, zoning, and existing land use. A year later they produced a simple but eloquent 20-page booklet entitled "Charles River Profile" which described the geology, biology, history, politics, land-use, and other significant aspects of the river. Rita Barron, the CRWA's first executive director explained in the booklet's preface, "Knowing the river leads to caring for the river, and caring leads to action."

Barron makes an important point. Not many people have a comprehensive knowledge of the river they seek to save. But the more they know the more they'll care, and the more they care the more they'll do. So there's an extra bonus in doing a river survey: You learn a lot and your campaign gets fueled with special energy and power. Discovering your river's biological rhythms, its history and geology and hydrology, may sound like a lot of work, but it can also be a lot of fun. And the work diminishes in direct proportion to your ability to spread it around. Because a good river survey implicitly calls for some technical expertise, it offers your first opportunity to recruit volunteer experts to help carry the load.

Surveying a Concrete Ditch

In 1988, the Los Angeles River had long been given up for dead. Paved by the Army Corps of Engineers for most of its 55-mile length, the river was an open sewer full of old cars, shopping carts, broken bottles, and other urban debris. One Los Angeles politician began promoting its use as a rush-hour truckway. Almost no one took it seriously as a river.

But then a visionary group, appropriately led by a poet named Lewis MacAdams, formed Friends of the Los Angeles River (which at first blush sounds like an oxymoron) and launched a campaign to convert sections of the much-abused waterway from a concrete ditch back into a living river. To do that, they applied for an Urban Stream Restoration Grant from the state of California and, to make their application more credible, they conducted their own preliminary survey of the river. With a volunteer botanist and an Audubon Club field trip leader, they gave the state a detailed (and astonishing) inventory of the plants and bird life inhabiting what most people believed to be a lifeless, cement ditch. The survey revealed 29 species and 49 genera of plants along with 177 species of birds.

With support from the Los Angeles mayor's office, they then got a $50,000 legislative grant to conduct a full biological assessment of the river. That work was completed in 1993 and is now being used to fuel a campaign against plans by the Army Corps of Engineers to further channelize the river bed.

Friends of the Los Angeles River had powerful support for their survey from key legislators and from the office of L. A. Mayor Tom Bradley. Their ability to find help in high places is not unique. It is likely that one or more public agencies will have sufficient interest in your river to provide some resources, even financial support for a survey.

That's what happened with the Mattole Restoration Council, a grassroots group on the isolated North Coast of California which made the ambitious commitment to restore an entire 306-square-mile watershed decimated by logging and road construction. The Mattole River hosts one of the last purely native stocks of salmon in California, fish untainted by inferior hatchery genes because the river is too remote to stock. But the fishery has been all but obliterated as a result of erosion and siltation caused by over-logging and road cuts on steep and unstable soils. The Mattole Restoration Council decided to reclaim the river, and to do it not with high-paid specialists and government bureaucrats but with residents of the watershed, volunteer energy, and sweat.

As part of that effort, they knew they needed to conduct a survey. It would be impossible to restore spawning habitat without an inventory of significant erosion sites responsible for silting up tributary streams.

A newspaper article about their work caught the eye of the California Resources Secretary which led to a $50,000 grant and a contract from the California Department of Fish and Game to undertake the survey. The result was a 48-page tabloid newspaper report which mapped 956 soil disturbances, 165 of which were visited in the field. It was a stunning piece of work and provided the first real picture of the state of the Mattole watershed. And it was a major step toward recovery of a bioregion ravaged by human abuse.

Freeman House, one of the founders of the Council, describes another benefit of this kind of work: "It is also part of the process of recovery," he wrote in 1990, "that we learn the things we need to know to live in places. Our crisis response becomes more effective as we come to know more about our particular places than *they* do."

Getting the state to pay for a river survey may be an exception to the rule, but don't overlook the potential willingness of fish and wildlife agencies, state and federal park services, and other governmental departments to provide help. Most threatened rivers have never had a comprehensive survey conducted and the information gathered can benefit a wide variety of interests.

There is, however, one important caveat about river surveys supported by public funds: Sensitive and controversial issues may be avoided and key information may be omitted if it involves an issue your public supporters don't want addressed. The best example of this pitfall occurred on the Sacramento River where a comprehensive management plan was developed by a public–private Advisory Council in response to the radical decline of spawning salmon and the general deterioration of the river.

Water flow in the Sacramento is the single most important influence on health of the salmon fishery, and water flow is the most controversial issue facing the river. Agricultural and municipal interests want to take more water out of the river and environmentalists want to leave more water in it. The result: recommendations for water flows weren't included in the management plan, a fact that upset many environmentalists, including Steve Evans, the conservation director of Friends of the River. Said Evans, "All 20 of the action plans regarding the management and restoration of the fisheries deal with issues involving water flows."

The Sacramento River experience should not, however, be interpreted as a reason to shun the support of public agencies, many of which will have a predisposition to being very helpful and sympathetic to your cause.

However you conduct it, a river survey has two complimentary purposes: To educate you, and to educate the public. The information you gather, therefore, should ultimately be compiled in terms easily understandable by the people you are trying to persuade.

The elements of a river survey are pretty standard, although they may vary in emphasis and scope from river to river. Among the basic points any survey should cover are:

1. *A basic description of the river.* This is the overview that provides a context for the more detailed information to follow. It provides a general picture of the location, length, and special features of the river, along with a discussion of the issues confronting it.

2. *An inventory of plant and animal life.* This does not have to be a definitive listing of every species of flora and fauna, but it should describe the significant fish, wildlife, plant, and tree species in both the riparian zone and the larger watershed. A listing of threatened and endangered species is obviously of premier importance.

3. *A description of the geology and topography of the river.* An earth sciences perspective places the river in its terrestrial context and gives you and the public an idea of the watershed which feeds it, the channel it has created, its age, and its structural health. Include types and quality of soil in the floodplain.

4. *A hydrological description of the river.* Hydrology presents at least three important considerations for a river survey: flooding, erosion, and sedimentation. Evidence of streambank erosion and channel downcutting is important to record, as is the condition of the flood plain and forested watershed. Since erosion is a major issue in heavily logged and overgrazed watersheds, and is usually not adequately surveyed, erosion impacts should be documented, including the effects of sedimentation on water quality, streambeds, and spawning gravels. An often overlooked issue is erosion of ocean beaches caused by dams that block sediment transport to the sea.

5. *A review of history and archaeology.* River corridors are the focal points of human history and they are often rich in archaeological evidence. A river survey should touch on at least the high points of the historic record. Some rivers, like California's American—where the Gold Rush began—and Massachusetts' Merrimack—where the industrial revolution began in America—have played a major role in state or national history. But whether your river is famous or obscure it has a story worth reviewing.

6. *A description of land use and ownership.* You can't mount a successful campaign until you know who owns the river corridor and watershed. It's crucial to know who has a stake in the river. Find out which parcels are privately owned, which ones are publicly owned, and what they're being

used for. The extent of mining, logging, and recreation should be reviewed. Be sure to provide an estimate of the populations which live in the river corridor and watershed. Later on this information will be important as you build a constituency for your campaign.

7. *An inventory of development on the river.* Carrying the previous point a step further, it may be appropriate to compile a more detailed description of development which affects the river, particularly where significant industrial, agricultural, or forestry impacts occur. Many eastern rivers are heavily impacted by riverside industries, as well as by coal mining. Western rivers are frequently affected by grazing and agricultural development, mining, and logging. Since most rivers have already been heavily developed, a detailed inventory of that development helps explain why any further impact on the river is inappropriate and it tells you the economic interests you will have to contend with.

8. *A summary of recreational use of the river.* Virtually all rivers have some recreational use, some of it easily quantifiable, some of it not. Boating, fishing, and swimming are obvious uses easily described. But so is nonspecific visitation, a bureaucratic way of saying that people are drawn to rivers to stand beside them and just look, to picnic on their banks, to wade in their waters. User-day figures are often available from agencies with jurisdiction over the river and provide a useful, if one-dimensional, perspective on recreation.

9. *An economic analysis of the river.* The economic value of development projects that degrade rivers is often exaggerated, partly because the economic cost of river degradation is usually underestimated or ignored. A preliminary survey may not deal exhaustively with economic analysis but in countless river campaigns it has been a major, sometimes decisive, factor.

10. *An assessment of the special and outstanding features of the river.* Above and beyond the information listed above, some rivers have special features which demand special mention. If your river has a blue ribbon trout fishery, or a spectacular waterfall, or legendary whitewater, or a site of historic importance, build that information prominently into your survey.

Once you've developed all this information, you're going to have to decide what to do with it. That can be a bewildering proposition unless you limit the focus of your campaign.

Focus on an Issue

The Locust Fork of the Warrior River winds some 90 miles through northwest Alabama, the second longest free-flowing river in the state, host to an abundance of riparian life including 10 or more species being reviewed for endangered status by the U. S. Fish and Wildlife Service.

Despite the environmental and recreational value of the Locust Fork, and despite the nearby presence of at least four other reservoirs with surplus water available, a local utility, the Birmingham Water Works, has proposed building a major water supply reservoir on it with a dam that would flood 4000 acres and cut the river neatly in half. Opposition to that plan followed swiftly and soon a number of conservation groups formed the Coalition for a Free Flowing Locust Fork.

The spearhead of the coalition is Alabama's largest river conservation group, the Cahaba River Society, which adopted a well-focused strategy to fight the dam. The CRS could have aimed its activist guns at any of a host of negative impacts that would result from the proposed reservoir. "There were a thousand issues to choose from," says Don Elder, executive director of the organization, "it took us quite a while to pick a path." But after a careful analysis of the project, they decided to focus their primary attention on a single question: Does the Birmingham Water Works really need the water?

Narrowing their primary focus to this one issue allowed the Cahaba River Society to more effectively focus their limited resources and to challenge the need for the project before any permits were granted. The result of this strategy was a 46-page analysis of the Birmingham Water Works' own rationale for the reservoir which convincingly demonstrates that the project is unnecessary.

With technical support from the Rocky Mountain Institute, the CRS prepared a meticulous review of water need projections based on anticipated improvements in water use efficiency and a reduction in per-capita consumption. The CRS analysis made good use of improvements in water efficiency technology and in the concept of demand-side management, which holds that it is cheaper, and safer environmentally, to reduce demand than to increase supply. Their conclusion: Birmingham doesn't need the water and won't in the foreseeable future.

At this writing, the Birmingham Water Board is in retreat, searching for a new rationale to build the dam. Elder is convinced the dam threat will remain, however, until public values and political realities change.

The lesson learned from the Locust Fork fight is that, unless you've got an unlimited budget and a huge staff, you have to pick your issues very carefully and then stay focused on them. To be sure, some river campaigns aren't amenable to a single-issue focus and every river has a multitude of values which make it worth saving. The trick is to limit your efforts to the issues you can effectively deal with and which combine urgency, simplicity, and popular interest.

When the U. S. Army Corps of Engineers revealed plans to funnel the Gauley River below Summersville Dam into a hydropower tunnel, it wasn't hard for opponents to focus on one issue: whitewater boating, and the tourist dollars it generated for West Virginia.

Much could have been made of the environmental impacts resulting from a massive diversion from the streambed. But Gauley River activists knew that the whitewater industry was a significant source of revenue, and they built their campaign around that fact. With the help of a study on the economic impacts of whitewater recreation, Citizens for Gauley River concluded that the boating industry was worth $10 million to $16 million per year. The Army Corps proposal, they argued, would dry up the river and dry up the money.

Given West Virginia's depressed coal economy and the growing belief that tourism represented the state's best long-term hope, the economic message caught fire. Local congressman Nick Rahall eventually won passage of legislation which compelled the reoperation of Summersville Dam, making whitewater recreation a project purpose of the facility. As a result, the Corps was not only prohibited from diverting water below the dam, they were required as well to guarantee 21 days of recreational flow each autumn, without hydropower interruptions. Never before, and not since, have releases for whitewater recreation been mandated by legislation.

If you don't have an issue as clear cut as recreation on the Gauley and you're having trouble finding a single focus for your river campaign, consider the following questions:

1. **What is the threat you want to address?**   On the Gauley, this was an easy question to answer, but sometimes that's not the case. California's Russian River once had a world-famous steelhead fishery and spectacular salmon runs. Today the river is in serious decline; its water has frequently been fouled by sewage and agricultural run-off, its flow diminished by too many diversions, its bed gouged and scarred by years of gravel mining and its fishery decimated by all of the above. Efforts to restore the Russian River have been focused on numerous issues: water quality, fishery decline, gravel mining, bank erosion, turbidity control. In a context like this, choosing one issue isn't easy. Which leads to the second question:

2. **What is the winning issue?**   First and foremost, the winning issue is one you can win. Little victories lead to big ones, they build enthusiasm, confidence, and credibility. So start with a modest objective and achieve it, then move on. In general, winning issues are those which have the best chance of capturing public support, generating media attention, and providing strategic success. Choosing a winning issue leads directly to another question:

3. *How do you want to frame the issue?*   Strategists at the Cahaba River Society decided the public was ready to embrace the message that greater efficiency of water use is an idea who's time has come. They presented a convincing argument that, through the use of new technologies, the installation of more efficient plumbing, and the commitment to a per-capita reduction in demand, the existing water supply could be stretched far into the next century, precluding any need for an expensive and environmentally destructive dam. They framed the issue in terms of water use efficiency, rather than water conservation, because efficiency suggests common sense and fiscal responsibility while conservation suggests sacrifice and a reduction in the standard of living. That is a crucial distinction.

Politicians call this "spin" and the point here, of course, is that whatever issue you choose to focus your campaign on, you should be able to frame it in such a way that it captures public interest. Ideally, your issue should be:

    a. *Urgent*   If something isn't done soon the river or the fish or the ducks or the clean water will be lost.

    b. *Simple*   Complicated issues confuse people and when people are confused they tend to avoid getting involved and are more inclined to leave things the way they are. Your issue should be reduced to the simplest, most basic and easily understood terms possible.

    c. *Popular*   A lot of people should care about it. That means you have to identify a constituency for this issue and be confident it is broad enough to give you the support you need.

After you've decided on the focus of your campaign, you need to learn everything you possibly can about your river and the threats to it.

Do Your Homework

In 1975, the Bureau of Reclamation was busy building the foundation for a concrete arch dam on the American River in the Sierra Foothills near Auburn, California. The thin, highly stressed structure was to be the longest "eggshell" type dam in the world. Suddenly a 5.8 magnitude earthquake hit the recently completed Oroville Dam and Reservoir 50 miles away. The earth and rock-filled dam held, but the quake shook the confidence of many geologists who had assumed that foothill fault systems were inactive. Many geologists came to believe that the newly filled reservoir, through the sheer weight of impounded water, triggered the quake.

Ten months later the Bureau's ill-designed Teton Dam in Idaho, built over the timid objections of some of the agency's own geologists, collapsed, releasing an enormous wall of water. The disaster took 11 lives, wiped out most of three towns, 4000 homes, and 350 businesses. Damage was estimated at $2 billion.

In the face of these developments, the Bureau of Reclamation was forced to reexamine its project on the American River at Auburn. The dam it was building would be rigid but fragile and highly sensitive to lateral displacement. Downstream, directly in the path of the dam, was the city of Sacramento and close to a million people. But after Bureau geologists studied the site, a Bureau division head pronounced that the "Auburn Dam site is incredibly stable." The Bureau wanted to proceed with the project.

In fact, the Auburn Dam site was found to be riddled with a network of faults, and expert opinion on the "stability" of the site varied enormously.

Friends of the River, which had an office in Sacramento, immediately immersed itself in the nuances of Foothill geology, reservoir induced seismicity, maximum credible earthquakes, and lateral displacement. F.O.R. staff members interviewed geologists and force-fed themselves enough information to speak knowledgeably and credibly about a complicated issue that the Bureau was trying to make disappear.

They learned, among other things, that the dam the Bureau still wanted to build could withstand no more than three inches of lateral displacement. They learned that the Bureau had dismissed an independent consulting firm when that firm concluded that a large reservoir at Auburn had the potential for triggering an earthquake of 5.7 or better. They learned that if Auburn Dam were to be built and then collapsed, its full reservoir would wipe out a downstream dam and flood waters could rise 40 feet around the State Capital. They learned that inundation maps for the city of Sacramento revealed that 260,000 lives might then be lost. They learned that Auburn Dam could be, in effect, a loaded gun aimed at the heart of Sacramento, that if it failed, if the Bureau was wrong again, the result might be the worst civil disaster in U. S. history.

Friends of the River did their homework, they made a lot of noise about earthquake safety and the message got through. Ultimately, even though the Bureau continued to insist (as they had before the Teton tragedy) that the original dam design was safe, the Interior Department demanded a redesign capable of withstanding a 6.5 earthquake. The dam has yet to be built.

The point of this story is important to any river activist who, in the course of a campaign, confronts powerful and well-paid professionals with years of expertise in subjects she or he can't even pronounce. To be effective, to be taken seriously, you have to do your homework. You have to research your issue exhaustively and understand it completely. The information you develop has to be accurate, free from hyperbole and exaggeration, and reliable enough to earn the trust of a cynical media.

The fruits of your homework serve your campaign both internally and externally. The information you unearth gives direction and substance to your campaign and it provides you with propaganda to feed the public.

The research you conduct should not gather dust on your desk; it should be translated into fact sheets, action alerts, and press releases; it should be the fuel you constantly feed into the engine of your campaign. What you research depends, of course, on the nature of your campaign, but it should always include the following:

1. *The threatening project or activity.*   What is the nature of the project, the development, the discharge, the diversion, the dam? What is it that someone is doing, or proposing to do to your river? The more you know about the threat the better equipped you are to stop it.

2. *The rationale.*   What are the arguments for the project or activity threatening the river? Is the need real? Ideally, you will come to know the other side's arguments as well as your own. Admittedly, that's not always easy. Don Elder says the Cahaba River Society struggled long and hard to pry loose from the Birmingham Water Board information on actual water use and projected needs. They succeeded, he says, in part because "we had on staff a person uniquely talented in extracting public information from people not inclined to give it."

3. *The impacts.*   The parties responsible for degrading rivers almost never acknowledge the full impacts of their actions. Environmental reviews are often arbitrary in scope. If you want to protect your river, you need to know the full extent of the impacts, or potential impacts, caused by the threatening project or action.

4. *The alternatives.*   For virtually every river-damaging project or activity, there is a less-damaging alternative. And for some projects there is no real need. Because environmental impact studies for river projects are often done by the project proponent, they usually give alternatives short shrift. River activists, therefore, frequently have to research alternatives themselves.

5. *The key players.*   You always need to know who you're dealing with, which means making an inventory of every person and organization who can help or hurt your campaign. Some campaigns use wall charts listing key players and the actions being taken to deal with them. In the end your success in recruiting support and countering opposition will depend on how much you know about both.

6. *The solution.*   The end product of all this research is a solution to the problem and, as we'll discuss in greater detail later on, the solution you choose is a key decision for the campaign.

Choosing the right solution will be a challenge because of the range of possibilities. If, for example, the threat to your river is encroaching land development, the range of possible solutions could include: protection under a state river program; protection through state land-use laws; protection through local land-zoning laws; adoption of a river corridor ordinance; creation of a river greenway; adoption of a flood plain ordinance; implementation of an environmentally sensitive, low-impact development design, or some combination of the above.

And you not only have to choose the right solution, you have to know how to use it. If you decide you want to seek Wild and Scenic protection, or a Clean Water Act intervention, or a conservation easement, or if you want to block some land development or challenge a timber harvest plan or appeal an FERC permit, you'll need to know the necessary steps to do those things.

In analyzing impacts, exploring alternatives, and choosing solutions, it will help if you can find people with the appropriate expertise.

Recruit People with Technical Expertise

When the Army Corps of Engineers decided to enlarge the reservoir at Abiquiu Dam on New Mexico's Rio Chama, they were proposing an engineering solution to a previous planning mistake. Thanks to a tunnel punched through the Continental Divide in Colorado, the Chama is capable of carrying water diverted from the San Juan River and delivering it to Albuquerque, which sits downstream on the Rio Grande. The problem with this complex work of plumbing is that Albuquerque never used the 48,000 acre feet of water it contracted to buy each year. Engineers and planners had radically overestimated the need, so the city's water stayed in the San Juan, flowed into the Colorado, and was eventually pumped into the irrigation ditches of California's Imperial Valley.

This gift to California was hard for some people in New Mexico to accept, so they decided Albuquerque's water should be captured and stored. After some timely modifications to Abiquiu Dam, a flood control facility on the Chama, the Corps of Engineers proposed to impound the unclaimed San Juan water in an enlarged reservoir. The result would be up to 1,000,000 acre feet of additional storage and the drowning of several miles of scenic river, including the Chama's best reach of whitewater.

Beyond the environmental damage the project would have caused, there were several other things wrong with this plan, but it took some professional expertise to figure that out. Phil Wallin, who was then a Santa Fe whitewater boater and regional director of the Trust for Public Land, had put together a coalition to protect the Chama, but Wallin was a lawyer, not a scientist. So he recruited an environmental engineer named Neil Williams and, together with sympathetic staff members working for various New Mexico resource agencies, they conducted a comprehensive and sophisticated analysis of the Corps' plan. Williams and his collaborators were able to make a convincing case for the fact that increased water storage at Abiquiu Dam would provide Albuquerque little real benefit and cost the city a lot of money. Most of the water stored in the massive reservoir, Williams demonstrated, would simply evaporate.

While Williams was debunking the logic of using Abiquiu for water storage, Fred Berry raised the specter of a catastrophic earthquake. A former geology professor at the University of California, Berry owned land on the Chama and had mapped the geology of that region. From his mapping he knew that significant faults ran near Abiquiu Dam, which was built into severely fractured rock. Berry believed the Corps of Engineers had greatly underrated the potential for seismic damage to the earth-filled dam, and he wasn't afraid to say so.

The Rio Chama coalition went public with Berry's earthquake analysis and the public, in turn, went ballistic. At hearings for the reservoir project, the Army Corps was eaten alive by angry citizens worried that the enlarged reservoir would endanger their homes and their lives.

People like Wallin, Williams, and Berry are absolutely essential ingredients for most successful river campaigns. If you're lucky, you'll have some experts on your staff or board. But most campaigns are started and staffed by generalists, people with no technical expertise. The Cahaba River Society's Don Elder has more than a decade of professional experience, but not in river protection; for 13 years he was a trumpet player with the Alabama Symphony Orchestra. So if you don't have the expertise, you'll have to go out and find it.

Recruiting technical expertise may not always be easy, but it is a lot less difficult if you've got a college or university at hand. During the Gauley campaign, David Brown made much use of a study done by West Virginia University on the "Economic Impacts of Whitewater Boating on the Gauley River." That study was commissioned, ironically, by the Army Corps of Engineers. As mentioned earlier, Brown and Citizens for the Gauley built a campaign around the enormous economic value of whitewater recreation.

Shooting Holes in a Cost–Benefit Analysis

Economic analysis is one of the most important tools of a river campaign and it often requires technical expertise. When two California irrigation districts floated plans to construct a hydropower dam in the heart of the Tuolumne River's free-flowing lower gorge, the rationale was purely economic. The dam was designed to be a hydraulic cash register and the cost–benefit ratio touted by its promoters was on the healthy side of one to one. But the economic justification for the dam did not take into account any environmental impacts on the river canyon.

To correct that oversight, The Tuolumne River Preservation Trust helped fund an independent cost–benefit analysis by the Environmental Defense Fund. EDF then conducted a sophisticated assessment using the latest methodologies in applied and theoretical economics. Their study factored in to the economic equation two environmental impacts that dam proponents hadn't bothered to consider: the virtual elimination of whitewater boating from 18 miles of the Tuolumne and the near-total degradation of an outstanding trout fishery.

With just those two environmental impacts "internalized" into the cost–benefit equation, EDF discovered that the cost–benefit ratio of the dam project plummeted. At best, said EDF, the ratio would be .877 to 1, meaning that for each dollar invested in the project, society would get about 88 cents of benefit in return. The dam would not only fail to make a profit, EDF concluded, it would cost society $26 million per year.

Finding this kind of technical expertise may sound daunting, but a service offered by River Network can make the job much easier. The service is a database called DORIS (Directory of River Information Specialists) which lists more than 500 river specialists recruited from conservation organizations, state and federal agencies, and a national network of river guardians. If you're having trouble finding the expertise you need, or just want to expand the technical horizons of your campaign, give River Network a call at (800) 42-DORIS.

Find a Long-Term Positive Solution

In some circles, environmentalism and obstructionism are synonymous. River conservationists, in particular, are often accused of being perpetually *against*—against dams, against diversions, against hydropower, against flood control. And it is often not enough for us to argue back that we are *for* wild rivers and healthy fish and clean water. We need to argue back with well-reasoned and long-term alternatives to the developments and activities harming rivers. We need to demonstrate a different way of doing things. Which brings us to the Charles River.

The Charles is a small but important river, meandering 80 miles from the hills of eastern Massachusetts through 35 municipalities and down into Boston Harbor. Flowing through the historic Back Bay of Boston, the

Charles borders parts of Boston University, Harvard, and MIT and carries on its usually tranquil waters racing shells from all three universities.

In 1955, Hurricane Diana slammed into New England causing some of the worst flood damage in American history. The Charles River watershed was particularly hard hit. For a decade after that, various plans were considered to tame the Charles and provide greater protection for the highly developed urban centers in the lower watershed. Simultaneously, citizen concern began to grow about the sad state of the river, which was heavily polluted with industrial, municipal, and agricultural waste. In 1965, after *The Boston Globe* ran a series of articles profiling the river's condition, a citizen's organization was formed to restore the Charles. It was called the Charles River Watershed Association. That same year Congress authorized the Corps of Engineers to conduct a study of various options for comprehensive flood control on the river.

For the lower reach of the Charles, which has an intimate hydrologic relationship with Boston Harbor, a new dam at the mouth of the river was the only answer. But that addressed only half of the flood control equation. Something had to be done about flood waters in the upper watershed. Conventional wisdom at the Corps would have been to channelize the streambed, rip rap the banks, and throw in a flood control dam. The operative word in the Corps' title, after all, is "engineer." But that scenario would have cost $30 million, it would have required the acquisition and permanent inundation of 10,000 acres, along with relocation of hundreds of private facilities and the replacement of numerous bridges.

Natural Valley Storage

The Corps examined this dilemma long and hard and then, against all odds, chose to do something totally different, something innovative, environmentally sensitive, and relatively cheap. They decided to let nature handle the water of the Charles, to maintain and preserve the wetlands which serve as a giant sponge or, as the Corps describes it, "Natural Valley Storage." Although the lower reach of the Charles had been virtually stripped of natural habitat, the upper watershed still had some 20,000 acres of wetlands. The Corps estimated the storage capacity of that acreage during Hurricane Diana at more than 50,000 acre feet. Preserving it would cost a third of the price for a "structural" solution.

The Corps' 1972 report on this proposal should probably be chiseled somewhere in stone: "The logic of the scheme is compelling. Nature has already provided the least cost solution to future flooding in the form of extensive wetlands which moderate extreme highs and lows in stream flow. Rather than attempt to improve on this natural protection mechanism, it is both prudent and economical to leave the hydrologic regime established over the millennia undisturbed. In the opinion of the study team, construction of any of the most likely alternatives, a 55,000 acre-foot reservoir or extensive walls and dikes, can add nothing."

While the Corps was developing its Natural Valley Storage idea, the Charles River Watershed Association was embarked on the herculean task of implementing a loosely defined state plan for a mile-wide public park the full length of the Charles. They understood that, while the Corps plan would preserve wetlands and preclude a dam, it would not alone protect the whole river. For that, a comprehensive river corridor plan was needed.

While a river corridor plan, properly done, represents one of the best long-term solutions for a degraded or endangered river, the multitude of interests that have to be accommodated make it an enormous challenge. That was certainly true on the Charles, where private property rights created a sensitive issue for both the corridor plan and the Corps. With the CRWA helping to promote the plan and smooth the way, the Corps eventually acquired about 8500 acres for wetland storage. The fortuitous timing of the Corps' scheme, which won congressional approval in 1974, and the CRWA river corridor plan, helped create a public–private partnership that drove both efforts toward success.

Today, the Corps' Natural Valley Storage plan is a rare example of cost-effective, environmentally sensitive flood control. And after more than a decade of effort, the CRWA corridor plan won official approval from the Commonwealth of Massachusetts in 1983. One of the key lessons to be learned from the Charles is that a positive alternative can sometimes emerge through collaboration with public agencies.

Taking Down a Dam

In other parts of the nation, the record of the Army Corps of Engineers, as any river activist knows, has been somewhat less enlightened. Take, for instance, the Oklawaha River.

By any measure, the Oklawaha is a river to cherish and preserve. "The sweetest water lane in the world," said poet Sydney Lanier in 1876. Bordered by oaks and cypress, palms and magnolias, the Oklawaha is a vital part of America's vanishing heritage of southern canopied rivers. The river (and its mile-wide riparian forest) has served as vital habitat for cougar, bear, manatee, and more than 100 species of fish. It was one of the most biologically important and diverse waterways in Florida until 1966, when the Army Corps of Engineers began building Rodman Reservoir.

Rodman was an essential link in the chain of artificial waterways the Corps was constructing across the waist of Florida north of Ocala. That chain was called the Cross Florida Barge Canal and it was rivaled only by the Tennessee–Tombigbee Waterway as the worst public works boondoggle in the nation. The barge canal, which was designed to provide a shortcut for shipping between the Atlantic Ocean and the Gulf of Mexico, never made economic sense, but like a public works vampire, it kept sucking the life from Florida's rivers while refusing to die.

Although President Nixon stopped construction in 1971, it took until 1990 for Congress to deauthorize the project and by then Rodman Reservoir had become a shallow, eutrophying, weed-choked, ecological embarrassment. Rodman wiped out 9000 acres of floodplain forest and 16 miles of the free-flowing Oklawaha. There was no swimming, sailing, water skiing, or recreational power boating because the reservoir is choked with stumps, floating logs, and water weeds.

But when the barge canal was killed, Floridians had what looked like a clear shot at repairing the damage the Corps had done. The Oklawaha could be restored with one simple, cost-effective fix, the perfect long-term positive solution: remove the dam and drain the reservoir letting the river restore itself. The idea made perfect ecological and economic sense. Nature, with a little human intervention, could bring the river back to life, and the cost of maintaining the deteriorating reservoir—$1,000,000 per year—could be eliminated.

That proposal, championed by a group called Florida Defenders of the Environment, became so popular that Governor Lawton Chiles and his cabinet backed it unanimously. With further support from most of the state bureaucracy, a campaign was launched. The Florida Natural Resources Department fashioned legislation to restore the Oklawaha and include it in the new Cross Florida Greenway Conservation Area. Logically, the plan should have been an automatic win.

But every dam and reservoir has a constituency and supporters of Rodman Reservoir, though small in number, have managed to stall restoration of the river. As this book went to press, reservoir supporters, with the help of a powerful state senator, had stalled legislation to remove Rodman by insisting on an 18-month study of the consequences.

Other Alternative Solutions

Rodman Reservoir is, of course, an anomaly. It is rare to find so elegant and simple a solution to a river problem. But there are rivers in Washington (the Elwha), California (the Tuolumne), and Maine (the Kennebec)—and others scattered around the country—where similar alternatives exist—where the removal of obsolete dams will bring damaged rivers back to life.

More typical scenarios demand long-term alternatives to hydropower projects, flood control dams, water supply reservoirs, or flood plain development.

The campaign to protect the Rio Chama didn't just shoot down plans for a larger reservoir, it offered a cost-effective, ecologically benign alternative. Instead of storing additional water at Abiquiu Dam where it would flood the river and then evaporate, the Chama Trust proposed that the City of Albuquerque should divert the water through collector wells and filter it back into the underground aquifer where most of the community's water comes from.

The two most common arguments for dam projects are the need for clean, cheap energy and the need for more water supplies. Flood control is often thrown in as a sweetener. Opposing either kind of project demands that you provide some alternative solutions. If you find yourself fighting a hydropower plant, it will probably be a privately financed investment venture promoted strictly for profit. The promoters will have no incentive to explore alternative, efficiency-driven methods for capturing the same energy they can produce from the river. That will be your job and a lot of research on the subject has already been done. Particularly useful is the work of efficiency expert Amory Lovins and the Rocky Mountain Institute in Snowmass, Colorado.

Water supply reservoirs are usually promoted in even more urgent terms, because many parts of the country experience genuine water shortages. But those shortages are often the result of management problems, not supply problems, since most of the country has only started to address the issue of efficient water use. Look beneath the surface of a water shortage and you almost always find patterns of inefficiency, misallocation, and inappropriate use which, if changed, could free up substantial quantities of water. The challenge to a river campaign fighting a water-supply project is to present a convincing alternative based on efficiencies and policy changes instead of more plumbing.

The Rocky Mountain Institute (RMI) has begun to focus its formidable expertise on this subject as well, and one of its research projects provided valuable ammunition to help defeat the ill-conceived Two Forks Dam on the South Platte River in Colorado. Two Forks was an obsession of the Denver Water Board for years and came perilously close to being built. It would have drowned 21 miles of state-designated Gold Medal wild trout water at a cost of $1 billion. In 1989, RMI released a 13-page analysis of the role water efficiency could play in meeting Denver's water needs. In 1990 the Environmental Protection Agency killed the project. The summary of RMI's research is worth quoting here:

> Full use of new water-saving equipment in Denver
> households would save more water than the proposed
> Two Forks dam would supply, and at about 20 percent of

the dam's cost per acre-foot. The hardware required—high-performance toilets, showerheads, faucet aerators and lawn-watering equipment—is all commercially available . . . Using this water-saving equipment involves no changes in lifestyle: it works at least as well, and looks at least as attractive, as the equipment Denverites use today.

The essential point to remember from all this is that long-term solutions need to both eliminate the immediate threat and foreclose future threats. As Phil Wallin points out, "It's not enough to beat back a dam or remove one source of pollution. You need to establish a framework for conservation—like Wild and Scenic designation, or a National Recreation Area, or a river ordinance. After all the sound and fury over Two Forks, for example, the river is still not protected, it has no designation at all. You've got to put a stake in the heart of the vampire, or it will return."

At this point in your planning you will confront some threshold issues which will define the format, strategy, and direction of your campaign.

Choose the Best Forum for Action

Before you go any further in the planning process you need to ask an important tactical question: In what forum of action do you want to focus your campaign energy? Where do you want to stage the fight? Picking the best forum for action means that you have to figure out what governmental arena or political process is most likely to produce the results you want. You may well end up engaged in more than one forum, but it's tough to ride two horses at the same time.

The Locust Fork River is an ideal candidate for Wild and Scenic protection, but the Cahaba River Society decided instead to challenge the Birmingham Water Board and its projections for water need. That decision made strategic sense because stopping the water board was a quicker short-term solution to the immediate threat. Later efforts could focus on a long-term solution, which necessarily needs to follow.

Finding a Forum for the Sacramento

Because river campaigns often involve a maze of issues and governmental jurisdictions, deciding where to start is important. In 1984, the Sacramento River Preservation Trust (SRPT) was formed to stop the Army Corps of Engineers from rip-rapping the last natural stretch of river between Chico and Red Bluff. Attacking the Corps head-on might have felt good, but the effort would probably have been as successful as trying to move an elephant with a hand truck. So instead of attempting the impossible, the SRPT focused on a less formidable opponent, the State Reclamation Board, which was the local sponsor for the project.

Attacking the Reclamation Board, on the grounds of inadequate environmental review, gave the SRPT several immediate advantages. It could promote the issue in an arena where everyone knew about the terrible decline of the river; it had far more support in the state legislature and among state regulatory agencies than it did in Washington; and it could employ the California Environmental Quality Act which provides better protection than the National Environmental Protection Act.

The SRPT strategy paid off. Challenging the Reclamation Board won the Trust time, during which the declining state of the winter run chinook salmon triggered an endangered species listing and a major public–private initiative to restore the Sacramento River.

Sometimes, when you're dealing with two states, various municipalities, and two different offices of the same federal agency, the best forum for action shifts from one moment to the next. That's what happened on the Clark Fork River in Montana.

When Americans think about river pollution, their minds usually turn to Eastern and Midwestern rivers like the Nashua and the Cuyahoga, which have come to symbolize the worst excesses of industrial abuse. It often comes as a shock, therefore, to learn that the nation's largest Superfund site, measured in geographic terms, is 140 miles of the Clark Fork River between Butte and Missoula, Montana. Arsenic, lead, zinc, cadmium, and other heavy metals from mine tailings, along with silt from clear cutting and agricultural wastes have made the beautiful Clark Fork something of a toxic soup. That such pollution could occur in Big Sky country is testimony to the unrestrained exploitation of western minerals over the past century. And while some of the mining rules have been changed and pollution has declined, the legacy of the past still leaches into the Clark Fork like the steady drip of an intravenous poison.

In 1983, in response to a pollution threat from a Champion paper pulp mill, the Clark Fork Coalition (later to become the Clark Fork–Pend Oreille Coalition) was born. It united a disparate group of environmentalists, property owners, and sportsmen's groups who resolved the pulp mill problem after a two-year study and a series of direct negotiations with Champion. But greater challenges remained, including the millions of cubic yards of poisonous waste littering the headwaters of the river, and the nutrient pollution from farmlands and urban development.

To deal with nutrient loading, which was sometimes so bad it turned the river a cloudy green, the Clark Fork Coalition decided to go to work

Clark Fork River, Montana. (Photo courtesy of Tim Palmer.)

in the arena of the EPA. It was a logical choice since water quality is the issue uniting the coalition, and the EPA has the most clout to address that issue. But sometimes this meant getting the state of Idaho, into which the Clark Fork flows, to force EPA to prod the state of Montana to clean house. And sometimes it meant having the state of Montana prod EPA to take action. And sometimes it meant having local governments wave the EPA club at the state.

Peter Nielsen, the former executive director of the Coalition, says the EPA was particularly effective in forcing action when the State of Montana was dragging its heels, most notably in winning state agreement to enforce a nondegradation policy for the Clark Fork. But he cautions against letting a river campaign become stuck in one arena. "My advice is to keep open minded for the best venue for action . . . you're not stuck with one."

Where Will You Win?

The best criterion for picking a forum for action is the likelihood of success. In what political, legal, or governmental arena are you most likely to win? Implicitly you are deciding where you will have the friendliest reception and the most allies. But picking a forum for action does not mean that all your campaign effort will be confined to that forum. If you decide that state or federal legislation is necessary to protect your river, you still have an enormous job ahead of you building enough local support to convince Congress or your legislature to act. If you are appealing to the Federal Energy Regulatory Commission not to license a destructive hydropower project, you also need to organize opposition to the permit among state agencies with jurisdiction over the threatened river.

Of course, one forum often leads to another. During the late 1960s and 1970s, the Snake River in Hell's Canyon was the focus of one of the nation's epic river battles. That campaign, which sought to block construction of a massive dam in the heart of North America's second deepest gorge, began as a Supreme Court appeal of a Federal Power Commission permit and ended in legislation making Hell's Canyon a National Recreation Area. Supreme Court Justice William O. Douglas had issued a landmark ruling requiring the FPC to expand its review to include the basic question of killing the river or, as Douglas wrote, "the desirability of its demise."

Environmental attorney Brock Evans was then Northwest Representative for the Sierra Club, and he responded to an urgent plea from an Idaho jet boat pilot looking for a way to save the Snake. With the opportunity provided by Justice Douglas, Evans intervened before the FPC and introduced what may have been the first witness to ever testify in court about the scenic and aesthetic values of a wild river. Adams knew the FPC intervention was only a holding action; like its subsequent incarnation, FERC, the FPC had no record of recognizing or caring about environmental impacts. But by taking the campaign into this legal forum, he was able to buy time.

Ultimately, the FPC granted a license for the dam but with an unusual caveat: the permit would be delayed for three years to see if river defenders could get Congress to pass legislation protecting the canyon. The legal forum led to the legislative forum and the campaign succeeded in the end.

Once you've chosen an arena in which to fight for your river, it's time to choose your weapons.

Pick the Right Tool for the Job

Just as there are numerous forums for a river campaign, so there are numerous river-saving tools available to work with. As any carpenter knows, there's a right tool for every job. But picking the right tool can be a challenge and sometimes you have to create your own. That's what happened on the Wildcat River.

The Wildcat River (it is known locally as a brook) flows out of the White Mountains of New Hampshire and tumbles down a spectacular staircase waterfall in the town of Jackson. The river is clear and clean and postcard pretty. It's also a perfect place to build a hydropower plant, if your interests run more toward megawatts than meandering brooks.

That was the case for a Massachusetts power company which applied to the Federal Energy Regulatory Commission for a permit to develop the Wildcat and destroy, in the process, Jackson's famous waterfall. The Selectmen of Jackson (a colonial term referring to the town council) were, to put it mildly, taken aback. They registered their disapproval loudly and officially during the FERC review process. Three times they protested the project and three times they were turned down. Over their protests FERC granted a preliminary permit for the power plant.

The agency should have known better. The FERC permit galvanized the town of Jackson and there may be no political force more formidable than a New England town council united around a cause. This is, after all, the Motherlode of grassroots democracy. No avaricious, out-of-state corporation was going to steal their river and no faceless federal bureaucracy was going to be allowed to let it happen.

Consensus in Jackson was nearly universal: the Wildcat River had to be saved. Not so clear was how to do it. The same fierce independence which fired local residents to oppose the hydropower plan, also made them shy of a river protection solution imposed on them by Washington. These are people who prize their independence.

But state and local restrictions on river development have no standing in the halls of FERC, which enjoys a kind of jurisdictional autonomy in licensing hydropower projects. Only federal intervention could stop this power play. So the obvious tool for the job was a Wild and Scenic campaign, which usually means the river is administered by a federal agency. And that's the kind of government involvement in land use decisions the people of Jackson would instinctively resist. At least six miles of the threatened river corridor lay inside the town and much of it was privately owned. What to do?

To answer that question, to fashion the best tool for the job of saving the Wildcat River, the people of Jackson created an innovative river corridor protection program, based on a mix of local initiatives. After Congress authorized a study of the Wildcat for Wild and Scenic consideration in 1984, the town got crucial help from the National Park Service in assessing the feasibility of creating a Wild and Scenic river plan developed by local interests and managed by state and local government.

The plan had three primary components. First, it would seek conservation easements from private landowners to protect against further development of the riparian corridor. Second, it would initiate changes in the town's zoning ordinances to add further protection from inappropriate de-

velopment. And finally, the plan would initiate an ongoing riverbank restoration effort near the town center.

The plan was ultimately successful. Private interests and the public good
were somehow woven into the fabric of a solution that protected the river
without disenfranchising the citizens of Jackson. It worked in no small part
because of a fundamental commitment on the part of all the organizations
involved to work cooperatively and to seek mutually acceptable objectives.
The National Park Service played a big role in mediating differences and
guiding the plan toward completion. And the Jackson Board of Selectmen
recruited a town resident and riverfront landowner (with a resource-
management background) to coordinate the activities of a citizen's advisory committee which participated in every step of the plan.

With this innovative plan in place, Congress had no qualms in granting
the Wildcat River Wild and Scenic status, with a cooperative management
formula that protects local interests.

The lesson of the Wildcat is that the tool you use to save a river has to
fit both the needs of the river and the political realities surrounding it.
The citizens of Jackson created their own tool, a hybrid Wild and Scenic
campaign which turned potential political opposition into a potent and
unified force for preservation. It remains a model for protecting rivers
flowing through private lands.

Saving the Smith

At the opposite end of the country, in the northwest corner of California, the Smith River offers a very different example. Draining the Siskiyou
Mountains in a web of emerald waterways, the three forks of the Smith
carve stunning canyons framed by old growth redwoods. The Smith has
the dubious but important distinction of being the only free-flowing river
system left in California; all its branches are free from dams. It is also one
of the most beautiful rivers in the nation and its rare value has been honored by both state and federal Wild and Scenic protection.

But a Wild and Scenic River is not free from risk, since the watershed it
drains can still be logged, mined, and developed. The river itself is usually
protected along only a narrow, half-mile wide corridor. For the Smith,
which intersects some of the most coveted timber land in the country, Wild
and Scenic protection was not enough.

In 1985, William Penn Mott, the visionary environmentalist who
headed the National Park Service, launched a campaign to designate an
entire river system, including its forested watershed, as a national park.
The Smith was the ideal river to fulfill Mott's dream. Almost 75 percent of
its watershed was federally owned and administered by the Forest Service,
and it adjoins Redwood National Park and two state parks. Most of the

watershed was still free from clearcutting and full of wildlife, including eagle, elk, bear, and mountain lion. The Smith has one of the finest salmon and steelhead fisheries in the West.

To the casual observer, making the Smith a National Park was a stroke of genius, the perfect river-protection tool. But to many citizens of the Smith watershed, where logging is a way of life, the idea was cause for revolt and they opposed it bitterly. The Forest Service quickly followed local sentiment and announced opposition to a Smith River park. The Smith was cut from a list of 12 candidate rivers and then, when Mott was squeezed out of the Park Service, the whole idea was killed.

That left a lot of frustrated river savers casting about for another protection tool. Some of them had been skeptical all along that the Smith could be turned into a national park while a firestorm of opposition raged all around it. The key to protection, some people argued, was a plan that could win the support of at least a significant part of the local population, including the business community. The logging industry, most people agreed, was beyond reach.

And so a joint effort began between a coalition of conservation groups called the Smith River Alliance and the Save the Redwoods League to shape an alternative scenario for saving the Smith. The tool they came up with was a National Recreation Area and they sold it feverishly to anyone willing to listen. It took a lot of selling, and it took some important compromises, but in the end a plan was hammered out acceptable to almost everyone but the logging industry.

Introduced in Congress and guided through the legislative thicket by area Representative Doug Bosco, the Smith River National Recreation Area bill created the highest level of overall protection granted any river in the country. Among its landmark provisions: prohibition of large-scale surface mining in the watershed; elimination of Forest Service plans for a major logging road through sacred Indian lands; addition of numerous tributary streams into the Wild and Scenic plan; protection of much of the remaining old-growth redwood forest; closure of 153,000 acres to all logging; promotion of "new forestry" sustained yield logging practices where timber harvesting is allowed; restoration of landscapes and waterscapes damaged by past mining, logging, and road building; protection of wildlife species and their habitat.

Signed into law by President Bush in 1990, the Smith River bill established a new standard for river protection and underscored the need to pick carefully the tools you use to save a river. The success of the NRA tool was due in part to the fact that it held the promise for economic benefits to the region. A major focus of the legislation is the development of recreation services and facilities in the watershed. Many local residents who would normally have been suspicious of more government regulations in their forests bought into the plan because of its promise to promote tourism.

Chapter 5 discusses in greater detail the variety of tools available for river protection and we don't need to review the whole list here. But the important point to remember is that a tool which works beautifully in one river campaign may be totally inappropriate or counter-productive in another. Invoking the Public Trust doctrine, which served the Mono Lake Committee very well, probably wouldn't get much mileage on the Los Angeles River.

Once you've picked your forum and selected the right tools you're ready to plan a strategy.

Define a Strategy

If you've followed all the steps outlined above, you're ready to construct a battle plan. But just to refresh your memory, let's review the planning stages you've already passed through.

So far you have thoroughly surveyed the river; you've focused on a key issue and decided how to frame it; you have researched the issue thoroughly; you have recruited people with technical expertise to help analyze the threat and propose alternatives; you have framed a long-term positive solution to the threat; you've decided in what forum it's best to launch your campaign; and you've chosen the best tool with which to do it.

The strategy you adopt is your blueprint—it defines the steps needed to reach your campaign goals and objectives.

A good campaign strategy is worthy of a full day's planning session with all the relevant campaign members participating. You'll be following this map for a long time and, even though it will change as events and political realities change, it demands thoughtful development.

What Worked on the American River?

There is no perfect model for a campaign strategy, but the one below contains most of the important elements, and it worked. It was developed by Friends of the River during its campaign to stop the most recent version of Auburn Dam on the American River. It should be noted that this was neither the first nor the last strategy plan to address the Auburn Dam issue. Not all of the strategies listed below were employed to the extent the organization would have liked, largely because of a lack of resources. There was, for example, no video produced and none of the activities were funded to the levels desired.

The Auburn Dam Campaign Strategy (1991)

A. Campaign Mission
   To permanently protect the canyons of the American River.

B. Campaign Goals
   1. Creation of a river-based National Recreation Area for the Middle and North Forks of the American River.
   2. Passage of flood control legislation which provides reasonable, cost-effective protection for Sacramento without threatening the environmental integrity of the American River.
   3. The legislative elimination of future dam threats to the canyons of the American River.

C. Campaign Objectives
   1. Passage of river-based National Recreation Area legislation.
   2. Defeat of any legislation to construct a gated, expandable or multi-purpose dam on the American River. (Circumstances later led the organization to oppose any dam on the river.)
   3. Development and promotion of viable flood control alternatives for the Sacramento area.
   4. Promotion of public awareness about the irreplaceable resource that the American River represents.

D. Campaign Strategies
   1. Develop credible, cost-effective flood control alternatives to Auburn Dam.
   2. Discredit Corps of Engineers flood control analysis and assumptions with independent hydrological analysis.
   3. Discredit the environmental impact conclusions of the Corps of Engineers feasibility study using critical EPA analysis and other independent expert opinion.
   4. Develop grassroots lobbying/letter writing campaign to generate popular pressure on key elected officials to support the no-dam alternative and protection of the river. Activate the activist list.
   5. Build grassroots support in Sacramento County by undertaking door-to-door canvas.
   6. Begin Washington lobby campaign to convince key committee chairs and agency personnel that local controversy, massive environmental opposition and protracted political/legal battle awaits any legislation to authorize construction of a dam at Auburn.
   7. Undertake a public information campaign in Sacramento area to publicize the natural resource value of the American River, publicize the local cost of a flood control dam and the existence of

cheaper, less destructive alternatives. Produce American River video.

8. Summarize and publicize Corps history of failures, cost overruns and boondoggles.
9. Prepare and publicize answers to key questions worrying the public about the need for Auburn Dam flood control.
10. Lobby Sacramento Area Flood Control Agency to reject Corps flood control plan.

Following this strategic plan was an analysis of the campaign's assets, which included staff, organizational allies, funding, and issues favoring the campaign. This was then balanced with a list of liabilities—including shortage of funds and staff, the compelling need for flood control, and the powerful support of local legislators for the dam. The result of this inventory was a ledger of sorts, allowing the organization to weigh the strengths and weaknesses of the campaign.

Each one of the campaign strategies listed here also has its own set of objectives and timelines. The grand strategy at the time this plan was written was twofold: to win passage of legislation creating a river-based (as opposed to a reservoir-based) National Recreation Area, and to defeat legislation authorizing the proposed dam. Ultimately, the NRA legislation became a subsidiary issue in the frenzy to defeat the dam.

When you develop your own campaign strategy, there will probably be a variety of different strategic elements in your plan. But remember to keep the focus centered on the strategy that serves your goals and objectives most efficiently. River campaigns can drain energy in a hundred directions and unless you are very clear about where you need to focus the resources of your campaign, you run the risk of doing a lot and achieving a little.

After you've decided what you're going to do, the next big challenge is deciding who's going to do it.

Set up a Team

It is part of the magic of grassroots activism that so much can be done with so little. The Clark Fork Coalition in Montana, one of the best managed river conservation groups in the country, has a staff of five. The Charles River Watershed Association, 28 years old and going strong, is run by three people. Idaho Rivers United covers the state with a staff of five. And scores of grassroots river organizations have no paid staff at all.

Whatever the size of the staff, there are never enough people to run a river campaign and there is always too much work to do. Given that basic rule, setting up a campaign team can be a little like building a house without having enough lumber; it may look a little unfinished and the wind will probably blow through. But if you allocate the building materials intelligently, the structure will stand and the roof will keep the rain out.

Who Does What?

When you're setting up a team, it's important to decide first what the most important tasks are and then who is best equipped to do them. Young campaigns sometimes evolve spontaneously with each team member doing what he or she most enjoys. That can be a mistake, not because people shouldn't do what they enjoy, but because what they enjoy doing may not be what's most important to the campaign.

All of this begs at least two questions: Who is on the team? And who leads it?

A river campaign team usually consists of a mix of volunteers, staff, and members of the organization's board. Young campaigns may be run entirely by volunteers. Older campaigns may rely primarily on staff. Board members should always be intimately involved, or they shouldn't be on the board. Whatever the focus of your campaign, there are likely to be some tasks requiring special expertise. If the first step of your campaign is a lawsuit, you're either going to need a lawyer on staff or find a volunteer to do *pro bono* work. If you're dealing with pollution and toxic waste, you'll need someone with scientific credentials to decipher technical data and respond to them, as well as an attorney to initiate action.

The Clark Fork Coalition deals constantly with complex pollution issues caused by mining, so it was logical for them to hire a staff scientist with experience in environmental issues. The town of Jackson hired a local resident with experience in resource management to coordinate a citizen's advisory committee. When Friends of the River launched a statewide campaign to win federal Wild and Scenic protection for more than 100 segments of river flowing through public land, they recruited a veteran land-use and wilderness specialist to lead the effort.

Sometimes the obvious jobs go begging because they aren't given enough priority. Publicity and promotion are key elements in any campaign, but media management is often handled randomly and haphazardly by whomever is available at the moment. Rarely does a river campaign put the hiring of a media director high on its inventory of staff needs, and that is often a big mistake.

Who Leads?

There's no mystery to setting up a good team; it's just good planning. The mystery lies in the chemistry that makes it all tick and that, like it or not, often depends on the quality of leadership at the top. Which brings us to the second staffing question: Who leads?

If you started this campaign it is logical to assume that you will lead it, but it's also logical to ask if you're the best woman or man for the job. Some organizations split responsibilities by having an executive director for the organization and a campaign director to lead the fight. Making that judgment without the influence of ego isn't easy.

The question of who's in charge is sometimes answered by the budget and boils down to someone's willingness to be responsible. Leadership doesn't have to be paid, but it does have to be totally committed. The Rio Chama fight was waged with no staff and a volunteer coalition. A core group of some 25 people participated in a coalition to successfully protect Oregon's Deschutes River. They got by with one part-time staff person for eight months.

While political correctness might suggest that campaign leadership should be a collective, consensus-driven process, reality suggests otherwise. The record of successful river campaigns bears witness to the importance of a focused, dedicated, and visionary leader. Marion Stoddart, who became known as Mother Nashua, held an unflagging vision for a clean and healthy river when everyone around her had written it off. Rita Barron helped rescue the Charles from a similar fate with the strength of her committed leadership. David Brown provided forceful direction to campaigns that saved both the Ocoee and the Gauley from terminal dehydration. Wendy Wilson not only led the fight to save the Payette, but forged her success into a statewide organization to protect all of Idaho's endangered rivers.

None of these people worked alone and their success was the success of thousands. But for each of these campaigns, there was one person who ultimately made it happen.

Having said that, however, it's important to be clear that rivers aren't usually saved by individuals, or even by individual organizations. One of the keys to success is coalition.

Form a Coalition

Lift the curtain on a victorious campaign to protect a river and you'll find the stage crowded with players. Behind the protection of the Tuolumne River was a coalition representing more than 20 organizations. The Rio Chama campaign drew together more than a dozen powerful groups and individuals. The Clark Fork Coalition unites environmentalists, businesses, landowners, and sporting groups in an unusual but highly effective alliance. The message is simple: you can't do it alone.

As soon as your organization is up and running, if not before, you should be reaching out to other organizations for guidance, cooperation, and support. You should be trying to build or join a coalition. Coalition building can be as modest an enterprise as recruiting local businesses and civic organizations to support your cause. And it can be as ambitious as joining a national effort comprised of the nation's leading environmental organizations.

A good example at the modest end of the spectrum is the Mattole Restoration Council which has 14 member organizations ranging from the local high school to a variety of watershed groups, a salmon support group, and a land and cattle company. Membership in the Council is open to organizations "whose mission is compatible with the Council's."

At the other end of the spectrum is the American River Coalition, a collection of some 30 local, state, and national conservation organizations herded together by Friends of the River to provide a united front in opposition to construction of Auburn Dam. Some members of the coalition have been actively involved, others have simply given moral or symbolic support. But when a dam bill was before Congress in 1992, their collective presence and their national reach greatly magnified the strength of F.O.R.'s voice and helped provide the margin of victory.

When the legislative battle was fought on the floor of the House, several groups—including American Rivers, the Wilderness Society, and the Sierra Club—played key roles in helping to swing the necessary votes. And throughout the campaign, the Environmental Defense Fund worked the issue behind the scenes. Friends of the River would never have prevailed without the support of the Coalition.

Coalition Caveats

Coalitions are important, but before joining or forming one make sure that your goals are compatible with those of the other members. Not all environmental groups work well together and even groups with compatible goals sometimes differ passionately on appropriate strategies and priorities. Be clear that you and your coalition partners are in harmony before cementing the relationship. One way to do that is to put in writing the expectations and responsibilities of each coalition member.

As in all relationships, money can sometimes be an issue in coalitions. It is wise to spell out in advance what the financial expectations for coalition members are so that campaign expenses (and income) can be equitably divided when they arise. Finally, a good coalition is a valuable working partnership if you make use of the expertise and experience available in it.

Chapter 3
Building Public Support

Okay, you've convinced me. Now go out and bring pressure on me!

FRANKLIN DELANO ROOSEVELT

In 1963, the environmental movement was in its infancy, Rachel Carson's *Silent Spring* was only a year old, the word "ecology" was confined to classrooms and textbooks, and environmental law hadn't been invented. It seemed safe to assume, therefore, that when Consolidated Edison, one of the nation's biggest energy utilities, applied for a permit to build a hydroelectric plant on the Hudson River, 40 miles north of New York City, the licensing would be routine, the opposition nonexistent. What happened instead is testimony to the power of public support for a river.

Con Ed was big and rich and used to getting its way. And the Hudson, one of the nation's premier rivers, had become a shabby, polluted waterway. (An indication of the River's decline was the flavor of its striped bass; while the Hudson harbored at least 10 percent of the Atlantic coastal run, few people ate the fish because they sometimes tasted like the oil and gasoline dumped into the river.)

Con Ed wanted to gouge a storage reservoir into the top of Storm King Mountain, a promontory overlooking the river in the scenic Hudson Highlands. A pumping station and powerhouse built into the side of the mountain would push water up a two-mile tunnel, filling the reservoir during periods of low power demand. The water would then be released through generators during periods of peak demand, creating as much as two million kilowatts of electricity. Storm King was to be the biggest pumped-storage project in the world.

While most people living along the polluted Hudson knew little about the river's ecology, some residents, including a number of prominent New Yorkers with homes around Storm King, feared the aesthetic impacts of the project. If complex ecological issues were still largely beyond public understanding, natural beauty was something everyone cared about, and it was clear that the reservoir, pumping plant, and power lines Con Ed had in mind would deface the scenic beauty of Storm King Mountain and the river it overlooked.

Hudson River above West Point, New York. (Photo courtesy of Tim Palmer.)

Opposition was led by Leo Rothschild, a Manhattan attorney and conservation chair of the New York–New Jersey Trail Conference whose members frequently hiked through the Highlands, and by Carl Carmer who had written a book on the Hudson in the 1930s. Spurred on by Rothschild and Carmer, irate property owners on both sides of the Hudson rose up in angry protest and were soon joined by a coalition of hiking and sporting groups, garden clubs, and conservation organizations. The rapidly growing opposition caught Con Ed by surprise. Many of the newly inspired Storm King activists were prominent and wealthy citizens. Before long a top New York ad agency was hired to counter Con Ed's P. R. campaign. Out of this uprising there emerged the Scenic Hudson Preservation Conference which, some people would argue, was one of the seminal events in the birth of the modern environmental movement.

Public support began to swell like a spring flood. When the Con Ed license application was heard by the Federal Power Commission in 1964, a throng of agitated citizens filled the normally vacant hearing room. Later that year a flotilla of small boats gathered in symbolic protest at the Storm King site, and villagers in Croton-on-Hudson turned off all their lights one night to demonstrate opposition to Con Ed's plans. Some citizens distributed bumper stickers proclaiming, "Dig They Won't" and launched the motto "Better dead than Con Ed." The Hudson became a touchstone for celebrities with environmental sensitivity. Robert Kennedy, Aaron Copland, and James Cagney joined the ranks of Hudson River supporters opposing Con Ed.

Scenic Hudson was plowing new ground with every action it took, and the result was a series of legal precedents which helped lay the foundation for environmental legislation. In 1965, just two years after the fight began, Scenic Hudson won a landmark decision in the U.S. Court of Appeals which affirmed the legal standing of citizens to seek preservation of natural beauty in rulings made under the Federal Power Act. That decision led to a 1970 court ruling upholding citizens' rights to sue for environmental protection in federal courts. The same principle was incorporated in the National Environmental Policy Act, passed by Congress in 1969.

The Storm King case dragged through the courts for 15 years while Scenic Hudson built a wall of public support around the mountain. Along the way a host of other environmental issues were dealt with, including a $20 million PCB removal project, a fisheries act aimed at restoring commercial and sport fisheries in the Hudson, and numerous other riparian enhancements.

In 1980, the case was finally resolved in favor of the mountain and the river. In a narrow sense the river's fate was decided through a series of legal decisions, but in reality the Storm King hydro plant was stopped, and the Hudson River was nursed back to health by an outpouring of public indignation and love. When the fight began there were no environmental remedies written into law, there was only public opinion, and public opinion prevailed.

The experience of Scenic Hudson highlights the most important rule in a river campaign: public support is key. Find a way to get the public on your side, and the current of opinion will carry you forward.

Create an Image for the River

An important first step in building popular support is the creation of an image for the river that communicates something appealing, important, and threatened.

During the 14-year battle to save North Carolina's New River from a twin-dam hydropower project, one image emerged which caught the nation's imagination: despite its name, the New River is a billion years old, it's the oldest river in North America, the second oldest river in the world. The New is a geologic treasure unique in the nation. That fact, translated into a campaign message, helped galvanize a national constituency which responded with one of the most massive and sustained lobbying efforts ever mounted for a river. The very old New River finally received federal protection in 1976.

The image you create for a river is an emotional bridge between the resource you're trying to protect and the public you're trying to recruit. So it's obvious you need to focus on something people care about. For New Hampshire's Wildcat River the choice was obvious: the spectacular waterfall tumbling through the town of Jackson.

It's often easier to arouse public interest in the protection of natural beauty than in complex and confusing ecological issues. The Tuolumne River Preservation Trust made much of their river's roots in Yosemite National Park, and Trust literature proclaimed that saving the Tuolumne was "like getting another Yosemite for free."

During the Rio Chama campaign, an aerial photographer produced a spectacular photo of the river canyon which was converted into a color brochure and distributed in every corner of New Mexico. That one photo became the image of the campaign, telling people at a glance why the river was worth protecting.

The Wildest River

The Tatshenshini, which carries glacial melt from the subarctic Yukon through British Columbia and into the Gulf of Alaska, has been touted as the wildest river in North America. Its watershed embraces the largest remaining undisturbed grizzly habitat and it flows through a wilderness of staggering size and beauty. Tatshenshini Wild, the group that spearheaded the successful effort to save the river from an enormous open-pit copper mine, promoted this image of pristine wilderness to great effect. International support for the Tatshenshini poured in and helped persuade the provincial government of British Columbia to protect the river in a mammoth national park.

Fish and wildlife also make appealing images and the endangered status of salmon on both American coasts has been used to generate support for numerous rivers, including the Sacramento and Mattole in California, the Penobscot in Maine, and the Sandy and John Day in Oregon.

Some largely urban rivers are less about wildlife than about people. The Charles River in Massachusetts flows through a heavily populated urban corridor and is a primary source of recreation and renewal for the hundreds of thousands of people who live near its banks. Rita Barron, the Charles River Watershed Association's former executive director, understood the importance of the river to all those people and she gave life to a term which came to define the Charles—"the people's river." The name fit so well it later became the title of a book about the Charles.

When Marion Stoddart decided to clean up the Nashua River the problem wasn't getting people to know the river was there—they could smell it from miles away. The problem was getting people to care. Congested with paper mill pulp and fouled with raw sewage, the Nashua looked, says Stoddart, "like a dirt road. Birds and small animals could walk across it . . . dead fish were lying belly-up, covered with flies." There wasn't much there to build a positive image around, but Stoddart had a vision of what the river could become. She tirelessly lobbied everyone she knew to promote an image of a restored Nashua with clean, clear water, green, tree-lined banks, and riverside parks. Then she set out to turn that image into reality.

The image you create for your river campaign may combine a variety of values, but the simpler you make it the easier it will be for the public to grasp it and for the media to hang stories on it. Which also means that the image should be aimed at the largest possible audience, not just at the people who know and use the river. You really haven't mobilized public support until you've reached beyond river lovers to the majority of people who never have and probably never will actually touch the river, who only see it from a highway or a bridge.

Try to make it clear that the natural values you are trying to protect in your river are irreplaceable; if they're lost they'll be lost forever. It helps, therefore, to have a clear and present danger.

Dramatize the Threat

There is an immutable law of human nature—we hesitate to act until a crisis confronts us. Building public support for a river campaign often means presenting the public with an impending crisis—the loss of something valuable, the possibility of an unacceptable risk, the payment of an inappropriate price.

Unacceptable loss was an underlying theme throughout the campaign for Sespe Creek. Keep the Sespe Wild made it clear they were fighting not just for the river but for species on the edge of extinction. A remnant of Southern California's last run of steelhead trout still migrated up Sespe Creek, and the handful of surviving California condors, reared in a captive breeding program, were being released into a wilderness area in the middle of the Sespe watershed. Nearly every newspaper and magazine article published about the river campaign highlighted the condors and their tenuous survival, suggesting that a threat to the Sespe was a threat to the condor.

Over time, the survival of both Sespe Creek and the California condor became entwined and that connection helped forge a powerful base of public support for the river.

There may be no other river with an icon species as endangered as the condor, but survival of the Pacific salmon has reached crisis stage on virtually all northwest coastal rivers, while the Atlantic salmon is struggling to stage a modest revival on a number of northeast streams.

Ongoing efforts to protect the Sacramento have been driven from the start by the threat to its fishery, which accounts for 60 to 70 percent of California's commercial salmon catch. The ambitious work of the Mattole Restoration Council—to rehabilitate an entire watershed—was initiated to preserve a salmon fishery. The Nature Conservancy and Oregon Trout are pushing a campaign to protect and restore 17.5 miles of the John Day River. "At stake," says a campaign brochure, "is the ultimate survival of native salmon and steelhead in Oregon." It would be hard to define a river threat more simply or powerfully than that.

To publicize the threat to a riparian species, you don't necessarily have to drag out the Endangered Species Act, which may be a useful tool in some river protection campaigns, but its record is mixed; it is usually invoked only after a species is already in crisis, and it is not always an effective method for building public support.

The infamous snail darter of the Little Tennessee River managed to delay completion of Tellico dam, but in the furor over a nondescript fish, the public debate ignored the real issues—which included the loss of a prized trout stream, inundation of a whole valley of prime farmland, and the burial of sacred Indian sites. In the end, the snail darter was perceived more as a red herring than an endangered species and the dam was built. Be wary, therefore, of relying on the ESA. It's hard to mobilize public support by dramatizing the threat to obscure species.

For some rivers, the threat isn't to a species or single, outstanding feature, but to the entire river corridor. When, in the 1960s, the Bureau of Reclamation tried to build two dams inside the Grand Canyon—dams which would have drowned two-thirds of the river corridor along with spectacular side canyons like Havasu—Interior Secretary Stewart Udall told the U.S. Senate that flooding the canyon could make it more accessible by boat. David Brower, then president of the Sierra Club, dramatized that threat with a full-page ad in the *New York Times* which asked, "Should we also flood the Sistine Chapel so tourists can get nearer the ceiling?"

Threats to the Human Species

Some river threats present unacceptable risks to the human species. Revived plans for a multipurpose Auburn Dam on the American River above Sacramento gave Friends of the River an opportunity to resurrect a threat the media had chosen to ignore: the potential for an earthquake-induced catastrophic flood. When project supporters got busy whipping up new interest for the dam in 1990, Friends of the River recruited two geologists and held a press conference on the steps of the historic Capital. Directing television cameras to a spot 40 feet up the stately building, they demonstrated where floodwaters would reach if the proposed dam broke. The geologists then released a detailed report challenging the safety of the Bureau of Reclamation's design and questioning whether any dam could be safely built at the site.

The health and safety of both fish and people was dramatized by the New England Coastal Campaign (NECC) during a fight against a coal-fired power plant on the Penobscot River in Maine. Critics of the power plant, including an environmental group called STOP (State Taxpayers Opposed to Pollution), argued that air pollution from the plant would endanger public health and that thermal pollution could damage the Atlantic salmon run, which is gaining a foothold in the river. At the time, NECC released an annual "Terrible Ten" list of the worst pollution threats along the New England coast and in 1990 STOP got the Penobscot power plant added to the list. This received widespread publicity and helped persuade the local planning board to reject the plant.

A Gift to the Governor

When Marion Stoddart wanted to demonstrate how filthy the Nashua River had become, she put it in a bottle and gave it to the governor of Massachusetts. Stoddart was trying to get Governor John Volpe to support passage of the state's first clean water legislation, a goal most observers thought was impossible so late in that legislative year. But in 1966 her Nashua River Cleanup Committee collected 6000 signatures on a petition, gathered together an entourage of local elected officials and business people, and descended on the governor's office. There they gave Volpe the bottle of filthy river water and told him they wanted the clean water bill passed. Volpe was shocked by the quality of the sample and promised to keep it on his desk. By the end of the summer he had signed the legislation into law.

Whatever means you use to dramatize the threat to your river, there are three important points to keep in mind.

First, you should make it clear to the public that the threat to their river isn't being addressed by their government, that nothing will happen to save their river unless they get involved. Only a handful of rivers have been protected through the initiative of government agencies.

Second, however you dramatize the threat, you've got to back it up with solid research. Don't make claims until you have reliable data to make your case. When STOP got the Penobscot added to the NECC's Terrible Ten list, they buttressed the listing with reams of expert analysis and public testimony.

Third, keep the threat alive in the public's mind. Don't let people forget that the river is in danger until the danger is gone. That's a tough challenge for a campaign that could last for years, but one of the keys to building public support is maintaining it over a long period of time. Successful campaigns do that by learning to conduct the media like a marching band.

Cultivate the Media

Media exposure is the key to building public support. Without it, your campaign and your cause are virtually invisible. It's a harsh reality but it's true. The good news is that rivers are "mediagenic"; TV cameras love them and print reporters tend to wax euphoric when writing about rivers they've just run. Put reporters on your river and you'll start generating stories.

That's what Pete Lavigne did on the Merrimack and the result was a blizzard of media coverage, including a week-long series of front-page newspaper articles detailing the state of the river. The Merrimack is the birthplace of the industrial revolution in America. Its banks and its tributaries were once lined with factories—mile upon mile of red brick mills powered by moving water. It was the most important working river in the nation, teeming with industry and reeking with filth. It took the Clean Water Act, and about $600 million to clean up the Merrimack, and while its waters aren't yet pristine, they are much improved. So much improved that cities along its 116-mile length are withdrawing drinking water in ever-increasing volumes, which is putting a new kind of strain on the river.

To highlight the problems created by development in the watershed, and to call public attention to the needs of the river, Lavigne organized a 16-day "Source to Sea" canoe trip from the Merrimack's headwaters in north central New Hampshire to its Massachusetts mouth on the Atlantic. Lavigne, then executive director of the Merrimack River Watershed Council, milked the trip for maximum media exposure by organizing press conferences en route, doing daily radio interviews, and inviting journalists along for a paddle. That single canoe trip reaped incalculable benefits in free publicity and it cemented positive relationships with numerous members of the media.

Cultivating relationships with key members of the media can have profound results. The *Los Angeles Times* is the biggest and most influential newspaper in the West. Until the early 1980s, the *Times* had a mixed record

Merrimack River at Lowell, Massachusetts. (Photo courtesy of Tim Palmer.)

on issues relating to rivers and water policy. That was partly because no one on the editorial page staff had a passion for the subject. No one that is, until veteran journalist and assistant editorial page editor Jack Burby began running rivers. Burby went down the Stanislaus, he went down the Tuolumne. He began talking to Friends of the River, who were happy to cultivate him. When he learned that the Tuolumne was targeted for a trio of dams, he was galvanized. His editorial voice rang out from the pages of the West's biggest newspaper with passion and eloquent conviction: the Tuolumne must be saved.

But Burby didn't stop there. He spent months researching river issues and water policy. He became an expert on the subject and his new-found authority transformed the editorial tone of the *Times*. One man falling in love with rivers influenced the editorial direction of the most powerful newspaper in the state.

Putting media people on the river is the easy part. Finding the right ones takes some work. But it's worth the effort to find people in the media with some predisposition to listen to you sympathetically, or at the very least neutrally. Not every newspaper and TV station has an environmental reporter and not every environmental reporter is competent to cover the subject intelligently. But you can usually find the best prospects by consulting with other environmental organizations and reviewing their lists of media contacts. Look for reporters with a track record of thoughtful coverage on environmental issues. Seek out reporters who are also anglers or boaters or backpackers.

If you're not sure about the prejudices and politics of a major media outlet, it may be better to postpone personal contact until you've had time to ferret out the most promising members of the staff. Media relationships are among the most important you will develop. Cultivate them carefully.

When you develop a media list make it comprehensive. Don't limit your scope to the big metropolitan dailies and the network stations. The first newspaper to endorse protection of the Stanislaus River was a weekly. For a long time it was the only newspaper endorsement Friends of the River had and they made good use of it as a reprint. Local television stations are thirsty for low-budget news stories and graphic footage. The coverage will more than likely be superficial but the exposure is free. And don't forget radio, which provides a substantial portion of the public's news diet.

Making a Media Kit

Once you've put a list together, it's time to make contact. In an ideal world you will have assembled a complete media kit before you announce your campaign. In the real world you'll do it as soon as you can find the money. But this is one thing not to scrimp on. A sloppy, poorly organized media kit suggests a sloppy, poorly organized campaign. Reporters and editors are cynical; they deal with reams of information daily. To get their attention, your information has to stand out.

Journalists will respond positively to a package of information that is professionally presented, well organized, and, perhaps most important, not overwhelmed with hyperbole. Don't call your opponents bad names, don't make wild claims, just state the facts. A good media kit announces that you are credible and quotable, that you know what you're talking about and that you can provide valuable information on an important subject. Be sure to include in each media kit an invitation for a personal tour of the river.

Typically, a media kit will contain at least the following:

1. A general press release announcing the organization's purpose, details about the campaign, people to contact.
2. A fact sheet describing in greater detail the river and the problems confronting it, including your best description of a long-term alternative solution. A question-and-answer format is sometimes useful. This is the most important part of the package.
3. Carefully selected newspaper clippings and/or background papers relating to the river and the issue in question.
4. A map of the river and a good black-and-white glossy photo, if you can

afford to have some printed. (It's important to place the river and the threats to it in geographic and pictorial context.)

5. A page of quotes from prominent and professional people saying nice things about your river and your cause.
6. A selected bibliography to facilitate the self-education of dedicated journalists.
7. A list of your board of directors and staff with brief biographies of key people, along with addresses and telephone numbers of those who will serve as media contacts.

This last point leads us to a fundamental rule: you should assign the role of representing your organization and river campaign to only a few people. Media inquiries should be directed to those people exclusively, and those people should be clear among themselves about the organization's agenda and its position on sensitive or complex issues. More than one environmental organization has been impaled by the ego or ignorance of the wrong staff member who, seduced by the media spotlight, offers inaccurate information or an inappropriate opinion.

In the world of your dreams, of course, you will have enough money to hire a media coordinator to ensure that all these things happen smoothly. In the real world you'll probably depend on volunteers or already overworked staff members. Whichever world you live in, be sure to list one or two names on each press release and media message for reporters to call for further information.

Videos and Slide Shows

In this age of images it may not be enough to have just a press kit; some people would argue that you also need a video or, at the very least, a slide show. For organizations of modest means, a video may seem out of the question, although broadcast-quality work can be done with a simple Hi–8 camcorder and editing deck. If you have to hire out, a professionally produced video will cost you at least $1000 per minute.

A simpler course of action is a slide show converted to video with a musical sound track and narration. With a good volunteer photographer, access to a sound studio, and a script you write yourself, it's possible to put a decent slide show together for a few hundred dollars.

A slide show or video is, of course, a basic organizing tool and something you're going to need anyway to make public presentations. But its value as a media handout can't be exaggerated; if the images are stunning and the message is gripping, a good video is better than the best press release. And if you shoot broadcast-quality tape, or at least Hi–8, you may find local television stations willing to use your footage in their coverage.

After you've fired the first broadside of information into the media swamp, wait long enough for the information to arrive and then follow with a phone call. Ask for a brief face-to-face meeting with the reporter or editor or producer in question. The goal here is to establish a personal relationship. If you have a technical expert available, take that person along to buttress your credibility. Go to the meeting with a number of specific story ideas the person you're cultivating may want to pursue. Make it clear that you and your staff are always available for background and perspective on any stories relating to rivers and water issues. The people you see quoted repeatedly in newspapers and on television are there both because they have some special expertise and because they have some special media relationships.

An Annual Media Pilgrimage

From all of this it should be clear that good media coverage doesn't just happen, it is carefully cultivated. One of the best examples of that rule is the relationship developed with local media by the Olympic Rivers Council in Washington. To maintain a strong relationship with newspapers on the Olympic Peninsula, members of the Council schedule an annual "pilgrimage" to meet with their staffs. Carol Volk, a Council member, explains the process: "We present them each with a current media packet—up-to-date documents on our organization and river-related issues, plus the never-outdated 'standard' information like a copy of the Washington State Scenic Rivers Act, the federal Wild and Scenic Rivers Act . . . so this information will be at their fingertips for easy reference.

"We wrap this all up," Volk continues, "with a nice cover letter inviting them to please call on us if they have any questions and, most importantly, to please call us for a second opinion on controversial subjects, to hopefully avoid printing incorrect information. When an incorrect statement *is* made, we immediately provide an editorial with correct information, and also remind the author to use the reference provided and/or call us in the future . . . The newspaper folks appreciate having a reliable reference in ORC, and feel comfortable calling upon us for information and opinions."

Developing and nurturing media contacts is the first step in working with the media. We'll discuss the second step—utilizing those contacts in a fully orchestrated media campaign—in the next chapter.

Produce a Basic Brochure

Think of a brochure as the business card for your organization and river campaign. Like a business card, it should tell the reader a lot with very few words. It should be informative but simple, compelling but brief. Almost anyone can knock out a quick brochure on a Macintosh, but if you want a professional job, hire a professional to do it. Unless you know a trained graphic artist willing to volunteer her or his talent, accept the fact that this will cost you hard money.

Before you start on a brochure, decide the specific purpose you want it to serve. Most organizations need a basic piece to introduce themselves to the public. But if your organization is planning a variety of different programs, or will be confronting a number of different issues, you may find you need more than one brochure.

A basic brochure should be general enough to avoid early obsolescence, which is why it's not wise to include references to pending legislation, legal decisions, or other time-sensitive events unless they are the principal focus of your campaign. Frequent revisions are expensive and time-consuming, although some groups get around this problem by printing inserts updating old information. While there's no single model for a river campaign brochure, the following formula covers the basics.

1. *Dramatically describe the river.* Tatshenshini Wild created an excellent brochure that opened with these words: "Tatshenshini is North American wilderness on the grandest scale: a river 6 times larger than the Colorado, peaks towering almost 3 miles high, the world's largest non-polar icefields, and everywhere countless glaciers." Your river isn't likely to warrant such grandiose language but you should summarize its attributes as dramatically and succinctly as possible.

The cover statement, or headline, should be short and catchy. The Nashua River Watershed Association's brochure states, "A good river is hard to find . . . help save it." A Friends of the River brochure asks, "How much is a wild river worth?" River Network's brochure says simply, "Helping people save rivers."

2. *Describe the problem.* State the facts with minimum emotion and maximum clarity; river threats are usually sufficiently disturbing to need no rhetorical embellishment. And avoid professional jargon like "nonpoint source pollution" and even "riparian", which simply confuse many readers.

3. *Describe the solution.* Without committing yourself prematurely to promises you're not yet prepared to make, briefly outline an alternative which could solve the problem and still save the river. You don't need a lot of detail, just the basic idea.

4. *Describe the organization.* At this point you'll be glad you've already developed a mission and goals statement because this is a perfect place to use it.

5. *Invite membership.* Never, never, never hand out campaign literature without offering people a way to support you. Every brochure should have a box on the back with basic membership information and donation options.

6. *Include pretty pictures.* Photographs will describe your river in ways words never can. There are exceptions to this rule (the Westport River Watershed Alliance has a very attractive brochure illustrated with pen and ink drawings) but, in general, photos are a must. Which leads directly to the Great Color Debate. All brochures should have full-color photos. Unless you don't have any good color photos. Unless you can't afford color. Unless you believe color is a waste of money that should be spent on the campaign.

A full-color brochure will cost two to four times as much as one in black and white. Many people would argue color is worth the price. Others disagree. The Tatshenshini Wild brochure works very effectively with black and white photos and a one-color accent. Your decision will be dictated in part by your budget, but most graphic artists would agree that good paper, even more than color, should be a top priority. A creatively designed brochure printed on cheap paper looks like a cheap brochure. And speaking of cost, don't ever print anything without getting at least three bids. Printing prices can vary as much as 200 percent for the same job.

When it comes to design and format, the best advice is to steal what you like from other people's brochures. Go to the nearest environmental center, or attend an environmental conference, and collect samples. Or stop by the local chamber of commerce which will have a rack full of brochures from local businesses. And River Network has a whole file of river brochures you can sample from. Find what you like and have an artist adapt it to your needs.

Format is usually a foregone conclusion. The vast majority of brochures are multiples of a four-by-nine inch fold, with as many panels as are necessary to include the desired information. The size is dictated by the shape of a number 10 envelope. The next most popular option is 5.5 by 8 inches, for which there is also a standard envelope. If you want to create a brochure with a more distinctive format, be sure there's an envelope to fit it. Nonstandard brochures are usually more expensive because printers have to trim them out of standard-sized sheets of paper.

Maybe the most important decision about a brochure is having one. If you don't, your campaign lacks a handy calling card and you lose a simple and effective method for spreading the word about your river. A brochure is one of those fundamental resources a successful campaign relies on. The real question isn't whether you need one but how many you can afford.

Foundations and large donors are often willing to fund production of brochures.

Get VIPs on the River

It's a little-known fact that Moses once paddled the Tuolumne. So did Dr. Kildare. And both men took part in the campaign to protect the river. Or at least the actors who played them did. Charlton Heston didn't exactly part the waters as he plunged through the big hole at Clavey Falls, and Richard Chamberlain performed no riverside surgery, but each man played a role in the campaign to win federal protection for the beleaguered river, and they both generated a flood of media attention.

Their separate trips occurred during the Tuolumne Wild and Scenic campaign at a time when then-California Senator Pete Wilson was still sitting on the fence. Heston, a personal friend, emerged from his Tuolumne trip convinced the river should be saved and shared his revelations with Wilson. Chamberlain made a special visit to Washington to testify before Congress on behalf of the Tuolumne. It was one of his better performances, an impassioned plea for "one of the most magnificent natural wonders I've ever experienced or seen."

Very Important People are valuable assets for any river campaign and they don't have to be Hollywood idols or famous rock stars to be effective. Anyone with prominence and power is a VIP and capable of drawing public attention and support to your cause. That includes elected officials, legislative staff, media, performers, writers, filmmakers, financial supporters, even clergy, whose sermons have on more than one occasion preached the gospel of river protection.

In the fight to save the Gauley, commercial outfitters funneled VIPs by the boatload down the river. One of those VIPs was West Virginia Congressman Nick Rahall who (with his legislative assistant Jim Zoia) was responsible for engineering Congressional protection. Rahall ran the Class IV–V Gauley several times and became a passionate supporter of river recreation.

Magic Spun on a River

The river itself is always more persuasive than any amount of lobbying in the corridors of power. David Brown credits a key encounter on a river trip for victory in a three-year fight to protect in-stream flows on the Ocoee. The Tennessee Valley Authority, which was completing renovation of a hydropower diversion flume, was preparing to shut the tap on the Ocoee, which had become the third most popular whitewater river in the nation. Brown knew that the one person who could turn the TVA around was Tennessee Senator Howard Baker, the Authority's best ally in Washington. And Brown also knew that the one man who could turn Baker around was Tennessee governor Lamar Alexander. Alexander was close to Baker, he had been down the Ocoee, he had voiced support for the river. But, as the deadline for TVA's planned diversion approached, he hadn't taken action.

Brown, who was then executive director of the Ocoee River Council, heard that the governor was going to take a vacation trip on the Colorado River through the Grand Canyon. Knowing the magic that can be spun on a river, Brown worked his way onto the trip and, at an opportune moment while standing on a sandbar, explained to Alexander the urgency of the situation. TVA was about to complete the diversion project and dewater the Ocoee "forever."

It's hard not to agree that rivers are sacred when you're in the bottom of the Grand Canyon. Alexander told Brown, "I'll call Howard Baker when I get back."

The governor was true to his word and Senator Baker engineered a $7 million appropriation to compensate TVA for guaranteeing the release of recreational flows 116 days per year for 35 years. Commercial outfitters are reimbursing the U.S. Treasury, and so far are ahead of schedule.

Stuart Udall, who served Presidents Kennedy and Johnson as Secretary of the Interior, had an on-river revelation of historic importance. As an Arizona congressman, Udall had supported dams in the Grand Canyon, but as Interior Secretary he began having second thoughts, despite his comments about dams increasing access for tourists. Ambivalence turned to solid opposition after a raft trip through the Canyon. "When I came off the river," Udall told author Tim Palmer, "I knew we were going to abandon the dams." (James Watt, Interior Secretary for Ronald Reagan, proved the exception to more than one rule: After the first two days of a Grand Canyon raft trip he announced he was bored and was helicoptered out.)

The Rio Chama Preservation Trust had among its members numerous commercial outfitters and private boaters and thus had the resources to organize countless river trips. Central to the Trust's strategy was convincing U.S. Senator Pete Domenici to support Wild and Scenic designation. And the only way to convince Domenici was to convince the City of Albuquerque it didn't need water storage on the Chama. To do that, the Trust took every member of the City Council, along with their families, on overnight Chama float trips. "In the end," says former Trust Chair Phil Wallin, "what saved the Chama was our ability to show it to key people on overnight trips."

Friends of the River has been benevolently brainwashing VIPs with river trips for almost 20 years and now has an ongoing program of putting important people on endangered rivers. Jerry Brown was running for governor of California in the early days of the Stanislaus campaign, and F.O.R. guided him down the river during a campaign swing through the Sierra foothills, an experience that helped make him an important ally when he was elected governor. (Brown ended his Stanislaus trip by shaking the hands and asking for the votes of a throng of Hells Angels camped at the take-out.)

Most rivers are navigable to some degree and if you can float a canoe you can organize a trip, even if it's brief. Friends of the Los Angeles River staged a "first descent" float trip on Earth Day 1990 to attract media and to give a key state senator a little time on the water. The trip down the mostly concrete channel lasted less than 100 yards, but the media got good images and the publicity was priceless.

During the Merrimack Source-to-Sea trip in 1989, New Hampshire's Governor and Attorney General, the New Hampshire Commissioner of Environmental Services, the Massachusetts Secretary of Environmental Affairs, a Massachusetts state senator and state representatives from both states joined the flotilla for a series of paddles downriver. The VIPs were part of a throng of more than 300 people who paddled the river, and they helped boost press coverage, which totaled some 35 newspaper articles, 12 radio interviews, and included television footage.

Putting important people on your river should be a carefully organized, continuing campaign strategy. One of the reasons Tatshenshini Wild was successful in generating worldwide attention for a little-known watershed in a remote part of British Columbia is that they relentlessly recruited important people to paddle down their river.

Doing the same for your river means making lists of influential people whose support you need, courting those people, and finding the appropriate guides and equipment to get them safely on the water. Whenever possible, utilize commercial outfitters that have the professional expertise, and the insurance, to guarantee that the trips are well-run and safe. The last thing you want to do is drown an important supporter.

Cultivate Alliances with Political Leaders

Without Pete Domenici, the Chama fight would have been lost. Without Senators Alan Cranston and Pete Wilson, the Tuolumne would have been dammed. Without the conversion of John Volpe, the Nashua wouldn't have been restored. Without the intercession of Ted Kennedy and Tip O'Neil, the Natural Valley Storage plan on the Charles River would have died. Without Nick Rahall, the Gauley would be dry.

It doesn't matter whether you're fighting a dam, stopping pollution, challenging development, or promoting a river management plan, you can't do it without support from political leaders. And it doesn't matter whether you're dealing with a U.S. Senator or a county commissioner or a member of the town council. At some point you may be dealing with all those people, so it's a fundamental part of building public support that you cultivate relationships and build alliances with them.

When Edward King was elected Governor of Massachusetts in 1980, the Charles River Watershed Association organized a ceremony on the banks of the river making King an honorary resident of the watershed. They did so despite the fact that King had a prodevelopment record inconsistent with watershed protection. That strategy paid off a few months later when a developer began pressuring King to relax rules for a sewer permit. CRWA told the Governor's office they objected to relaxation of permit requirements, the Governor then refused to intervene, and the developer had to follow the permit rules.

It's harder for elected officials and other public servants to be sensitive to your issues if they don't know you personally. Rita Barron says it's important to "build friendships with public officials so that when you go to ask them for something, they see a friend coming through the door. Otherwise they will dive under the desk." So part of the process of building public support means an aggressive outreach campaign to political leaders, meaning prominent lawyers, union executives, big donors, realtors, in short, people who know and influence people.

You can use almost the same strategy for political leaders as you do for the media. Put together a list of key contacts, prepare information kits and set up appointments. Your key contacts should include all the power brokers capable of influencing the fate of your river and your list should be relentlessly bipartisan. These are the political leaders you need to keep in contact with, whether you have their initial support or not. Some activists even mount flow charts on their office walls with the names and status of all political leaders they need to work.

Start Early, Research Positions

The outreach process should begin early in your river campaign. As soon as possible, set up meetings with key political leaders to brief them on the threat to the river, to explain your goals, and to solicit their support. (In the long run you'll deal more with staff members, but whenever possible insist on meeting with the leader directly.)

Never go into these meetings without first researching your politician's background, interests, record, and probable position on river protection.

Shape your presentation to fit the politician's interests and look for ways to make protecting your river a politically attractive proposition. If your politician can appear visionary and take credit for a major environmental victory, all the better.

If there are prominent people involved in your campaign (and if there aren't, get some), trot them out for initial contact with the politicians you meet. If your organization has developed a significant membership base, or has support from other organizations with big memberships, make it clear to the politician that a large number of her or his constituents support river protection.

Several things will result from these meetings. Some politicians will enthusiastically embrace your cause, will offer to carry legislation, influence other politicians, and lobby on behalf of your river. Others will be cautious and noncommittal, waiting to see which way the political winds are blowing and what their constituents think. Still others will openly oppose you. All this feedback is valuable, and is important to have early in the campaign so that you can tailor your strategy to political reality. Even people openly opposed to your river protection campaign will give you valuable insight into the political hurdles ahead.

As FDR suggested at the beginning of this chapter, some political leaders will express sympathy for your cause but will ask you to generate evidence of popular support before they take action. "You generate the letters," a powerful member of Congress once told Friends of the River, "and I'll generate the support."

You can also generate letters to change a politician's mind or push her or him off the fence. Be careful, however, not to attack political opponents personally. Today's adversary could be tomorrow's ally, unless you've already scorched the common ground you might someday meet on.

A case in point: During the 1990 election, one of the nation's leading environmental organizations chose not to endorse the reelection of a prominent U.S. Senator. But rather than leaving the issue there, a top spokesman for the group denounced the senator in the media. The senator, who won the campaign handily, was incensed by the remarks and vowed in private not to cooperate with the group again. The climate between the parties has since warmed somewhat, but unnecessary damage was done.

Build Local Support through Public Events

The Grand River wanders for 256 miles through south-central Michigan before emptying into Lake Michigan west of Grand Rapids. Although the city of Lansing, through which the Grand also flows, holds an annual festival to celebrate the river, ignorance about the Grand is widespread, as are the classic problems of poor land use planning in the watershed, illegal discharges, polluted runoff, and erosion.

That lack of public familiarity makes solving the river's problems more difficult. To address that issue, Verlen and Valerie Kruger organized an epic canoe trip on the Grand. It was an appropriate step for the Krugers, both because they live on the river and because they have made epic trips their life's work. Verlen won international fame with Steve Landick for a 28,000 mile paddle around and through North America. Verlen and Valerie later paddled 21,000 miles from the Arctic Ocean to Cape Horn.

The Krugers conceived this trip, which they called Grand River Expedition '90, as a means of raising public awareness about the river. They were astonished by the level of interest. A total of 125 people in 55 canoes joined the 14-day float. Along the way they picked up trash, conducted water-quality surveys, developed educational displays, collected oral histories, and generated enormous publicity. Four Campfire Girls conducted a turtle count while a member of the Soil Conservation Service did a streambank erosion survey. The Expedition also gave a healthy boost to the efforts of a local environmental group to launch the Grand River Watershed Council, with the aim of creating a network of river protection interests.

Festivals, Races, and Auctions

The Grand River Expedition is only one of numerous examples around the nation of events which brought people together and built public support for a river. Many river conservation groups conduct regular events to involve and educate the public, have fun, and raise money. For example:

We've already mentioned the Gauley and Ocoee River Festivals, which built support, raised money, and gave paddlers and activists a sense of community and a feeling of power.

Montana's Clark Fork Coalition has raised both money and public interest through a unique triathalon in which contestants have to paddle upriver half a mile, then hook some form of "trash" fish within 30 minutes, and finally run back to the starting line collecting a requisite amount of trash en route.

The Charles River Watershed Association hosts an annual canoe race which draws upwards of 2000 paddlers and culminates in a riverside celebration with information displays, music, and food. There is also a popular swim designed, says Rita Barron, "to show people that they can go into the Charles and not come out with two heads and looking purple."

The South Yuba River Citizen's League gathers significant support in the Sierra foothills from an annual auction that nets as much as $20,000 and provides a social focus to the organization's river protection activities. Auctions, because they often involve months of volunteer involvement in planning and organization, as well as cooperation from the business community, are an effective way of getting the public involved in your campaign.

Friends of the River, which has developed valuable relationships in the Southern California entertainment community, has had its greatest success penetrating Hollywood through the organization of an annual auction. The money raised is an important benefit, but equally important have been the friendships and contacts developed through auction activities which have helped build a much stronger base of public support in Southern California.

Several river groups have organized public school projects to involve and educate school children about river issues. One of the most ambitious of these programs is conducted by a group on the Fox River in Illinois. Friends of the Fox River has developed a monitoring program which now enrolls 110 classes at 30 different schools whose students adopt a site on the river, sample and test it four times a year, and then report the data. Teachers incorporate the program into their curricula and students become budding activists.

One group of Fox River students, freshly charged with their river-monitoring training, caught a company illegally dumping construction waste in the flood plain of the river and alerted authorities.

River clean ups are being organized coast-to-coast and have taken an interesting new twist with formation of the Divers Environmental Survey, a group of SCUBA divers in Massachusetts who have begun cleaning rivers from the bottom up. River clean ups are also good for networking and coalition building because they are labor-intensive and provide a convenient excuse for a variety of groups to work together and strengthen ties.

Annual events, reliably repeated every year, help provide an ongoing support base of volunteers and provide public evidence of the organization's continuity. Conferences, while time-consuming and complicated to produce, can have a major impact on public awareness. One of the biggest river conferences in the nation was started by Friends of the River some 14 years ago as a modest attempt to unite the river community and promote public support. Today it draws more than a thousand people to three days of workshops, speeches, exhibits, swap meets, dinners, dances, and non-stop schmoozing. The whole thing is produced by a volunteer committee with one staff coordinator, and the experience has given birth to an extended community of committed activists.

Identify and Recruit Your Natural Constituency

When you set out to build public support for a river, you are really doing two different things; on the one hand you are building a broad political base among the general public so that when an issue is put to a vote, when public opinion surveys are taken, when candidates run for office, when there is an opportunity for the general public to express itself, that expression will favor your river.

On the other hand, you are also inspiring and recruiting activists, you are building a community of people who care enough to take some form of direct action, which may be as simple as writing a letter or making a phone call to an elected representative or as complex as volunteering to work in the campaign. And while activists may emerge from any corner of the political map, most of them will come from constituencies with a direct interest in the river. Identifying and recruiting those natural constituencies is, therefore, a vitally important and highly rewarding step.

On the Stanislaus and the Tuolumne and the Payette and the Chama and the Gauley, a key constituency was recreational boaters—whitewater lovers unwilling to surrender their playgrounds. They turned out by the hundreds and they made a major difference. On the Great Whale in Quebec it is the Cree and Inuit, whose homeland and culture is literally being drowned by the world's largest hydropower project. On the Sandy River in Oregon, the natural constituencies are property owners seeking protection for a watershed threatened by too much development, and fisher folk who prize the river's abundant salmon runs.

Natural constituencies are usually a latent force, hibernating until someone wakes them up. The vast majority of people with a vested interest in a river will not spontaneously act to protect it, often because they don't know quite what to do. If they did, most river threats would be nipped in the bud.

When California gravel companies, which had already ripped apart the bed of the Russian River, began moving up onto the terraces above the river, they encountered an angry activist named Martin Griffin. Griffin owned a riverside winery and vineyard and he knew that the only way to stop the gravel companies was to organize other vineyard owners along the river. In the late 1980s he gathered together a constituency with a vested interest in protecting the river corridor, secured a court injunction, and initiated ongoing political and legal resistance.

Recruiting support from other environmental groups makes obvious sense, although the obvious is sometimes overlooked. Always remember to contact local chapters of the Audubon Club, the Sierra Club, the Native Plant Society, Trout Unlimited, Ducks Unlimited, and other conservation organizations. And don't be shy about asking for space in their newsletters or time at their board meetings to pitch your cause.

Landowners, as we will explore in greater detail below, are a natural constituency without which many river campaigns would fail. In the Northeast, where millions of people live close to their rivers, riparian landowners are the biggest single constituency for river protection. There is an assumption among some activists that riverside landowners will be hostile to efforts to protect their river, and contact is therefore avoided. While such hostility sometimes exists, without landowner support, efforts to protect private land rivers are doomed.

Find Some Unlikely Allies

It's more than a hackneyed cliche: Politics makes strange bedfellows. Among the unlikely allies who have had major impacts on river protection campaigns are the Army Corps of Engineers, the United Mine Workers Union, two of California's biggest agribusiness water users, the National Taxpayers Union, and an army base.

In September 1992, it was crunch time for the American River. A Congressional bill authorizing construction of an expandable flood control project—the "dry" version of Auburn Dam—had cleared every committee hurdle and was being debated on the House floor. Construction and operation of the project would have wrecked part of the American River canyon, destabilized upstream slopes, and laid the foundation for a river-killing multipurpose reservoir.

Friends of the River, American Rivers, and a host of other environmental groups had been combing the Capital for last minute muscle to oppose authorization of the dam when someone suggested the National Taxpayers Union. By no stretch of the imagination an environmental lobby, the NTU is nevertheless devoted to battling boondoggles and government giveaways. Since the proposed Auburn Dam would have provided twice the level of flood protection required by federal regulations, and since far cheaper, nonstructural alternatives were available, the NTU found the authorization bill an irresistible target to oppose. That opposition wasn't the only reason the dam was voted down, but it certainly helped and it illustrates the value of looking for unlikely allies.

If the National Taxpayer's Union seems like a strange source of support for a river campaign, think about the Army Corps of Engineers. After all, Arthur Morgan's authoritative history of the Corps was titled, "Dams and Other Disasters." But, as you will recall from the last chapter, the Corps of Engineers actually initiated a flood control plan on the Charles River based not on dams but on the natural storage capacity of wetlands.

The alliance between the Corps and the Charles River Watershed Association didn't stop with this enlightened proposal. It took a working partnership between the two to bring the idea to life. Getting the Corps' Natural Valley Storage plan approved in the face of resistance from the Nixon Administration's Office of Management and Budget took political arm twisting the Corps couldn't do by itself. So Rita Barron, an arm twister extraordinaire, enlisted the help of Senator Ted Kennedy who did a legislative end run to authorize the plan. Later, when appropriation money was being held up, Barron twisted Tip O'Neil's arm to clear the road block. Lobbying for the Corps of Engineers, instead of against it, could give hard core river savers an identity crisis, but the Charles River experience teaches us never to write off anyone.

Labor unions have a pattern of favoring dam projects for the construction jobs they create, but that pattern is by no means universal. During the Gauley campaign, the United Mine Workers union became a staunch ally of the river. That happened after Nick Rahall's congressional staff showed the union that hydropower developed by the Gauley would displace coal mining jobs. And in another example, the Grain Millers Union helped persuade a major food processing plant to oppose construction of a hazardous waste landfill on the banks of the Weldon Fork of the Grand River in Missouri.

A far stranger political alliance occurred during one of California's epic water wars when two powerful agricultural companies helped defeat a water project they actually wanted. A statewide referendum in 1980 sought voter approval for a massive canal project to divert water to Southern California around the Sacramento–San Joaquin Delta, the most important estuary on the west side of the western hemisphere. Although a companion measure would have provided significant environmental safeguards, most environmental groups opposed the so-called "peripheral canal" fearing it would allow Southern California water interests to drain Northern California's already overworked rivers and take too much water from the Delta. Most farmers, on the other hand, supported the canal, thirsting for ever more irrigation water.

In August of that year public opinion polls showed the canal plan ahead by 46 to 27 percent, with 26 percent undecided. Three months later the canal was overwhelmingly defeated at the polls. The dramatic turn-around in public opinion can be credited in no small part to the massive infusion of anticanal money by two giant agricultural companies who wanted the canal, but without its environmental safeguards. Their reasoning was that water development interests had the legislative power to eventually get what they wanted and there was no reason, therefore, to settle for a canal plan which limited the water available for export. It was a cynical strategy but environmentalists were willing to dance, at least this time, with the devil. And, so far, it has proven to be a failed strategy; numerous efforts to revive the canal since then have failed.

From the Army with Love

Equally unusual but far more positive was the working relationship that developed between the Nashua River Watershed Association and Fort Devens, a major military reservation through which the Nashua River flowed. After initiating the effort that would eventually clean up the Nashua's waters, Marion Stoddart moved on to the task of creating a permanent greenway along the river. Out of the blue she got a call from General Jack Cushman, commanding officer of Fort Devens. Recalls Stoddart, "He told me that Fort Devens has a vested interest in cleaning up the Nashua River. He said to me, what can I do to help?"

What he could do turned out to be a lot. Stoddart had never been to Fort Devens and had never thought of it as a potential ally in her Nashua crusade. But Cushman had eight miles of the Nashua in his reservation and was interested in improving community relations. So Fort Devens gave the Nashua River Watershed Association not just an office, but an entire two-story building, cleaned up, painted and maintained just for them. With the office came civil engineers, landscape architects, a lawyer, a CPA to help set up the new organization's books, a car, and a limitless supply of Vietnam vets to perform all manner of volunteer work.

Later on, with sponsorship from the EPA and the Department of Labor, Fort Devens hosted an environmental education program for disadvantaged teenagers, coordinated through the NRWA office. The program was called Project CURB (Clean Up Our River Banks) and that's precisely what the kids did, by the hundreds, over five months. "Fort Devens," says Stoddart, "provided 13 Green Berets and 13 big trucks that the Green Berets would drive around to pick up these kids to take to their work sites along the river."

Despite the Fort Devens experience, unlikely allies rarely just walk in the door; more often they require careful recruitment. A good course of action for finding them is to make a list of all constituencies with any kind of interest in the river, and then search for even the smallest common ground you think you may share with any of them. This will require, among other things, that you set aside some of your own prejudices. We are divided as much by attitudes as we are by actions, and our impressions of each other are often wrong. You may well find that by listening to fears and objections you haven't considered, you can resolve some of your opponents' concerns without compromising your campaign.

On some issues, of course, there is no middle ground. If Hydro Quebec goes forward with its massive power project on the Great Whale River, the result will be ecological and cultural genocide. But most rivers face issues less black and white, more responsive to solutions fashioned from the concerns of several different interests, some of them very unlikely allies.

Talk with Private Landowners Early

Rivers that flow through predominantly private land present a profoundly different conservation challenge than rivers on public land. If the river you are trying to save is bordered by a significant amount of private property—as are most rivers in the East—you will get nowhere without enrolling the owners of that property in your campaign. And unless you enroll private landowners early in the process, before media coverage begins and rumors start to fly, you may not be able to enroll them at all.

The reason is simple: any activity which appears to have even the slightest potential for restricting private property rights will be viewed with suspicion, if not angry opposition. In 1991, while Friends of the River was campaigning for a National Recreation Area on the North and Middle Forks of the American River, landowners along the South Fork of the American began hearing rumors that their reach of river would also be included and that condemnation proceedings would therefore follow. Public sentiment in California's Mother Lode still has frontier overtones and government intrusion is highly unwelcome. In a series of meetings and rallies, local residents erupted in a frenzy of opposition to the NRA. Had such a reaction been anticipated in advance, the groundwork for a better understanding of the real facts could have been laid.

Many people in New England—even people in Massachusetts—don't know where the Westport River is. Its modest watershed drains an appendage of land at the extreme southeast corner of the state, hard up against Rhode Island. The Westport is more estuary than river, its two arms opening into the mouth of Buzzard's Bay. But it is a special and fragile resource, an enclave of rural tranquility and natural beauty where one of the nation's largest concentrations of osprey nest, where bald eagles occasionally roost, where people fish and swim and revel in the meeting of river and sea.

The Westport's problems are pollution and urban development. Some 30,000 people living in its watershed rely exclusively on septic systems to dispose of their sewage, and many of those systems are old. Dairy farms leach cattle manure into the watershed. Toxic dump sites threaten groundwater. It is a classic case of nest fouling, on a grand scale. Shellfish production in the estuary, an important commercial resource, is threatened by human and agricultural pollution, and accelerating growth promises to exacerbate all these problems.

But if riparian property owners are the problem for the Westport River, they are also the solution. The Westport River Watershed Alliance is a home-grown organization with more than 2000 members, most of whom live in the watershed. Many of them have a direct personal interest in the river because it flows past their back yards. They often collaborate with the Westport Fisherman's Association, a group of commercial and sport fishermen who also have a clear vested interest in the health of the river.

Members of the Westport River Watershed Alliance know that while confrontation with riverside residents is sometimes necessary to stop the pollution threatening their river, cooperation is usually a more desirable and effective strategy. Their efforts lean heavily, therefore, on education and outreach and their board contains riverfront landowners.

The Wild and Scenic management plan developed for the Wildcat River by the National Park Service and the people of Jackson, New Hampshire required zoning amendments which could have alienated some private landowners. But those landowners were brought into the planning process and their concerns were addressed from the start. As a result, when a town meeting was convened to adopt the necessary zoning amendments, the vote was unanimous.

Oregon's Sandy River is the kind of waterway people dream of having in their back yard, and for Rob Galasso the dream is a reality. Close to Portland, the Sandy drains the west side of Mt. Hood through a pristine canyon still home to otter, elk, bear, osprey and spotted owls. Because he lives on the river and kayaks it regularly, Galasso is acutely aware of abuses to it, some of which result from overdevelopment and underregulation. County zoning laws aren't enforced and urban growth threatens to encroach further into the river corridor.

To address these problems, Galasso and a few others formed Friends of the Sandy River. One of their first acts was to circulate a petition and survey among riverfront property owners explaining problems facing the watershed and asking them to support both state and federal Wild and Scenic protection. Galasso got 300 signatures.

He also began a newsletter to educate property owners about river issues and to explain little-known zoning laws—including setback requirements—that many of them didn't know about. To field questions about Wild and Scenic designation and to build more support for the effort, he held a series of public meetings.

All these efforts helped ensure a broad base of landowner support for Wild and Scenic designation, but also resulted in something else Galasso hadn't counted on. Some property owners, fearing a Wild and Scenic river would bring land use restrictions, have stepped up the pace of logging and other development. Galasso says he knows of one large riverside clear cut of several hundred acres he believes the owner harvested to beat Wild and Scenic designation. "If I had been more aggressive in approaching land owners early and proposing alternatives to harvesting, things like land swaps or easements, I might have been able to prevent some of this." he says. "I'm afraid my worst fears were realized because I took only partial action."

Wise Use or Resource Abuse?

Underlying the strategic importance of addressing the concerns of landowners is the growing threat of the so-called "wise use" movement. An outgrowth of the "Sagebrush Rebellion" and the James Watt theology of natural resource exploitation, this rapidly growing phenomenon might more accurately be called the resource abuse movement. In the past five years "wise use" groups have sprung up all over the country with the message that environmental protections are an infringement of private property rights and that the public should have unlimited access to forests, waters, minerals, and range.

Wise Use activists think they have a winning strategy in exploiting the private property issue. In 1993 they succeeded in stopping what had looked like an easy Wild and Scenic designation for New Hampshire's Pemigewasset River by arousing vague fears of a federal take-over. Under the guise of the New Hampshire Landowners Alliance, Wise Use extremists made wildly inaccurate statements about Wild and Scenic designation, distributed "wanted" posters of the National Park Service project coordinator leading the Wild and Scenic study, and even showed up at a study committee meeting with members of a motorcycle gang to intimidate the participants. Seven towns along the river had to vote on adopting the locally developed plan and six of them rejected it.

The best response to this kind of frontal attack is careful and patient education. Because Wise Use zealots are unlikely to crawl out from beneath their rocks until your river-saving efforts are fairly public, you should have

Pemigewasset River, New Hampshire. (Photo courtesy of Tim Palmer.)

time to reach landowners first with an accurate and appealing message if you act early.

It is important to remember, however, that the Wise Use movement is touching a sensitive nerve. Riparian landowners are genuinely concerned about surrendering freedom of action on their properties and suffering a loss of property value. They're also afraid of regulations they don't understand, they're afraid of trespass and vandalism from increased public access, they're afraid of liability, and they turn pale at the very thought of eminent domain.

So when you go out of your way to involve landowners early in your river protection process, you can satisfy most of these concerns at the outset and, equally important, incorporate their suggestions into your river plan.

Both River Network and The Nature Conservancy have excellent background material on the resource abuse–Wise Use movement. Forewarned is forearmed.

Advertise the Economic Value of the River

As you work at building public support for your river, remember that financial interest is one of the driving forces in society. So while you develop eloquent arguments for protecting the ecological, aesthetic, and recreational values of the river, address the economic value as well.

In the bad old days when the Nashua River was, as a popular cliche often put it, "too thin to plow and too thick to drink", riverfront property was worthless. The Nashua's stench drove people away from it and the FHA put a zero value on one home sitting too close to the river. Bill Flynn, then mayor of Fitchberg, Massachusetts even got a letter from a business that had decided against relocating there because the city, which sits by the Nashua, had so little respect for its river.

But that letter became a powerful piece of propaganda as the Nashua River Watershed Association campaigned for a greenway along the restored river corridor. Today, says Stoddart, riverfront property is among the most valuable in the whole watershed.

Twenty years ago economic arguments for river protection were mostly speculative and anecdotal; today they're rooted in research. Evidence from all over the country demonstrates that protected river corridors and greenways enhance adjacent property values, and increased property values result in increased property tax revenues for local governments. Financing for many park and open space plans is predicated on the economic assumption that they will pay for themselves through increased tax revenues. When California floated a $330 million park bond, the state estimated that $100 million would be returned to local economies each year from increased business income and enhanced property values.

The dollar value of river recreation, in all its many forms, is seldom given appropriate recognition or measurement. But 140 million people participate in wildlife-related recreation each year and a lot of that recreation is on or around rivers. The Forest Service estimates that in 1985 nearly 60 million American anglers spent $28 billion on their sport. Even birdwatching is a significant economic activity; California birdwatchers contributed $27 million to the state's economy in 1987, supporting nearly 2000 jobs.

River floating, which generally means using gravity instead of motors for propulsion, has exploded in both popularity and economic value in recent years. Use of Wild and Scenic rivers in national forests more than doubled between 1976 and 1984. Commercial river outfitters pump more than $70 million into the Colorado economy each year and canoeists contributed more than $20 million to the Arkansas economy in 1988.

During the Gauley campaign much was made of the value of the river's whitewater recreation which is now estimated at $20 million per year. That's a remarkable figure for one river with a 21-day season, and when you compute it over the life of a hydropower project, the economic value of whitewater recreation becomes highly competitive. A similar analysis for the Penobscot revealed that whitewater recreation on that one river represented a $375,000,000 net value to the state of Maine. That information helped defeat a planned hydropower project.

The Price of Beauty

The beauty of unspoiled rivers is one of their main attractions and it should be no surprise to learn that, according to a poll done for the President's Commission on Americans Outdoors, natural beauty is the single most important criterion for tourists selecting a site for outdoor recreation. And thanks to new sampling techniques, even natural beauty can be assigned a dollar value. Through a survey concept called "willingness-to-pay", dollar values can be arrived at for the estimated benefits of any natural resource. The survey process simply asks people how much they would be willing to pay for a specific recreation activity rather than forego it.

The National Park Service has folded results from a number of studies into a composite table of willingness-to-pay values for a variety of outdoor activities, including nonmotorized boating and anadromous fishing. Those two activities, interestingly enough, average almost twice the willingness-to-pay levels of any of the other activities listed. The surveys indicated people were willing to pay $51.52 per day to fish for salmon and steelhead and $48.68 for nonmotorized boating. This is, of course, over and above the equipment costs of such recreation.

Benefit–cost analysis, which is used for the justification of water-development and hydropower projects, can and should be applied to natural systems and environmental quality. Willingness-to-pay surveys can be performed for the presence of wild and endangered animals, scenic vistas, biodiversity, and clean water. One California survey established that households in the state would be willing to pay between $42 and $94 annually to keep Mono Lake full enough to preserve its natural qualities. The cost of the hydropower and water that would be needed to replace water left in the lake came to only $2.64 per household per year. On that basis, preserving the lake becomes an easy choice.

Establishing this kind of data is no small task, but there is a substantial amount of information already available. The Rivers, Trails and Conservation Assistance Program of the National Park Service has produced a resource book entitled, "Economic Impacts of Protecting Rivers, Trails and Greenway Corridors" which provides a good, nontechnical review of these issues.

There is a wealth of information on the economic value of rivers in the *River Valuation Bibliography* prepared by Chiara Dolcino and Stephen Andersen. This comprehensive literature survey includes an annotated bibliography, an alphabetical bibliography, and a list of whitewater recreation valuations for some 41 rivers. The compilation is updated periodically and Andersen is available for consultation at (703) 836-6149.

Another useful resource is *An Annotated Bibliography of Economic Literature on Instream Flow* available from the U.S. Fish and Wildlife Service's National Ecology Research Center in Fort Collins, Colorado. And River Network's free DORIS service (Directory of River Information Specialists) offers support from more than 500 river specialists, available through a toll-free number at (800) 42-DORIS.

River valuation is no more precise a science than are most cost–benefit analyses for multipurpose dams. Many people would say that no price can be put on a free-flowing river. But river valuation does give us a rough set of numbers to work with and allows us to counter the economic claims of river wreckers with economic claims of our own.

Remember to apply economic analysis in both directions—for the river and against the threatening development. As discussed earlier, the Environmental Defense Fund blew holes in the cost–benefit ratio of a hydropower dam proposal on the Tuolumne River by factoring in the value of whitewater boating and fishing that would have been eliminated by the dam.

When pollution is the problem, the cost of cleaning it up may be enormous, but so will the benefits. More than half a billion dollars has been spent to clean up the Merrimack and $200 million has been spent on the Nashua—but the value of clean water for drinking and recreation, the appreciation of property values, the enhancement of recreation and wildlife, year after year after year, far exceeds the expense.

Among the many compelling arguments for cleaning up the Westport River is an $800,000 per year commercial shellfish industry which is now threatened by polluted runoff. The long-term economic benefit from having viable stocks of Atlantic salmon in the spawning streams of New England could be calculated well in excess of the short-term clean-up costs.

Seek Support from the Business Community

In some pockets of the environmental movement there remains a kind of vestigial resistance to the idea of doing business with business. That's too bad. Business and industry may be responsible for a lot of environmental abuse, but the climate has radically changed and the popular imperative today is to demonstrate environmental correctness. An increasing number of businesses even *believe* that environmental protection is both the right thing to do and good for the bottom line.

For example, several river campaigns have found more than a loan available at their local bank. When the Nashua River Watershed Association developed a comprehensive greenway plan for the preservation of the river corridor, they needed support to print the half-inch thick document. So they went to a local bank and to a large paper company, which had once been among the river's polluters. The beautifully printed greenway plan ended up costing the Watershed Association nothing, and it created some important allies. "Those people from the bank," recalls Marion Stoddart with glee, "they came in and they collated this thing in their free time on a Saturday."

When Rita Barron needed money to publish her *Profile of the Charles River* she went to a bank too, not for a loan but for a gift. The bank's support made the profile possible and helped cement support in the local business community. Because banks market image and community relations as much as interest rates, many of them are willing to support mainstream environmental causes. Having said all that, it should be acknowledged that banks are inherently conservative so it's not likely you'll get one involved in a campaign that involves much public controversy. Still, if your goal is a comprehensive river corridor management plan, a greenway, or the cleanup of a befouled river you may find some common ground with a local bank. And because banks are deeply involved in the business of any community, if you get a bank on board other businesses may follow.

Penetrating the Chamber of Commerce

The single best way to penetrate the business community, however, is through the local chamber of commerce. Most chambers invite luncheon presentations from community groups, which provides a golden opportunity to meet the movers and shakers of your business community. Wendy Wilson carried her Payette campaign to the Boise Chamber of Commerce and the response amazed her. Because her initial anxiety may feel familiar to many of us, Wendy's account of the meeting is worth reading:

> When I first drove up to the Boise County Courthouse for a Chamber of Commerce meeting, the building was pitch black. Maybe no one was there, I thought, maybe I'd be lucky to get out alive. What if the lumber mill workers and cattlemen didn't like city girls with an attitude? What if they all secretly wanted to be construction workers and switch-flippers for a power company?
>
> Instead I found a Chamber of Commerce that cared about the future and considered the river a part of that future. Friends of the Payette won the approval of the first of over a dozen endorsing organizations at the Chamber meeting. Later, we became known as moderates in a state that hates radicals. The Chamber helped soften our image.

Before you make a Chamber of Commerce pitch, make sure you have your presentation together. A brief slide show is appropriate, but don't overdue the visuals. Put together a well-organized, precise speech long on facts and short on rhetoric, and leave plenty of time for questions. If you have an economic analysis for your campaign, lay it out; these are people interested in the bottom line.

Rivers with an active recreation industry always have potential for business support, albeit in a specialized niche. Commercial river outfitters have contributed more money to Friends of the River than any other source and, through their client lists, have provided access to an important constituency. They have also donated or discounted fund-raising river trips and have transported many a VIP down endangered rivers.

Because commercial outfitters on the Gauley generate substantial annual revenues, their income clout helped make it easier to recruit banks and local Chambers of Commerce to support the river protection campaign.

Winning support from businesses with no direct interest in rivers is an altogether more difficult challenge, but the Clark Fork–Pend Oreille Coalition has developed a successful program for penetrating the local business community which could be replicated anywhere. They call it the "Environmental–Business Partnership" program and it targets environmentally sensitive businesses in the Missoula area to solicit financial support or in-kind services. Participants are listed as business partners in *Currents*, the Coalition's newsletter, and are promoted at public events. Each business receives a window sticker and posters to advertise their partnership. Participants include a print shop, an ice cream shop and bakery, construction companies, and real estate firms.

Bring Business Leaders on Board

Another way to build support in the business community is to include business leaders on your board of directors. The Cahaba River Society has a 19-person board of directors and 11 of those directors represent a business. With the help of this well-connected board, the Cahaba River Society has made presentations to hundreds of local businesses and corporations. More than 65 of them have become Society members and by 1991 the young organization had already raised $20,000 from its business outreach.

Another good strategy for recruiting business support is to honor businesses which do environmentally good things. An easy way to do that is to inform the local Chamber of Commerce that you are going to initiate an annual award program and that you are soliciting candidate companies. Criteria can include any activities which have a positive impact on water quality, conservation, public education, or support for environmental protection of rivers.

Finally, when and if you complete an analysis of the economic value of your river, translate it into a popularly written, well-designed report and circulate it through the business community. Then ask for letters of support from companies who think saving your river is good for business.

Build a Membership

There are two reasons for having members: money and muscle. Building membership, besides being an obvious demonstration of public support, provides a fund-raising base, a volunteer pool, and political clout. Friends of the River, one of the largest river conservation groups in the nation, had a membership in 1993 of about 10,000. While that number pales beside the hundreds of thousands who belong to the National Wildlife Federation, the Sierra Club, and the Audubon Society, it is more than enough to impress the California legislators whose attention F.O.R. seeks. And it is enough to provide more than $200,000 per year in membership support.

The Westport River Watershed Alliance, on the other hand, has less than 2500 members, but that number represents about eight percent of the watershed's population. As a result, the Alliance wields considerable influence and is automatically consulted on issues affecting the watershed.

While absolute numbers impress politicians, the quality of membership can be as important as the quantity. Among F.O.R.'s 10,000 members are 500 to 1000 who can be counted on to write letters, make phone calls, or take some form of direct action on behalf of a river. Grassroots organizations with small budgets and few staff can still achieve great results with an active and involved membership.

Building membership is both a precise science and a mysterious art. Some organizations have the foresight or good fortune to begin life at an opportune moment when the focus of public attention is on their river. Others start from obscurity and work slowly upward. Whatever the case with you and your river, there are some important rules to follow.

First, define the role or roles you want your members to play. Do you want activists or just addresses? Do you want volunteers to help run the organization and its campaign? Do you want to give members a vote in organizational policy? What kinds of activities and opportunities do you intend to offer members? Answering these and other questions will help you decide how much energy you want to put into membership; it will also help identify potential members and shape the appeal you use to find them.

Build a Database

The first concrete step in building a membership is to create a database. If you don't yet have a computer, find one now. It isn't even worth trying to create and build membership without a well-organized database. Membership software is available, but if you can't find or afford it ask other membership groups, or River Network, for a template to set up your own. Besides each member's name, address, and telephone number, the database should include renewal date, giving record, and some way to flag activist involvement (writes letters, makes phone calls, etc.). Depending on the number of fields your database can handle, you may want to include other information as well, like a code denoting how each member was acquired, demographic information, political affiliation, special expertise, etc.

Once you've got a database, use it. That may sound obvious but some organizations are so slow inputting new members that months go by between receipt of the membership check and the first communication from the organization. When someone sends in a membership check their enthusiasm is hot; don't let it cool.

One of the biggest challenges to building membership is keeping members. A renewal rate of 70–75 percent is considered good, although really successful groups can top 90 percent during periods of high visibility. But you won't keep any members unless you service them. This means regular communications and activities which give members a sense of participation and belonging.

Some members will join simply because they believe in your cause. They don't want to attend meetings or volunteer, but they do want periodic updates on the progress of your campaign. Other members join because they want to be involved and participate in the campaign, if only now and then. Those members need activities to get involved in, a tangible opportunity to make a difference.

Good membership programs respond to each new member with both a receipt acknowledging arrival of their check and some printed material offering further information about the group and the river campaign. Renewal reminders, automatically flagged in your database, are then sent out anywhere from one to four times, beginning a month before the membership expires.

If you have a newsletter (and, as we will discuss below, you should) it will become the strongest connecting link between your organization and its members. The newsletter helps keep members tied into the progress of your campaign, acknowledges members' contributions and gives them a sense of family.

Actively building membership (sometimes called prospecting, or mining for members) can take a variety of different paths. While direct mail returns have declined in recent years, many organizations still rely heavily on this system. It requires a mailing list and enough money to cover printing and postage. A return of 2 percent is good for a cold list, containing names of people not already aware of or interested in your organization. Much higher returns can sometimes be achieved from "warmer" lists.

If you don't want to handle this job yourself, it's easy to find a mailing house that will do it for a fee and a percentage of the return. Some mailing houses, especially those devoted exclusively to nonprofit clients, will take on direct mail prospecting without an up-front fee, but only if they think your issue and your message are hot enough for a healthy return.

Telemarketing, despised by many people confronted by dinnertime phone calls, has an impressive performance record, especially used in conjunction with direct mail. But telemarketing is also expensive, soaking up as much as 50 to 80 percent of donated revenues before reaching the recipient.

The Cahaba River Society built a membership of more than 2300 in less than 5 years in part by hosting a variety of events for members and the general public, including free canoe trips, dozens of river cleanups, and a river watch program. Perhaps most effective has been a series of town meetings held every three months in each of four towns along the river.

Membership growth is dramatically enhanced by media exposure. If the threat to your river is getting a lot of press, it's time to crank up a membership appeal. Sometimes the course of human events will propel an issue or organization into the limelight. When President Reagan named James Watt as Secretary of Interior, the Sierra Club discovered a golden opportunity to promote itself. Watt, perceived by many as an antienvironmental extremist, was the perfect foil and Sierra Club membership nearly doubled during his tenure. Next to John Muir and David Brower, some members have observed, James Watt was the best thing that ever happened to the Sierra Club.

Of course, timely events and human foils don't always come along when you need them, so you have to create your own. Some membership consultants argue you shouldn't start a membership drive until you have a media campaign underway. Certainly, the more media attention you can create before asking people to join, the more members you're likely to get. We'll explore this issue further in the next chapter.

Publish a Regular Newsletter

It is almost axiomatic that a river conservation organization should have a newsletter. The reasons are simple and pretty well understood: Every organization needs a voice, a means of communicating with its members and with the outside world. Every organization needs a platform from which to state its case. With the simplification of desktop publishing, newsletters can now be produced in-house by virtually anyone, even those with marginal computer skills. A cursory survey of newsletters published by river conservation groups reveals publications ranging from the dismal to the inspired. But almost any newsletter is better than none.

It may be inappropriate to lay down rules for newsletters since they work best when they are true reflections of the organizations behind them. But there are some universal qualities common to the best examples.

1. *They are informative without being boring.* Good newsletters have lively, concise articles on the issues the organization is most concerned with. Those articles should educate the readers without going into laborious detail.

2. *The articles are devoid of inside information, unexplained acronyms, and bureaucratic lingo.* Some newsletters sound like they are written by and for specialists, full of references the lay reader won't understand.

3. *They are free from hyperbole and exaggeration.* Some groups tend to view their newsletters as a means of confidential communication among their members. Remember that whatever you print will be seen by more people than you can imagine. Intemperate and inaccurate remarks will return to haunt you and weaken your credibility. Good newsletters are taken seriously and are sometimes quoted by the mainstream press.

4. *They are full of people.* People like reading about people, regardless of the issue, so put people in your newsletter. One of the best uses of a newsletter is the recognition of good work by staff, volunteers, board members, and supporters. Major contributors can be recognized and thanked, staff members can be profiled, and interesting experts can be interviewed.

5. *They invite participation.* Good newsletters make readers want to get involved with your organization. They carry schedules of events, they list activities needing volunteers, and they print letters to the editor.

6. *They are fun.* The prevailing tone of nonprofit newsletters is serious, heavy, and dull. Lighten up. make an effort to put some fun in your newsletter. Use humorous quotes, editorial cartoons, outrageous anecdotes, anything to relieve the tedium. Consider balancing dry articles on issues with juicier recreation pieces about your river.

Every newsletter should have a membership coupon inserted or printed within it, a list of staff and board members, and your mission statement. If you can afford it, print overruns so that you have a few hundred more than needed for the mailing list. Use those to promote your organization by dropping them off at other organizations, businesses, and schools. Be sure the local library has a subscription.

Format is a matter of taste and budget but, as with brochures, unless you have a brilliant graphic artist on staff, copy the format of another newsletter you like. River Network has a file of samples. However you design it, don't cram the contents of your newsletter. Leave some white space. Do use photos when space allows, particularly of people.

You will of course want to use your newsletter to promote upcoming events like auctions and river festivals and clean-ups. And, depending on frequency and timing of the publication, it is also a good vehicle for action alerts to your membership when letters are needed or expert testimony is being sought.

Some Good Examples

Before you put your first newsletter together, it makes a lot of sense to look at a variety of existing ones. Among the better examples currently being published:

1. *Housatonic Current.* Voice of the Housatonic River which flows thorough Massachusetts, Connecticut, and New York, *Current* is a polished, interesting, half-tabloid newsletter with numerous brief news items and a few longer features, including articles of general interest. It lists all new members and donors along with a map of the river and its watershed. [P.O. Box 28, Cornwall Bridge, CT 06754]

2. *Headwaters.* The quarterly journal of Friends of the River, *Headwaters* is a tabloid-sized newspaper printed on newsprint and laid out like a conventional paper. It is heavy on informational articles, river trip descriptions, legislative news, and photos. [128 J Street, Second Floor, Sacramento, CA 95814]

3. *River Voices.* The newsletter of River Network, *River Voices* is chockfull of how-to and anecdotal articles about river-saving strategies. Each issue focuses on a specific theme—such as the Clean Water Act, water efficiency, private land issues—and recounts the successful efforts of groups all over the country. [P.O. Box 8787, Portland, OR 97207]

4. *River Report.* A single sheet, front-to-back page, 8.5-by-14 inch monthly report by the Cahaba River Society which is both highly informative and a model of simplicity. The Society has also published one edition of a showcase full-color, tabloid-sized newspaper called *Cahaba*, which is filled with stunning photos and artwork and a few feature articles. [2717 7th Avenue South, Suite 207, Birmingham, Alabama 35233]

It's far more important to get something out on a regular, reliable basis than to attempt a version of the *New York Times* with each issue. Start small and simple and work up.

When you're ready for the printer, shop around. Printing prices, as mentioned earlier, vary radically. If you insist on recycled paper, as you should, your choices will be somewhat limited, but don't let that discourage you. If at all possible, find a sympathetic print shop interested in your river and ask for a major price break.

One way to soften the blow from the printing bill is to sell advertising, as is done in *Housatonic Currents* and *Headwaters*. Advertising in *Headwaters* comes mostly from whitewater equipment suppliers and commercial outfitters although clients have included an investment fund, a brewery, and an environmentally sensitive real estate firm. At one time *Headwaters* was mailed to 20,000 readers and Friends of the River committed a half-time position to selling advertising, which grossed about $25,000 per year. Regardless of circulation, your newsletter can provide business supporters with a means of reaching your membership. And the availability of advertising space also allows the organization to trade for auction items and commercial river trips.

Chapter 4
Getting It Done

Ya gotta do what ya gotta do.
SYLVESTER STALLONE IN "ROCKY IV"

After you've committed, planned, organized, and promoted, just one step remains to protect your river—doing it. And, as with everything else in this guide, there is a logical sequence of actions which, if followed, will help you do it successfully.

Form a Partnership with a State or National Organization

In 1986, Alasdair Coyne was an organic gardener and the president of a nonprofit recycling organization in Ojai, California. He was not a political activist, didn't know the first thing about river protection, and had never seen the giant jumbled boulders, the tar seeps, and the Chumash petroglyphs in the back country along nearby Sespe Creek.

But that Fall Coyne attended a public hearing on a Forest Service management plan and learned that two dams were being allowed for on the Sespe. He then spent three days hiking the remarkable canyon carved by the creek through one of the largest wilderness areas in Southern California. What he saw convinced him he had to do something to protect it. This was, after all, the very heart of the habitat for the condor recovery program and the last viable steelhead stream on the south coast. And while a local member of Congress had plans for a Sespe protection bill, the proposed legislation covered only half the creek and left the two dam sites free for development.

Coyne and a few friends created an organization and launched a campaign. But they had the wisdom to know what they didn't know, so they sought help wherever they could find it. At the state level, Friends of the River helped Coyne's Keep the Sespe Wild Committee appeal the dam-encumbered Forest Plan, research seismic safety issues, and generate publicity. Friends of the River included Sespe Creek in its statewide Wild and

Scenic "100 Rivers Campaign" and promoted protection among its 10,000 members.

At the national level, American Rivers' staff gave the fledgling Sespe Committee an understanding of the Washington legislative scene, through which the partial Sespe protection bill would soon be passing. American Rivers also helped with the Forest Plan appeal and gave Sespe supporters thorough briefings on the intricacies of Washington politics and lobbying.

In time, this partnership with other groups helped Coyne achieve what he and his Committee might never have done alone. Sespe Creek became a major environmental issue in California and a household name in Ventura County. A compromise Wild and Scenic bill was passed by Congress in 1992, expanding the protection of the original bill. Still, the dam sites weren't included and remain vulnerable to development, so Coyne continues to work with his state and national partners to win protection for the whole watershed.

Alasdair Coyne's experience translates into some simple advice relevant to any river organization: find a partner, find several partners, don't try to do it alone. And like Coyne, you'll get the most valuable start-up support from state and national groups that have experience with your issue. It's a waste of time to plow the same ground other groups have been farming ahead of you when you can reap the benefits of their efforts. And a growing number of statewide river organizations—like Friends of the River, Idaho Rivers United, New York Rivers United, and the West Virginia Rivers Coalition—are available to support and promote local river campaigns.

In 1993, New York Rivers United was organized and filing FERC interventions in a matter of weeks, thanks to partnership support from a number of organizations, including River Network which provided organizational advice and a $5000 start-up grant. Moving quickly out of the gate was particularly important in New York because nearly half the state's hydropower dams were up for relicensing that year and activists had to file a flood of interventions in order to steer the licensing process toward more beneficial treatment of the state's rivers. Partner support made it possible to cut the usual organizing time and get NYRU quickly up to speed.

A National Partnership of River Guardians

A good place to begin your search for campaign partners is in River Network's River Activists Directory, a 140-page (and growing) compilation of activists and organizations throughout the U.S. The Directory contains more than 2500 listings and is updated quarterly. It will tell you if there's a statewide river conservation organization where you live and it can guide you toward other groups and individuals in your area.

In 1993, River Network began organizing a National Partnership of River Guardians among the grassroots river groups and activists listed in the Directory. The goal was an integrated network of activists working collaboratively all over the country to protect river systems.

The Partnership offers one-stop shopping for an essential array of support services, including: A quarterly journal providing technical information and a river "bulletin board"; case studies of successful river-saving campaigns; special how-to publications; access to the River Activists Directory; access to DORIS, the database of 600 volunteer experts on river conservation issues; electronic conferencing; annual activist retreats; an 800 phone number for problem-solving consultations; workshops to develop campaign strategies and organizing skills; fund raising information and development planning, as well as some direct financial assistance for statewide river councils.

These Partnership services reflect the essential purpose of River Network, which was founded in 1988 by Phil Wallin with the simply stated mission "to help people save rivers." That mission is structured into four distinct programs:

The River Clearinghouse Program

Offers a variety of support services like those described above and compiles case studies of river campaigns. Five of the best case studies of river conservation success stories are available in a booklet entitled *People Protecting Rivers: A Collection of Lessons From Grassroots Activists.* New case studies are compiled each year.

Other River Network publications include *River Wise* and *River Wealth,* which present a variety of tried and tested methods for public education and fund-raising. Fund-raising videos are available on loan and copies of Lotus 1-2-3 software—which provide both a spreadsheet and a database—are offered free to any organization working on river protection.

The River Leadership Program

A nationwide effort to strengthen existing state and regional river advocacy organizations and to establish new river councils that advocate for river protection at the state level. It also provides a network link among local and state groups to keep them abreast of national legislation and important trends affecting protection and restoration of rivers and watersheds. And it contracts with state river councils to train grassroots river guardians.

In its first two years the River Leadership Program supported the efforts of groups in Idaho, California, West Virginia, Connecticut, New

Hampshire, Montana, and New York and was doing preparatory work in eight other states.

The Riverlands Conservancy

Purchases riparian land for preservation by public agencies or private trusts. By 1993, seventeen land purchases had been completed, totaling 17,174 acres of critical river habitat, and another 4,340 acres were under option. These purchases helped protect land along the Snake and Grand Ronde Rivers in Oregon and Washington; the Eleven Point in Missouri; and the Skagit, Sauk, Little Wenatchee, Icicle, and South Fork Stillaguamish Rivers in Washington.

The River Wealth Program

Offers fund-raising and development services aimed at giving river conservation groups the tools they need to support themselves financially.

While these programs can provide valuable, sometimes decisive, support for state and local river groups, River Network is by no means the only partner to seek as you start an organization and launch a campaign. State river councils like Idaho Rivers United, the West Virginia Rivers Coalition, and Friends of the River in California offer important advice and counsel, well-established local groups can be important allies, and several other national organizations provide outstanding support services.

Gateway to the Washington Bureaucracy

On a wide range of river issues, but particularly on small hydro projects, hydropower relicensing and Wild and Scenic protection, American Rivers is an essential partner. Headquartered in Washington, D.C., American Rivers is the nation's largest river conservation organization and, for hundreds of local river groups, it's the gateway to the Washington bureaucracy.

No one in the river movement knows the regulatory labyrinth better than the staff of American Rivers and no one has had more intimate contact with the Federal Energy Regulatory Commission and the U.S. Forest Service. American Rivers has a host of helpful services to offer local river groups in the context of what president Kevin Coyle calls "tandem relationships". Explains Coyle, "Our partnership involves guiding groups who lack the necessary expertise through the substantive issues. We help with litigation, agency interventions, appeals, and forest plans. We have hundreds of these kinds of relationships in the course of a year."

American Rivers was instrumental in educating the U.S. Forest Service about its administrative responsibility to include rivers in its forest planning process and has been a partner in countless forest plan appeals. Because the Forest Service often lacks the budget, the expertise and sometimes the will to properly assess rivers, American Rivers has worked with dozens of local and state organizations to monitor, comment on, and appeal forest plans which deal inadequately with river resources. The Sespe is a case in point and if you, like Alasdair Coyne, need help deciphering the forest planning process or lobbying the Forest Service to properly evaluate a river, American Rivers is the place to turn.

A big piece of the American Rivers agenda is committed to hydropower threats and the organization has its own National Center for Hydropower Policy, which uses education, lobbying, and litigation to steer hydro developers away from wild rivers. American Rivers has also fashioned a coalition of groups to intervene in hydropower relicensing proceedings before the Federal Energy Regulatory Commission. By mid-1993 the coalition was focusing on 160 projects involving 230 dams, and 90 interventions had been filed.

Since education is a fundamental part of the "tandem relationship" Coyle described, American Rivers has also produced a book that is required reading for any group fighting a hydropower license or intervening in a relicensing application. *Rivers at Risk* is the definitive guide to hydropower licensing and relicensing, and offers essential insights into the sometimes arcane world of FERC.

Other American Rivers publications include handbooks on state river protection programs, a state-by-state compilation of outstanding rivers, and a river conservation directory.

Besides expertise, education, issue development, and moral support, American Rivers has one other asset river organizations will find attractive: money. "We have seed grant relationships with numerous groups," says Coyle, and while the grants are small they have helped a number of river organizations through important stages of development. American Rivers also administers a river conservation fund provided each year by Recreational Equipment Incorporated, the outdoor equipment retailer. The R.E.I. fund totals some $70,000 and is distributed annually to 20 or 30 groups.

When Pollution Is the Problem

Of course, Wild and Scenic protection and hydropower threats aren't on everyone's river-saving agenda. If, instead, your problem is pollution you'd be wise to contact two other national groups doing grassroots work on this issue. The Izaak Walton League, which has been working to protect rivers since 1922, launched the Save Our Streams program in 1969 to teach local citizens how to test the biological health of their rivers. And River Watch Network, a Vermont-based organization, helps individuals and communities monitor water quality as the first step in restoring and protecting rivers. We'll take a longer look at both programs later in this chapter.

Numerous other partnerships could be productive for your river campaign; your challenge will be to find organizations with agendas that match yours. At the top of a list of particularly useful partnerships would be these: The Sierra Club (and its local chapters), National Audubon (and its local chapters), the Wilderness Society, the National Wildlife Federation, Trout Unlimited, Ducks Unlimited, the American Whitewater Affiliation, the American Canoe Association, the National Well Water Association, the Environmental Defense Fund, the Natural Resources Defense Council, and the Environmental Policy Institute/Friends of the Earth. The Sierra Club Legal Defense Fund is an invaluable ally on major litigation cases and has been especially useful in challenging hydropower permits. The Conservation Law Foundation (in the Northeast) and the Southern Environmental Law Center (in the South and Southeast) work with local groups on a wide array of environmental litigation as well.

While partnership with state or national groups may be fundamental to the success of your campaign, it is not always a risk-free ride. Unless you're clear on your own agenda and insist on following it, you may end up following someone else's. David Brown, veteran of the Ocoee and Gauley campaigns, agrees that "it makes a lot of sense to have a national group to assist you, especially if you don't have a strong feel for the game in Washington. But set your own agenda, don't let them set it for you." The prevailing advice on this subject is that no one knows your issue as well as you do so, while you seek advice, technical support and money, don't surrender control of your campaign and its agenda.

Most partnerships are casual and informal, an agreement to collaborate, to teach, to learn. But some involve a variety of specific expectations and obligations, and those partnerships should always be defined in writing. It's important to be clear, for example, on the division of responsibilities in a campaign, to know who is doing what tasks. Fund-raising, publicity, and strategic planning should be carefully coordinated and communication, particularly in the heat of a legislative battle, should be continuous and structured. (Nothing is more frustrating in a river campaign than to have partner organizations doing and saying conflicting things in public.)

If you raise money together you will want an agreed-upon formula for dividing and spending it. Since you are likely to be doing joint media work, you need to be clear about who speaks for whom on what issues. And, since disagreement and conflict is sometimes inevitable, it helps to have a system for resolution.

One of the advantages of having a more powerful partner is the leverage you acquire in promoting a credible alternative to the project or action threatening your river. A statewide or national voice will always be louder than yours alone.

Promote an Alternative to the Threatening Project

On Valentine's Day in 1986 a torrential deluge hit Northern California, filled the American River and blew out an earthen coffer dam built to divert the river during construction of the ill-fated Auburn Dam. A 40,000 acre-foot flood thundered into Folsom Reservoir downstream.

Folsom Dam provides the primary flood protection for the city of Sacramento, which sits in a basin at the confluence of the American and Sacramento Rivers. On this fateful day the Bureau of Reclamation miscalculated the run-off and kept the flood pool in the reservoir too full. When water from the broken coffer dam arrived, Folsom reservoir began to fill dangerously, threatening to over-top the dam's earth and rock-fill flanks. Had that occurred, the earthen portion of the structure would have rapidly eroded away, the dam would have been washed out and Sacramento would have suffered a catastrophic flood. The Bureau's critics charge that scenario came within a few hours of happening.

The near disaster frightened Sacramentans, who were already reeling from flooding in tributary streams. Local politicians began scrambling for some way to improve the city's flood protection, and the simple solution of choice was another dam. But most residents had no idea that human error, not Mother Nature, was the biggest problem in the '86 flood. Instead of acknowledging operational mistakes and developing new guidelines for Folsom Dam, both the Bureau and the Army Corps of Engineers began reviving plans for Auburn Dam.

Flood control remains the lifeblood of the U.S. Army Corps of Engineers, a formidable bureaucracy which has historically had such a devotion to justifying the construction of dams that critics have accused it of creating its own reality, much as a volcano creates its own weather. That's why Friends of the River, the Environmental Defense Fund, and other Auburn Dam opponents turned to an independent hydrology consultant to dissect the Corps' flood control plans and offer an independent analysis.

It will always be difficult to totally discredit the Corps' engineering analysis, but a high-quality rebuttal by an esteemed professional can at least cast the Corps' conclusions in doubt. That is what happened to the proposal to build a new dam at Auburn. Respected hydrologist Dr. Phillip Williams recomputed the Corps' own data justifying a flood control dam and reached an entirely different set of conclusions. Among other things, Williams persuasively demonstrated that Sacramento would have far more flood protection than the Corps acknowledged if Folsom Dam were operated according to original Congressional intent. Instead of spending upwards of $700 million on another dam, Williams argued, the Corps should reoperate its existing dam, coordinate storage with upstream dams, and improve downstream levies.

Williams' conclusions provided a credible alternative for an eleventh hour campaign which offered an entirely different vision for the American River. Auburn Dam opponents argued that flood control could be achieved through better management of existing facilities, improvements in levies, and limits on flood plain development. They also insisted that stopping the dam wasn't enough and that a National Recreation Area should be established to give the river some additional protection.

Thanks in part to a bizarre coalition of development interests who wanted a bigger dam and conservationists who wanted no dam, Auburn legislation was defeated in Congress in 1992.

The central point to this story is that a successful river campaign needs to promote both a credible alternative to the project threatening the river and a long-term solution that effectively removes the river from harm's way.

Two Levels of Protection

This suggests the need for addressing river protection at two levels. At one level, you are confronting the immediate threat—stopping a dam or diversion, eliminating a source of pollution. To combat the immediate threat you need to propose an alternative that provides another, preferably cheaper, way to achieve the desired benefit. Alternatively, you may be able to demonstrate that the desired benefit isn't necessary, appropriate, or worth the price that would have to be paid.

The second level of protection needs to address the fact that the river remains at risk as long as it is not sheltered from harm by some form of special designation. So you really have to look at protection in two different contexts; elimination of the immediate threat, which in itself requires a credible alternative, and development of a long-term scenario for the river that precludes any future threat.

The Gauley provides a good example. For that river, legislation was first passed to guarantee instream flows and preserve whitewater recreation, while later legislation created a hybrid National Recreation Area to preclude future development and provide long-term protection. On the American River this dual strategy resulted in defeat of a dam proposal but not passage of the National Recreation Area legislation that would have added a layer of protection. At this writing, new dam proposals are being launched and the river remains at risk.

As outlined in Chapter 2, the alternatives you propose for your river need to be exhaustively researched and totally credible. You also need to be able to describe your alternatives in brief and simple terms for popular media consumption. Bea Cooley, former executive director of the American River Coalition, insists that "you've got to have someone with credentials to present the alternatives. And if you don't have volunteer expertise, you've got to spend the money to get it. And then you have to find a way to make the other side look at your alternatives."

For some river threats, a credible alternative simply means debunking the opposition's claims. When the TVA wanted to shut down the Ocoee River to generate hydropower they claimed the electricity was needed, as David Brown puts it, "to keep little old ladies warm in the winter." But Brown had his own analysis conducted and discovered that the Ocoee diversion would represent just "7/10,000ths of TVA's generating capacity." Revealing the minuscule importance of Ocoee hydropower helped demonstrate the value of a free-flowing alternative.

Of course, the country is laced with lesser rivers and streams for which the threat is never as dramatic as a billion dollar dam or a river-killing diversion and for which viable alternatives are more readily available. Sugar Creek is a good example.

Flowing through northwestern Ohio, Sugar Creek preserves an important riparian corridor through a region of rich farmland intensively developed for row crops. The creek corridor provides vital habitat for migrating song birds, waterfowl, and other wildlife, and its waters host 41 species of fish.

Like many Midwestern streams, Sugar Creek had always been subservient to the interests of agriculture. When the creek became jammed with debris, causing floodwaters to inundate low-lying farmland in 1973, local farmers petitioned county commissioners to channelize the bed. (Under Ohio law, once a stream is channelized it must be maintained free of trees and shrubs so that stream blockage doesn't recur.)

In response to this threat, a group of citizens formed the Sugar Creek Protection Society. Their strategy was elegantly simple—rather than organizing opposition to the channelization, they proposed a long-term alternative by offering an environmentally sensitive plan to clear the obstacles from Sugar Creek themselves, and to keep it clear in perpetuity.

It was not a modest proposal. Sugar Creek was plugged with 46 massive log jams and an accumulation of waterborne debris. But with 1000 names on a petition to save the creek, the Society convinced the Board of Commissioners to let them try. With a modicum of donated heavy equipment and chainsaws, the all-volunteer crew got underway in 1975 and completely cleared the creek while preserving riparian foliage in a natural corridor. Today SCPS members continue to monitor and maintain the healthy stream.

Promoting alternatives requires knowing what it is you are offering an alternative to, and for that it helps to know in intimate detail the other side's plans.

Research the Opposition's Every Move and Respond

While we've been outlining a series of detailed steps for protecting rivers, laying them out like the blueprint for a house, it is important to understand that river campaigns, like rivers, aren't neat and orderly, they change as they go along.

So while a proactive campaign plan is fundamental to success, it's also true that you will have to react creatively to changing political realities. This means you can't simply create a game plan and follow it blindly from A to Z; you have to respond to some of the key moves your opposition makes.

It's therefore important to know what the other side is doing, to stay informed about their strategies, and to adapt your strategies accordingly. This means, among other things, having access to information inside the opponent's campaign, and while we're not suggesting ecological espionage we are suggesting the value of key relationships with agency personnel, opposition employees, elected officials, and anyone else close to the other side. Friendly moles can be a valuable asset, as David Brown discovered on the Ocoee.

As discussed earlier, Tennessee's Ocoee River, once drained almost dry by a hydropower diversion, surged back to life in 1976 when a rotting wooden flume was abandoned and water was allowed to return to the river. Boaters flocked to the new run and by 1982, annual river use reached 90,000 paddlers. Those people were understandably upset when the Tennessee Valley Authority announced plans to spend $26 million reconstructing the flume to divert the river again.

In the campaign against TVA's rediversion plan, David Brown took frequent advantage of changing circumstances to attack the credibility of the TVA, sometimes with valuable inside information. Early in the campaign, TVA employees circulated a petition against recreational use of the Ocoee and delivered it, with more than 2000 signatures of area citizens, to a local member of Congress. But a friend inside TVA gave a copy of the petition to Brown, who showed it to another friend who worked for the county. They discovered the petition was padded with dead people and names from an old school bond drive. It turned out that only about 200 names were valid and when TVA officials declared their employees had nothing to do with the fraud, a mole in the agency told Brown otherwise. The press had a field day with the news and TVA was publicly embarrassed.

But that's just one example; there are others. Since TVA was already embarked on rebuilding the diversion flume, Brown's strategy had to focus on securing guaranteed recreational flows from the restored project. That meant he needed to demonstrate that the hydro diversion made little economic sense. By talking to the project contractor, Brown discovered that construction was over budget with higher costs than TVA had announced. Brown got a member of Congress to initiate a GAO audit and later arranged for a technical analysis which demonstrated that project costs were 10 times higher than initially estimated, thus making Ocoee hydropower far less cost-effective than TVA claimed. Armed with that information, and the knowledge that TVA was canceling nuclear power plants because the whole system was already over capacity, Brown made a strong case for the irrelevance of Ocoee hydropower.

Adjusting to Changing Circumstances

Friendly contacts—with a project contractor, with members of Congress, with county officials, and with TVA staff—made it possible for Brown and the Ocoee campaign to adjust to changing circumstances with effective counter-strategies. The Ocoee example also demonstrates that no matter how carefully you plan a river campaign, it has to be flexible enough to respond to new events and opportunities.

Bea Cooley would emphatically agree. When Cooley directed the American River Coalition's fight against Auburn Dam, the campaign was complicated by multiple proposals and a horde of overlapping agencies and interests. One dam was being proposed by the Army Corps of Engineers for flood protection, but scenarios ranged from various versions of a dry-dam with no permanent pool to a "stageable" dry dam which could be converted to a permanent impoundment. Another dam was being proposed by the Bureau of Reclamation, with three different configurations, all of which would flood varying portions of upriver canyons.

Competing members of Congress were promoting varying versions of both proposals while the local flood control agency was trying to make sense of it all and developers were demanding that some dam be built so flood plain construction could continue. Meanwhile two county governments were lobbying for a big multipurpose dam so that they could cash in on subsidized water. And a pro-dam business group commissioned a cleverly slanted survey to demonstrate public support for a big dam.

"There was no fixed target," reflects Cooley. "Every time we would slay one dragon, or at least cut off a piece of him, another dragon would appear."

The only way to deal with such a complex and confusing scenario, Cooley says, is to develop a bullet-proof understanding of all the players and issues. Other than the effort to win Congressional approval for a river-based National Recreation Area, Cooley concedes, "Our campaign was completely reactive. But what we did well was gather together all the information we could and then focus it on each issue as it came along. To the extent that knowledge is power, we were able to focus quite a bit of power against each new target."

Veteran activists agree about the importance of following the opposition's every move, but warn that you shouldn't get in the habit of always reacting to the other side. Donn Furman, who has run successful campaigns for the Kings and San Joaquin Rivers in California, says it's "better to anticipate and foreclose" than to merely react.

The main point here is that, like any political process, the struggle to protect a river will always be, if you will, fluid. You need to be well enough organized to follow a plan of action, and flexible enough to adapt it to changing circumstances. And it's easier to adapt when you know what the other side is up to, when you're familiar with all the key players.

Work the Key Players

Picture a flow chart on the wall of your campaign office with the names of every organization, agency, and person who will, could, or should play a key role in the fate of your river.

If your river happened to be the American, the number of local, state, and national politicians, committee staff, agency officials, business leaders, and other assorted decisionmakers listed on your wall—both friendly and unfriendly—would be, at an absolute minimum, 34, not counting media. This includes county supervisors, state legislators, members of the House and Senate, Congressional committee staff, flood control agency personnel, Army Corps and Bureau of Reclamation officials, leading developers, labor leaders, regulatory agency staff, state agency staff, chambers of commerce, utility executives, and water contractors.

Add to that list the number of friendly environmental groups with which you are building partnerships, alliances, coalitions, and strategy and you now have more than 60 "key players" to work with.

While the average river campaign is less complex, this example nevertheless demonstrates the magnitude of the job of working key players. And the importance of that process can't be exaggerated—next to building support among the general public, it is the most important thing you will do to win your campaign. In fact, if you remember nothing else from this book, remember this: without support from key decisionmakers you will fail, and without support from the general public you won't get support from the decisionmakers. It's that simple.

A comprehensive list of your key players should evolve out of the organizing steps you've already taken. Refer back to the forum of action you chose, the tools and the strategies you've selected and list every person and organization you think could have a significant impact. Then thin the list until you've got it narrowed down to just those people you think you can influence and who you are sure will make a difference to the outcome of your campaign. Inevitably, your list will contain more names than you have the time or staff to work.

Of course, you might also follow David Brown's lead. "One of the first things we did on the Ocoee," he says, "was load up a van and drive around the state talking to anyone who knew anything about the river." That reconnaissance trip provided some crucial information and the names of numerous key people.

Three Categories of Key People

Key people fall roughly into three categories: supporters who just need ongoing encouragement, undecideds who need education or friendly persuasion, and confirmed opponents who need to be stopped or neutralized. Each category requires a different approach.

Key supporters, more than anything else, need not to be taken for granted. To be effective, they need to know what your campaign is up to on an ongoing basis, and to stay loyal they need continual encouragement and thanks. River campaigns typically take years, not months, and preserving the support of key allies over that span of time is a challenge.

Many of the key people in your campaign will be agency bureaucrats and politicians, which is to say they will be cautious and fickle, full of hesitation and indecision. Winning the hearts and minds of the undecideds and the morally or politically timid often means moving beyond logic and reason to personal persuasion and the exercise of power. When you are working key players who haven't made up their minds, one of the two best tools you can use is a friendly peer, someone on your side who knows the key players and agrees to intervene. David Brown kicked Ocoee protection into gear when he was finally able to get Lamar Alexander to work on Howard Baker.

While working key players requires working their friends, it may also require building public pressure through the orchestration of letters and phone calls, about which we'll speak more later. And when you are trying to persuade agency personnel and elected officials—the people who will make the key decisions about your river—Bea Cooley suggests continuous contact. "You have to stay in touch and keep the pressure on constantly," says Cooley. "And I think you have to communicate your position to them in writing, put it in their faces repeatedly, because you can't assume that they understand anything you tell them."

Volume as well as frequency is important in the cultivation of decisionmakers. While it's possible to over sell your cause, it's impossible for a public official to ignore an avalanche of mail.

There are of course key players you will never win over, powerful people who will remain completely opposed to your campaign. If it's clear they are beyond your reach, don't waste time on them; move on.

Working key players requires careful preparation. You don't just go out and do it. David Brown warns that you should never go after someone until you have carefully prepared the groundwork. "You can't work the key players until you have your information together and your ducks in a row," he says. "You can't just identify a key person and then run up and ask them to do something. You have to be sure you're ready."

Creating the Right Political Climate

That means you need to research each key player thoroughly enough to know his or her position toward, interest in, understanding of, and potential impact on your river. It also means you have to know your own issues thoroughly, that you have to do your homework. And it means you have to establish the necessary political climate to make your campaign viable, visible, and credible. Key people aren't likely to support you if you've got no public profile, if they don't believe you or if they doubt you can get the job done. A "comfortable" political climate might include some favorable media coverage, the public support of other prominent people, public poll results, or a significant number of letters. Public people are less likely to offer public support when they think they are standing alone on an issue.

When your list is together and the climate is right, a work plan or wall chart is a good way to organize the effort. Arrange your key names into the appropriate categories, briefly describe their roles and what your objectives for them are, then list a set of action steps with timelines for completion. You can then proceed in a systematic way to recruit support and respond to opposition.

One other important point about key players: whether you're confident of victory or resigned to defeat, don't cut the phone lines to the other side. No matter how polarized or confrontational your campaign becomes, there is tremendous strategic value in staying in touch, and on friendly terms, with the opposition. If they know you, and you know them, then it's much harder to hate each other. And if you don't hate each other, if you share a measure of mutual respect, it will be infinitely easier to negotiate a settlement or fashion a solution you both can accept. And even if you beat them cold on this river fight, the same bureaucrats and politicians may very well be around for the next one. So leave your bridges intact.

David Brown fought the Tennessee Valley Authority tooth and nail over the fate of the Ocoee. Now, as executive director of America Outdoors, an organization representing river outfitters, Brown deals regularly with his old adversaries. "Despite the conflict that occurred," he reflects, "TVA was an interesting agency, there were some people there who were very supportive of recreation on the river. As a whole, they are now a pleasure to work with."

Work Cooperatively with Public Agencies

There is a temptation, to which this book falls easy prey, to describe river campaigns in terms of combat. We tend to speak of conflicts and battles, allies and enemies, winners and losers. But the military metaphor is also misleading because it wrongly suggests that protecting a river means constant confrontation. As often as not it means cooperation and education, particularly with public agencies having jurisdiction over and involvement in your river.

Take, for instance, the U.S. Forest Service, custodian of millions of acres of federal land through which flow thousands of rivers, most of which have no designation to guide their use and many of which are threatened by various forms of development.

Until the mid-1980s the Forest Service was only dimly aware of its responsibility to include rivers in its forest planning process and to evaluate rivers for potential Wild and Scenic protection. In most of the 118 national forests around the country there were no clear guidelines for river assessments and no personnel trained to do the work. As a result, American Rivers began filing a flood of appeals against forest plans that inadequately evaluated river resources. In many cases, rivers that met the federal criteria for Wild and Scenic protection were completely overlooked; in other cases Forest Service personnel dismissed rivers because they didn't understand the assessment criteria.

After a period of bad feeling and mutual distrust, American Rivers President Kevin Coyle decided to approach the Forest Service, as he puts it, ". . . respectfully. We made a decision to resolve our appeals face-to-face." The result was three years of barnstorming around the country during which Coyle visited some 40 national forests. "We assume that government agencies know all the laws," says Coyle, "but they don't. My visits involved a lot of brow beating of Forest Service people about what a Wild and Scenic river is. I had to educate them. We'd go on all-day drives through the forest and I'd literally show them what made a river Wild and Scenic."

Coyle didn't stop with the Forest Service. "We went to the BLM (Bureau of Land Management) and did the same thing. We approached them cautiously and respectfully, we treated them as though they had overlooked something, not ignored it."

Inspired in part by American Rivers' Forest Service efforts, Friends of the River began a campaign in 1988 to identify and lobby for the protection of every eligible stretch of Wild and Scenic River in California. The project was first called the Forty Rivers Campaign, but as the inventory of eligible rivers grew it became the Eighty Rivers Campaign, and then the Hundred Rivers Campaign. The last name stuck although the inventory grew beyond 200.

Directed by F.O.R. staff member Steve Evans, the Hundred Rivers Campaign promises to be one of the most significant river conservation efforts ever. And while the Forest Service will never agree to recommend for protection every river on the F.O.R list, Evans has already managed to more than double the number of rivers the Forest Service says is eligible for Wild and Scenic protection. When legislation is passed and the campaign is complete, Friends of the River expects to have well over 100 new Wild and Scenic designations in California.

That campaign would have failed if Friends of the River had approached the Forest Service as an enemy. Its success is attributable in part to a process of patient education and lobbying, of working cooperatively with Forest Service staff instead of against them. Evans has developed numerous relationships with key personnel in most of California's 17 National Forests and those relationships have helped him help them see the light. Which is not to suggest that the Forest Service has stepped gaily onto the dance floor with Friends of the River. "All the national forests in California have had to be prodded to do full river assessments," says Evans. But the process of prodding was facilitated by considerable human contact and professional courtesy.

Having said all this, we should acknowledge that cooperation has its limits. Evans is the first to insist that working cooperatively with the Forest Service is only successful "when the agency is willing to make a resource-based decision. It's not successful when their decisions are political-based. And the U.S. Forest Service is incapable of making controversial decisions." When the agency fails to identify an eligible river, or refuses to recommend an eligible river for protection because competing interests want to develop it, Evans resorts to a show of strength—orchestrating a flood of letters, packing hearings, filing appeals.

Of course, it's one thing to work with the Forest Service in identifying rivers eligible for protection. It's something altogether different to work with an agency like the Bureau of Reclamation or the Army Corps of Engineers when a project is being planned that would profoundly impact a river. When Bureau engineers are promoting a high dam it's a challenge, at best, to work cooperatively with them, and perhaps the best advice in that situation is to keep channels of communication open, remain courteous, and develop as many contacts inside the agency as you can. Some of them may be on your side.

Get to Know Agency Allies

Thankfully, there are several public agencies with an implicit interest in helping you protect your river. They include your state water quality agencies, state fish and game departments, the Environmental Protection Agency, and the U.S. Fish and Wildlife Service. So, after you've made a list of every agency with some form of jurisdiction over your river, the first rule in working with them is simple: get to know them. If you can't put together a list of friendly agency personnel from your environmental allies, get copies of each agency's personnel directory and begin establishing contacts. That means friendly phone calls, brown bag lunches, invitations to a briefing. Always ask to be put on an agency's mailing list. Get in the habit of calling key agency people every few weeks just to keep in touch and to keep your issue on their agenda. Always attend key agency hearings and submit written comments.

As this process unfolds, you will probably develop some sympathetic relationships with agency people who also like rivers and share your conservation values. That's the ultimate point of this exercise. Get to know the people whose decisions can affect your river. Take them on river trips. Don't be dealing with strangers. In the end, the success you have working with public agencies may be as much a product of your personal relationships as it is the logic of your issue.

If a public agency begins playing a key role in your campaign, be sure you know the limits of its jurisdiction, resources, and policy. You can then shape your strategy to utilize that agency's support and you can avoid strategies which would offend the agency or invoke its opposition. The National Park Service, for instance, can be a valuable partner in the development of Wild and Scenic plans or greenway proposals, but working with it may dictate different tactics and a less political style than you would otherwise use.

Plan a Comprehensive Media Campaign

In the annals of river conservation literature its hard to find examples of a well-executed, comprehensive media campaign. That's not to say that numerous river crusades haven't generated lots of coverage, but there's more to a media campaign than headlines and soundbites and more often than not media management isn't given the attention it deserves.

But wait, you may well be saying to yourself, I know how to write a press release, I've assembled a media information kit, and I've put together a list of media contacts. What else is there to do? The "what else" is what we're going to talk about here, and it applies equally to existing organizations and the new one you've just created.

If, like most river groups, yours doesn't have the money, the time, the personnel, or the interest to mount a full-blown media campaign, you may have to pick and choose selectively from the possibilities outlined here, but remember that no one will know about your river if you don't market your message.

The operative word here is "market." Some people hate the "M" word, they find it distasteful to reduce their lofty ideals to marketing jargon. But like it or not, what you are about to do is market your river, to sell it, like a product.

The first step in selling anything is defining the product. Sounds simple, you say, my product is a river. But the definition has to be more precise than that. The people who protected the Tatshenshini sold it as "North America's Wildest River." The marketing message for the John Day River could be reduced to one word: salmon. On the Gauley and the Ocoee the product bought by the public was whitewater recreation. Your river may have several products worth marketing, but you should choose the one or ones you think have the greatest sales potential.

You also have organizational products to sell and you need to identify them as well. Those products could include river trips, slide shows, river literature, special events, T-shirts, technical expertise, and an ethical, conservation vision. And you have one exclusive product the public won't find anywhere else: the feel-good experience of protecting a river.

In short, when you sell your message to the media, be sure you know what you're selling.

Know Who You're Selling To

The next step in marketing is identifying a target audience. Most advertisers focus their message on that demographic slice of the public most likely to buy their product. So should you. You'll get more mileage from your message if you tailor it to the people you know you need to reach.

You've already identified the natural constituencies for your river, so the message you shape should be designed to appeal to them. If, for instance, a key product of your campaign is river recreation, make sure the media message you develop targets a recreational constituency.

Wealthy organizations target their audiences with the help of surveys and focus groups. Since even a modest-sized survey could set you back $5000 and a professionally arranged focus group isn't much cheaper, you'll probably have to use other tools to find out what your target audience thinks about your river. But that's not as hard as it may sound and there are several simple ways to collect public opinion, including town meetings.

As Don Elder explained earlier, the Cahaba River Society holds town meetings up and down the length of the river's watershed. The meetings are designed to build a basin-wide constituency and to find out what local citizens are concerned about. It's an easy, inexpensive process to organize and could be invaluable for targeting your campaign.

A questionnaire is another good tool for gathering opinion. Ask respondents to explain what their greatest concerns are about the river, what action they want to see taken, who they think should take it, and whether they are willing to get involved in the campaign. The questionnaire can be circulated at town meetings, distributed in your newsletter, in the newsletters of allied organizations, and by direct mail.

Another effective way to poll the public and build a constituency is the door-to-door canvass. Canvassing is slow and labor-intensive but it's a great way to get accurate and in-depth feedback on your river campaign. It's also a good way to put volunteers to work. If you can't find the volunteer labor, look into partnering with an existing canvass—they gather information for you and raise money for themselves. The League of Conservation Voters does extensive canvasses in many parts of the country and frequently seeks local issues to work on.

Some groups prefer to conduct phone canvasses because they're quicker and far more contacts can be made in the course of a day or evening. Friends of the River has established an ongoing, in-house telephone bank to activate and poll members, generate letters, and raise money. The main limitation to phone canvassing is rising public resistance to telephone intrusion.

Once you've identified your products and targeted your audience, you need to develop a message. If you followed the advice in Chapter 3 you have already done that. The key to communicating your message through the media is simplicity and snap. The message has to be short and punchy. No buzzwords, no jargon, nothing too complex. Far too many groups ignore this advice and it is worth a major commitment of time and creative energy to develop the words and the images that summarize your message in a way that even the most vacuous newscaster can understand and regurgitate accurately.

Running Your Media Campaign

Once you've done all this, you're ready to launch a media campaign, with as many elements as you have the time, the staff, and the money to develop. Those elements include:

1. The Press Release

Organizations that have their media act together make continuous but judicious use of the press release, which has three basic purposes: To respond to a recent development or to announce a position; to provide context and background information for breaking news; to announce an event and invite the press to cover it.

Press releases should not be used indiscriminately; send them out too often and the media will start to ignore you. On the other hand, don't pass up a legitimate opportunity for media attention and always be prepared to move quickly.

In 1991 a Southern Pacific train derailed in a narrow canyon along the upper Sacramento River. A tank car tumbled into the river and leaked thousands of gallons of a toxic herbicide. Within hours the river was biologically dead and within hours after that every environmental organization in California with any media savvy was issuing a press release. Friends of the River joined the chorus and reaped substantial publicity for its river conservation message.

Timing is everything. You should be prepared with a press release whenever you have an opportunity to make or respond to news.

Writing a press release is a simple skill, often done badly. There are a few hard rules, besides the basic who, what, where, when, why, and (often forgotten) how. The first paragraph (the lead) is all important. It should tell readers the basic facts but tempt them further. Sometimes a question works well:

> How many steelhead trout are left in the Russian River?
> No one knows, but the numbers have plummeted since 1970, and that's why Friends of the Russian River is sponsoring a conference at the Junior College September 30 to discuss the fate of the fish.

Never put your opinions in a press release unless they are quotes from the mouth of someone else. Avoid hyperbole, emphasize facts and, whenever possible, announce an action. If, for instance, you want to make public your opposition to a dam project, don't just send out a press release. Instead, write a letter to the dam-building agency stating your position and then announce in a press release that you have sent the letter. Even better, schedule a meeting with the agency and alert the press, with a copy of your letter attached.

Press releases should always be double-spaced, preferably on letterhead, with a date of issue and a time of release (usually "immediate"), along with a contact name and phone number. Put a brief headline at the top of the page and repeat a shortened version on top of succeeding pages. Press releases should rarely run more than two pages. Always describe your organization and its purpose clearly and succinctly toward the end of the release.

As important as knowing how to write a press release is knowing where and when to send it. We discussed the development of a media list in the last chapter. Now for a little etiquette. Never send the same release to two different people at the same newspaper or television station. Carefully choose one contact and send one release. It's embarrassing to have two different people at the same newspaper working the same story.

It's also embarrassing to send a release too late for use and it's a waste of time to send it too soon. Press releases received several weeks before the event are soon forgotten. For daily papers the rule of thumb is three to five days before you want to see it appear in print. For weeklies, which have smaller staffs and longer lead times, allow 10 days to two weeks. And after you've mailed it, always follow up with a phone call, at least to key media.

Press releases for radio and television stations should contain the same information as newspaper releases but in abbreviated form. Broadcast news is, of course, shorter and, except for background material, a broadcast press release should be limited to one page.

Often overlooked by media campaigns is the Daybook provided by the Associated Press. In major cities, AP puts out a complete listing of coming events which television, radio, and print media rely on. Check with the AP office in the nearest large city.

2. Media Kits

We described this package in detail in Chapter 3. Now you have to make intelligent use of it. Media kits are for distribution at press conferences; they're background information to give reporters interviewing you and to hand around at editorial board meetings. If you have the money, it's also good to mail one as a "backgrounder" to everyone on your media list with a cover letter offering yourself and your organization as a resource for future stories.

3. Feature Stories

The heart of your message only emerges when the news media decides to do a story on your river in-depth. That means a feature.

Getting a feature story for a river is seldom difficult, particularly if there's a dramatic threat involved—like a dam, a pollution scare, or a high-profile endangered species. This is the fodder of journalism and the more controversy there is the more the media likes it. Your job is to provide the background, the research, and the authoritative expertise for the story. And you do that by becoming a reliable source and a familiar contact. Keep a running list of ideas for feature stories and feed them to friendly journalists. In smaller towns and for weekly newspapers, you'll find editors willing to take freelance feature articles about your river.

When you're dealing with television and radio, remember that a feature story means three to five minutes of air time, so well-rehearsed sound bites and visual bits are crucial.

4. Editorial Meetings

To some degree, you get the media coverage you ask for and the best place to ask is at the top. That's why background sessions with editors and editorial boards are a fundamental part of any media campaign. The Olympic Rivers Council, as described earlier, has used this strategy with great success.

To set up a meeting send a letter and press kit to the editor, news director, or program director you want to meet with, explaining what you want to talk about and why it is important. Follow with a phone call and arrange to bring with you one or two of the most prominent and credible supporters you have. During the meeting resist the temptation to proselytize. Lay out the facts, answer questions, and offer expert analysis and background information for future coverage.

5. Letters to the Editor, Op-Ed Pieces, and Editorial Replies

Letters to the editor are one of the best-read features of any newspaper so you're missing a major audience if you don't make use of this free forum. You should, of course, invite your members and supporters to write letters on behalf of the river. But you should also orchestrate the submission of letters from key people—experts, political leaders, celebrities.

A massive outpouring of letters isn't necessary or effective since most newspapers limit the number of letters on any given subject or from any given writer. It's far better to have a fewer number of well-written letters from prominent people, timed to correspond with key campaign events.

Op-ed pieces provide another effective—and free—forum and they, even more than letters, should be carefully crafted by a prominent spokesperson for your campaign.

Television and radio stations routinely provide opportunities for "free speech" messages or replies to station editorials. If you stay on top of the news you can find opportunities to get on the air. To arrange a reply, contact the station's program director and ask for air time.

6. Talk Shows

The airwaves are awash with talk shows and in most markets they're fairly easy to get on. When shopping for a talk show, listen before you leap, become familiar with the host's interests and style, and structure a letter of request in response to what you hear.

Before going on the air, particularly for the first time, it pays to rehearse, even to role play what you are going to say. Have a friend play the host and practice framing short, succinct answers. It's also helpful to practice responding to hostile questions since you will almost certainly get your share.

7. Press Conferences

Press conferences are thinly veiled theater. You use them to get attention for an important announcement, an up-coming event, a lawsuit, the opening of an office, the opinion of someone important, to release new information. Alert the media with a press release 48 hours in advance and always follow-up with telephone calls. Have press packets and a general release available at the press conference.

Press conferences should have a clear and simple focus, they should start on time and they should be held in the morning, preferably by 10:00 a.m. A press conference that's over at 10:30 will make the news at 6 and 11 o'clock as well as the newspaper the following morning. Not withstanding the instant transmission of minicams, television reporters still work primarily off tape and aren't likely to cover an event they can't have edited and on the air that day.

Whenever possible plan your press conference at the river; it offers the visual impact television crews crave. Hang banners and posters to dramatize your message and turn out a throng of volunteers. Be on hand well before the event starts. It isn't always practical, but if possible have an amplified sound system available so that you can be heard above the noise of a crowd. Some rental units can be run off batteries.

8. Slide Show

Cheaper than a video and visually more effective, a slide show should be one of your basic media tools. It can range in sophistication from a loose collection of slides you project during a lecture to a fully scripted show with title graphics and a sound track. A slide show shouldn't run longer than about 10 minutes, which allows for more than 100 pictures, and a good one can easily be done in half that time. Its biggest advantage is the size and quality of the image projected. The disadvantage is the need for a projector and viewing surface.

9. Video

Everyone is doing video now and its very ubiquity has become an argument in video's favor. People have come to expect it. Video's biggest single advantage is convenience; it's easy to edit and update and you can carry a whole show in your pocket. It's also cheaper to copy than a slide show, offers moving images and greater graphic flexibility. But video is more expensive to produce, running upwards of $1000 per minute for a professional production.

There are some viable alternatives, however, that can make video affordable, even cheap. It's worth seeking out student filmmaking classes or volunteer amateurs interested in developing some credits. Sometimes PBS stations will produce a program which you can adapt for a campaign video.

When you've got a video, flog it. Make it available to schools and libraries and see if you can have it shown on the local public access cable channel.

10. Speakers Bureau

As word spreads about your campaign, invitations will start to arrive from business and civic groups, churches and schools to provide speakers on the subject of your river. Be prepared. Developing a speakers bureau requires identifying the people in your campaign who can make your case effectively in public. A well-run media campaign involves a continual series of public presentations and reaps twin benefits since you're educating your audience and, often, getting media coverage as well.

11. Theater

There are different points of view about political theater and some people are wary of it, worrying that it lacks dignity and mainstream appeal. The knock on theater is that it is sometimes done badly, in poor taste or with little sophistication, and therefore turns people off. The up side of theater is that more often than not it gets immediate media attention. When Earth First! unrolled a giant fabric crack down the face of Glen Canyon Dam there was no seismic shift in public thinking, but a picture of the crack made front pages all over America.

And when Friends of the River transplanted a Toyon pine tree from the Stanislaus River Canyon to the grounds of the state Capital in Sacramento, thereby making the point that all living things in the river corridor were threatened by New Melones Dam, the action got widespread and respectful publicity. If you decide to do some theater, make sure it isn't offensive to the general public and therefore counterproductive.

Not many groups will do theater with real theater, but the Mattole Restoration Council, in collaboration with other environmental groups, and with a National Endowment for the Arts grant, sponsored a musical comedy called Queen Salmon, which has been touring the West Coast to great acclaim since 1991. The "biologically explicit musical comedy for people of several species" chronicles the plight of Pacific salmon with humor and good music.

12. Top 10 Lists

The increasing popularity of this publicity device may or may not have anything to do with David Letterman. American Rivers began a list of the nation's 10 most endangered rivers (along with the 15 most threatened) in 1987, and while the idea took a while to catch on, an aggressive media campaign has resulted in extensive national coverage. The annual announcement is now made at a celebrity-festooned press conference and follow-up press conferences are held around the country for each of the endangered rivers.

The New England Coastal Campaign's Terrible Ten list was another media masterpiece, garnering widespread publicity and focusing public attention on threats to the coastline and estuaries of the Northeast.

The Art of Making News

Turning these basic elements into a media campaign requires constant creativity. Here are some suggestions for the fine art of making news.

Conduct a survey and announce the results; issue a report; organize a press tour of the river; announce the formation of an organization; make a prediction; arrange an interview with a public figure; adopt a river; hold a contest; make a speech; announce an appointment to your staff; respond to breaking news; present an award; celebrate an anniversary; prepare and release testimony for a hearing; release a letter you have received; praise a decision; protest a decision; stage a peaceful protest; host a debate; respond to outrageous claims by the other side; open an office.

Finally, when your campaign starts to reach critical mass, you may want to employ the oldest marketing tactic in politics—yard signs. Friends of the Payette put yard signs "all over Southwestern Idaho," says Wendy Wilson. "A legislator once asked why we had them—she saw them everywhere. We said that was why."

Once you've captured the public's interest, the next step is to put that interest to some creative use, like writing letters.

Organize a Letter-Writing Campaign

During the summer of 1983, the fight over the fate of the Tuolumne River hit a frenzied peak, with much of it focused on the heart and mind of Senator Pete Wilson. Wilson's support for a Tuolumne protection bill was essential for passage, but the senator had resisted a decision. Hoping to help him make one, Friends of the River and the Tuolumne River Preservation Trust launched a letter-writing campaign of epic proportions. At one point during that summer, Wilson's aides said, the senator was receiving up to 2000 letters a week. The unofficial letter count total is believed to have exceeded 10,000. Wilson, as you have read earlier, eventually backed the river.

If the fate of your river is riding on a legislative decision, letter writing has to become a key part of your campaign. A loose rule of thumb espoused by some members of Congress is that one letter reflects the views of 100 people. Whatever the accuracy of that formula, most legislators agree that, next to an opinion poll, constituent mail is the single best way to sample the views of voters. Former Arizona representative Mo Udall has said, "Mail to a modern-day Congressman is more important than ever before . . . my mailbag is my best 'hotline' to the people back home."

So, how do you generate ten thousand letters? Or even a hundred?

Friends of the River has orchestrated some of the most successful letter writing campaigns in the country and one of the key ingredients to their success is on-river organizing. Since the early days of the Stanislaus campaign, F.O.R. has used volunteers, river guides, and sometimes a part-time staffer to get river runners to write letters. Over the years, hundreds of river guides have been trained to give letter-writing talks to their passengers. The guides are armed with letter-writing kits, including paper, pens and envelopes, along with instructions on what their passengers should write.

The success of this program depends in part on the willingness of commercial outfitters to let their guides proselytize on the river; most do, and F.O.R. works closely with outfitters to keep their cooperation. Letter-writing tables are also erected at river take-outs and at virtually all F.O.R. events.

While the F.O.R. model has been highly successful, it's obviously limited to runnable rivers where people come to play. If yours isn't a whitewater river, it probably still supports some kind of recreation, and if people visit it in any significant numbers you have an automatic letter-writing constituency. You can tap into that constituency simply by planting a table and a chair beside the river, hanging up a poster or a sign, handing out literature, pens, and paper, and urging people to write a short letter on the spot while your message is still warm in their heads. People become even more willing to write a letter when you offer to add postage and mail it.

Off-river letter-writing campaigns depend largely on direct mail and phone banking. While the performance of direct mail seems to have dwindled as the avalanche of junk mail grows, if you have a good list, use it, and if you can borrow lists from other groups, use those too. The best list is a collection of names of people who have already given money or time for the river. One of the reasons for setting up a database, as we described during the membership discussion in Chapter 3, is to easily access activists who will write letters.

To do that you send out an action alert, which can be as simple as a bulk-mailed sheet of paper folded in half, announcing the urgent need for letters to protect the river. Contents of the alert should include the nature of the immediate threat and the action you are trying to get a legislator or agency to take, along with some sample language for a letter and, of course, the appropriate address.

Tell your supporters that letters should be short and simple, limited to about three paragraphs. Letters shouldn't try to make more than two or three basic points and they should never threaten or intimidate, as in "vote my way or we'll run you out of office."

Letters should also be personal. If the letter writer has seen the river, has had an important experience on the river, that direct experience should be conveyed.

At the end of an action alert leave room for a coupon the recipient can fill out and return. The coupon gives you an opportunity to ask for contributions to cover the cost of the mailing and to get confirmation that the recipient actually wrote a letter.

Phone Calls and Fax Attacks

Phone banking can also be an effective way to generate letters, although it doesn't put physically into people's hands the words of the message they need to convey. On the other hand you can reach more people quickly on the phone and it allows you to carry on a discussion and gather feedback. Phone banks also allow you to react to events in a hurry, while a mailed alert takes time to write, print, and mail. For an urgent letter writing push just before a hearing on Sespe Creek, Alasdair Coyne personally made 300 phone calls in one weekend.

Wendy Wilson is partial to the telephone as well. "I think the phone bank is the only way to get any letters in," she says, "we've had great success with it." But unless you can afford to hire phone callers, you'll need a dedicated crew of volunteers willing to work late afternoons and early evenings, when most people are at home.

Arguably, the best way to generate letters is with action alerts followed by a phone bank. Many campaigns have used this tactic and if the issue is really urgent (and you can afford the time or money it takes) the dual effort will probably produce the best results.

The fax machine has provided a techno-bridge between letters and phone calls and "fax attacks" have quickly become a standard weapon in the activist's arsenal. Since fax messages combine the written formality of a letter with the speed of a phone call, they serve particularly well in delivering last-minute messages. Some people argue, however, that letters delivered through the mail still carry more emotional punch. Increasingly, legislative offices will also be wired for E-mail, which is another useful means of instant communication.

Some letter campaigns rely on standardized cards with a printed message and space for a signature. Legislators may get the message from this mass attack, but they clearly put more stock in personal letters.

Always coordinate a letter-writing campaign with partner organizations to distribute the burden and broaden the reach of your effort. Time your letter campaign carefully to coincide with important hearings, votes, or agency decisions. The letter attack should peak just before a vote is taken or a decision is made and should be carefully targeted at key individuals.

Laying Siege to the Legislature

Finally, there's the eleventh-hour statehouse assault to drive your point home while legislators are debating the fate of your river on the very floor of the legislature. Many statehouses allow for messages to be delivered by pages to legislators during floor debate. It can be a very persuasive tactic to have a last-minute reminder placed in the hands of a state senator or representative on the verge of a vote.

In the closing hours of the epic battle over the Payette, when legislators were heatedly debating a bill to protect the river, Friends of the Payette organized an army of supporters who converged on the statehouse in Boise and fired a barrage of letters into the hallowed chamber. Between 11:00 a.m. and 1:00 p.m. they sent in 620 messages, more than had ever been delivered before. And, of course, they won.

Get Involved in Lobbying

The marbled hallways of the Congressional office buildings lining Independence and Constitution Avenues in Washington, D.C. are meant to be imposing, and they are. Newcomers can be excused a sense of awe, if not downright intimidation.

Only slightly less imposing are the statehouses in Albany and Sacramento, Boise and Boston. It is in these ornate halls of power and bureaucracy that you will inevitably find yourself during any river campaign looking for a legislative fix. And before you do, there are some important things to know.

First of all, resist the temptation to let someone else do your lobbying for you. If you've been fighting for your river and you've finally gotten a protection bill before Congress or the state legislature, be there. If a bad bill is in the works that would hurt your river, be there. You can and should get advice and support from state and national groups who know the ropes, but you know the river and you need to make its case. You also need to meet your legislators face-to-face so that they can attach a human being to the river they're being lobbied about.

Alasdair Coyne is now a comfortable and polished speaker, faint traces of his native Scotland coloring the edges of his words. He has testified before Congressional committees and lobbied in those big marble buildings, going so far as to don coat and tie. But none of this came naturally to Coyne, a man more comfortable in T-shirt and shorts who was, he confesses, "a really shy person. I had a really hard time doing it."

The Right People at the Right Time

Coyne is not unlike a lot of people unfamiliar with the halls of power. But being a lobbyist doesn't mean becoming hip, slick, and cool. More than anything else it means mastering your material and presenting it well to the right people at the right time.

The right time is as soon as you catch wind of legislation, or the discussion of legislation, you think will damage your river; or as soon as you are politically and organizationally ready to seek the passage of legislation to protect your river. It's never the right time to lobby if you aren't prepared.

There are probably three optimal lobbying time frames:

1. When your campaign is first gearing up and you want to communicate your concerns to elected officials and perhaps discuss the pros and cons of legislation;
2. When a bill is being worked up in committee and you want your opinions on it clearly understood;
3. When a bill is being voted on and you want to influence the outcome.

So, when the time to lobby comes, there are several steps to take.

1. Get Some Help

Unless you're already a veteran at this game, the first step is to find someone who is. That means contacting allied organizations—hopefully some of your campaign partners—with lobbying experience and a knowledge of the legislative body you're dealing with. Arrange a meeting and discuss issues and strategy carefully, giving particular attention to a review of key committees your bill will pass through and the legislators you need to lobby. If you have an effective working relationship with other groups, you may be able to muster teams of lobbyists working the bill together.

2. Be Organized

Lobby campaigns need to be carefully orchestrated. You can't just start throwing bodies at the legislature. When Friends of the Payette began a lobby campaign on the Idaho Legislature, they put together an eight-person lobbying team which divided up the entire House. They also conducted a lobby training session for volunteers, and everyone who talked to a legislator was required to report to the lobby team the results of every contact.

3. Team Up

Anyone who has done any lobbying will tell you there is strength and comfort in numbers. Two people are usually more effective than one, but more than three is a mob. Team up with someone you're comfortable with and confident in. Shyness is not necessarily a liability; you don't have to be polished, just sincere and well-informed. Whenever possible take along someone with prominence or professional credentials.

4. Be Prepared

The secret to effective lobbying is preparation. Learn everything you can about the legislators you plan to lobby and tailor your presentation to their interests and areas of expertise. Rehearse your presentation until you have it reduced to its elemental parts and you can repeat them quickly and comfortably. Limit your pitch to three or four points and remember the K.I.S.S. principle (Keep It Simple, Stupid). Among some lobbyists, the prevailing advice is to aim your message at a fourth grade level of comprehension. That may misrepresent the intelligence of some elected officials (both up and down), but the point is to refrain from a superfluous show of technical verbiage.

5. Ask for What You Want

One of the hardest things for some amateur lobbyists to do is close the sale. They will ramble on at length about their issue but hem and haw when it comes time to ask point blank for support. Don't ever leave a legislator's office without making it explicitly clear what you want. Don't leave room for the one thing most politicians do best—creative interpretation.

6. Leave an Information Package

Prepare a lobbying kit containing all the essential information about your river—along with your desired outcome—and have enough for both the legislator and her or his aides. Include some stunning photographs.

7. Demonstrate Constituent Support

Whenever possible, take with you some evidence of constituent support for the river. Petitions are always effective, but you can also take letters written by prominent people, newspaper editorials, and letters to the editor. Try to speak on behalf of as many people as possible and always look for ways to make your issue politically attractive to your legislator.

8. Schedule Ahead

Scheduling meetings will be one of your biggest challenges so plan your lobbying trip carefully in advance. It is always easier to meet with staff members than with their legislators and, if you have the time, doing so is often a good preparation strategy. Staffers can brief their legislators and prepare them for a more focused meeting with you. But when you have only one shot at a meeting and you want to deliver your message directly, be firm and insist on the legislator in person. Sometimes you'll succeed.

9. Plan for Drop-In Visits

No matter how well you schedule yourself, your schedule will fall apart. Legislators are seldom on time for meetings, partly because committee hearings and floor debates always start and end late and partly because, between any committee room and the legislator's office, there are hundreds or thousands of feet of hallway packed with other lobbyists, colleagues, and press all wanting his or her attention.

So when you have gaps in your lobbying schedule pull out a fallback list of people you want to see and do as many drop-in visits as you have time for. You'll often find an available staff person and sometimes you'll luck out with a legislator-in-the-flesh.

10. Prepare Testimony

Not all of your lobbying will take place in the relatively private confines of a legislative office. There are times when you will have to testify before a committee, with legislators imposingly ensconced behind a long dais in a big room, and that's when the faint of heart tend to faint.

Alasdair Coyne would tell you, "If I can do it you can do it," and he would also advise you to have some sympathetic bodies in the hearing room. Committee testimony is often done by twos and threes so you probably won't have to be alone at the witness table.

Committee testimony should always be prepared in writing and copies should be submitted to committee staff. Your spoken testimony should be brief, full of both feeling and fact and, if you can handle it, extemporaneous with notes to refer to. Always be prepared for questions following your testimony; they may provide the best opportunity to make your case. Some people like to role play the question and answer, and that's probably a good idea for anyone not experienced at a congressional witness table.

When Alasdair Coyne first prepared testimony for a hearing in Washington, he faxed a copy to American Rivers and they sent him back a comprehensive critique which he found enormously helpful. They'll do the same for you if you ask. "We do a lot of coaching," acknowledges Kevin Coyle. "It's a little like talking down an airplane when the pilot has died of a heart attack. We help them land in Washington."

One last word of caution: because other activists and organizations will often have more experience than you do, and because you will be intimidated at first by the halls of power, the process of lobbying is where you are most likely to lose control of your campaign. That's why it's essential that you establish and maintain a personal relationship with your elected representatives.

And when you lobby, remember this as well: you will almost never be given what you ask for. Usually, you have to negotiate.

Negotiate from a Position of Strength

Throughout this book you have been exposed to two competing messages, one soft, one hard. You have heard, on the one hand, about the need to seek and find common ground, to avoid polarization and confrontation, to work cooperatively with others. And then we have talked about the exercise of power, about selling a message, stopping a dam, winning a fight.

If the contradiction frustrates you, take comfort in the fact that it has been frustrating humans for centuries. Perhaps the best we can do about these conflicting objectives is pursue them both. When you negotiate the fate of a river, that's pretty much what you'll be doing; looking for common ground while exercising all the power you can muster.

Some people argue that too many rivers and other wild places have already been negotiated away and that it's time to take a stand for what is left. Besides, how can you negotiate the construction of a dam? Either it's built or it isn't. But the truth is that the majority of river campaigns aren't about a single, simple threat, or a single solution. They involve varieties of abuses and a tapestry of solutions, which inevitably requires negotiation.

When to Negotiate

At the very least you will probably have to negotiate a solution when:

1. Your river suffers from widespread pollution.
2. Diversions have eliminated adequate instream flow.
3. The riparian corridor and watershed slopes are being logged.
4. Development encroaches on the flood plain and river corridor.
5. Administrative agencies with jurisdiction over the river aren't doing their jobs.

Countless books have been written on the subject and it's not our intent here to train you in the art of negotiating. But we need to discuss a few basic points, the first and most important being not to begin negotiating until you can do so from a position of strength.

Steve Evans has had great success negotiating with the Forest Service for Wild and Scenic eligibility designations when there has been a tangible display of public support for a particular river, or when there has been the threat of an appeal or lawsuit in his back pocket. Negotiation, says Evans, "only works when you do it from a position of strength. That strength can be legal or political, but it has to be there."

That fact suggests that timing is a crucial part of the negotiation process. You don't want to begin negotiating until you have sufficient power to back up your position. Your power may come from a clear demonstration of public support (one of the reasons the steps outlined in Chapter 3 are so important), it may come from the threat of a lawsuit or the intervention of a public agency or the backing of a powerful politician. It may also come from a barrage of publicity supporting your cause. Wherever your power comes from, it's important to use it when you have it because power, like water, has a tendency to ebb and flow.

The Clark Fork–Pend Oreille Coalition has been successful negotiating agreements with mining and forest products companies, partly because they put together a powerful coalition of environmental, sporting, and business interests.

When Champion International sought a permit to increase its discharge from a paper mill into the Clark Fork, the Coalition objected and a lengthy review process began. That eventually included a two-year study, an Environmental Impact Statement, and a political stalemate that lasted seven months. Finally, Peter Nielsen, then executive director of the Coalition, entered into a face-to-face negotiation with the head of the paper mill and they managed to agree on the terms of a five-year discharge permit.

Nielsen's success in negotiating an agreement was due in part to the fact that a lobbying effort had forced the Montana Water Quality Bureau to hold up Champion's discharge permit. The Water Bureau's action gave the Coalition a position of strength and gave Champion a powerful incentive to settle.

Information, as the saying goes, is power and sometimes the right information can give you negotiating strength. When the Cahaba River Society researched the Birmingham Water Board's rationale for wanting to dam the Locust Fork River, they found it was full of holes. The CRS put together a persuasive analysis of Birmingham's real water needs which helped them counter the Water Board's plans.

Media muscle can also give you a position of strength. The New England Coastal Campaign's Terrible Ten list of prominent polluters was first and foremost a public relations gimmick (there often weren't even 10 offenders on the list). But during the 1980s it generated an enormous amount of media coverage, which translated directly into power. Pete Lavigne, who co-chaired the Campaign, recalls that, "Out of 12 or 13 cases nominated to the list, we won about eight hands down."

Have a Fallback Position

The question inevitably arises, "What if, despite our best efforts, the other side is clearly more powerful than we are?"

There are several pieces to the answer. First of all, never enter a negotiation without a bottom line, beyond which you won't go (and, of course, always ask for more than you expect to get). If you're involved in the negotiations with other partners make sure everyone understands and agrees on the bottom line. Secondly, always enter a negotiation with a fallback alternative; don't stake everything on the outcome of negotiations. Know what you'll do if you have to walk away from the negotiation. Knowing your fallback position allows you to honor your bottom line and empowers you with the freedom of walking away.

Finally, there is sometimes negotiating power in principle alone, and in any river campaign, principle is a potent force. Translated into a negotiating asset, principle allows you to occupy the high ground where media exposure and public opinion will back you up.

If you're looking for literature on the art of negotiation, perhaps the best place to start is with *Getting to Yes*, by Roger Fisher and William Ury. Fisher is an international negotiation guru who heads the Harvard Negotiation Project. His book is short, succinct, and packed with wisdom.

Be Prepared to Compromise

The history of river protection is littered with painful compromises—rivers and canyons sacrificed to development so that other rivers could flow free.

Lake Powell, which backs up behind Glen Canyon Dam, buried a section of the Colorado River which those who once knew it describe with awe and reverence. Glen Canyon was lost in the compromise that lifted the threat of dams from Echo Park on the Green and Yampa Rivers in Dinosaur National Monument.

The Clavey River is a spectacular tributary of the Tuolumne and was part of American Rivers' 10 Most Endangered list in 1993. That's because it was cut out of the Tuolumne Wild and Scenic bill during last minute negotiations and is now targeted for a major hydro project.

The Gauley River was saved from a hydropower dam by legislation that struck a compromise between Wild and Scenic designation and a National Recreation Area. The compromise left a river corridor ripe for commercial exploitation and that's what happened. Now some people fear the Gauley, saved from a dam, will die from development.

Protecting rivers is a political process and politics is, as they say, the art of compromise. So when you're negotiating the fate of a river, no matter how strong your position may be, you will rarely get everything you want. The challenge, therefore, is to get the most you can, to know what you're willing to give up and to be very clear about what your real objectives are.

David Brown, who engineered the Gauley campaign and now represents the interests of outfitters who own land along the river, thinks compromise is a relative term. "Some people wouldn't agree there was compromise on the Gauley. It depends on your point of view. On the Gauley, without acknowledging private land rights, there wouldn't have been protection."

The important thing to remember, insists Brown, is what your true objectives are and how they can best be achieved. "Are you trying to notch your pistol with another Wild and Scenic designation, or are you trying to protect a river?"

Negotiation guru Roger Fisher has constructed a whole system around the premise that reaching agreement is far more easily achieved when you defend your objective instead of your position.

Compromise demands that you acknowledge the interests of the other side. Acknowledgement doesn't mean agreement, but it means willingness to listen. Environmentalists in general and river-lovers in particular have a tendency toward self-righteousness which can be offensive to those not sharing the faith. That attitude can get in the way of agreement.

Ultimately, compromise is aimed at establishing a win–win solution which allows both parties to walk away with their agendas more or less intact. But win–win is usually possible only when both sides are willing to step away from their positions to explore alternatives that will result in the desired objectives.

There is, of course, one major problem with this scenario. While "win–win" has become a popular buzzword it's hard for some people to accept it as a legitimate environmental and river-saving strategy. Earth First! has popularized the phrase, "No compromise in defense of Mother Earth." The meaning of that message is that the environment has already been compromised too much, that far from giving up any more of the earth, we have to take back some of what has been lost. Applied to dwindling forests and ravaged rivers, that's a compelling argument.

However you approach the issue, never forget that in negotiating an agreement the ultimate objective isn't satisfying your ego or winning debating points, it's protecting the river. That's what negotiation and compromise should be about.

The Importance of a Bottom Line

As we discussed earlier, you should never begin negotiating without knowing your bottom line, and you should never compromise below it. Establishing a bottom line can be a major challenge, especially if you are negotiating on behalf of several other parties. Sometimes negotiating the bottom line among your allies is more difficult than negotiating an agreement with your opponents. There is always the danger that one of the parties on your side will be willing to give up more than is necessary in order to reach agreement. David Brower has lamented publicly for years his and the Sierra Club's willingness to surrender Glen Canyon in exchange for Echo Park.

Of course, your bottom line may change as circumstances change. In 1988, Friends of the River participated in a complicated negotiation that produced a memorandum of understanding which the parties involved thought was a workable compromise on the Auburn Dam issue. At that time members of the state legislature, two key members of Congress, Friends of the River, and other environmental groups were willing to accept the construction of a small "dry" dam which could not be restaged to impound water, in exchange for a variety of environmental protections including a river-based National Recreation Area in the canyons of the American River.

Accepting a dry dam was a major compromise arrived at by F.O.R. board members after a long, painful debate. But the political equation behind the agreement kept changing, the congressional sponsors shifted their position to embrace an "expandable" dry dam and the study for a National Recreation Area was stretched to accommodate a reservoir.

All of this exceeded F.O.R.'s bottom line, they pulled the plug and the compromise fell apart, along with legislation for the dam.

Sometimes compromise allows you to regroup and fight another day. After a Herculean organizing effort which created a broad popular constituency for Sespe Creek, Keep the Sespe Wild was still unable to win inclusion of the two prospective dam sites in the Wild and Scenic bill that was passed in 1992. The main obstacle was the local member of Congress, who carried the bill but wanted the dam sites left for possible future development. Sespe Wild swallowed the compromise, took what they could get and resolved to keep up their efforts until the entire Sespe is protected. Meanwhile, the Congressman was defeated in the next election, which changed the local political equation and may open the door for further protection.

Compromise doesn't always mean giving up. Sometimes it just means postponing. If you can agree to a compromise which postpones your ultimate objective while giving you a partial victory and the possibility of winning more later, it can be advantageous to get what you can a piece at a time. It's certainly an improvement over getting nothing.

And sometimes compromise simply means changing the terms of the debate. During the Rio Chama campaign, most members of the Chama Trust wanted Wild and Scenic protection right down into the existing reservoir pool at Abiquiu Dam, but one faction feared that a major flood could back up the reservoir into the Wild and Scenic segment, thus setting a dangerous precedent for impoundments on Wild and Scenic rivers. Finally, someone suggested a novel compromise: the portion of the Chama inside the flood pool would be protected as a "permanent Wild and Scenic study segment." No study would ever be done and no designation would be made, but because study rivers are protected until designation is made, that segment of river would have all the protection of the Wild and Scenic Act. Changing a few words achieved a compromise that got the desired result.

If compromise isn't possible without surrendering your bottom line, however, walk away. It's better to lose outright, to back up and regroup, than to give away too much. That's why it's so important to have a fall-back position you can retreat to.

Give Recognition to Public Officials

When California Congressman George Miller won passage of reform legislation which forced the Bureau of Reclamation to reallocate Central Valley Project water to benefit salmon and steelhead, supporters threw a lavish crab feed to say thanks. That was easy.

When he ran for Governor of California, U.S. Senator Pete Wilson, who had provided pivotal support for protection of the Tuolumne, Kings, Kern, and Merced Rivers, asked for and got the endorsement of Friends of the River. That was hard.

When Edward King was elected Governor of Massachusetts, the Charles River Watershed Association made him an honorary resident of the watershed, despite evidence his public position favored watershed development. That was smart.

Recognizing public officials is an essential part of the political process, although it is often overlooked and sometimes requires great delicacy. Honoring George Miller was easy because he has been one of the West's most consistent champions of water policy reform and river protection, and because he delivered on a difficult and controversial bill.

Endorsing Wilson was hard because his positions on some nonenvironmental issues offended F.O.R. board members, because some board members were suspicious about the depth of his commitment to rivers, and because his opponent had an excellent rivers and water platform. In the end, Wilson got the endorsement, partly because F.O.R. felt the need to honor a debt.

Honoring King was smart because, as recounted in Chapter 3, that friendly gesture helped inspire him to turn down a developer's request for relaxation of sewer permit requirements.

When an elected official supports your river, you have a certain obligation to support that official. And that can sometimes be difficult. You may find that the politician providing the key support for your river has a dismal record on other issues. An extreme example is Oregon Senator Bob Packwood, who has played key roles in river protection legislation but became a political pariah in the wake of sexual harassment charges. More commonly, a public official who supports river protection may oppose other environmental legislation you support. What to do?

There's no easy answer to this dilemma, but campaign professionals are adamant about the need to acknowledge public officials who help your campaign succeed. "Loyalty," says David Brown, "is a very important factor here. Politicians don't respect someone who changes horses after the campaign is over."

One expression of loyalty is political support, which is why Wilson asked for the Friends of the River endorsement. Brown agrees that if a politician helps save your river, you should help save his or her election. "Generate letters for them," he says, "support them in their campaigns, even when they may not be of your political persuasion."

Brown acknowledges that this can lead to some "delicate situations, like when your candidate runs against someone else you support."

David Weiman, one of Washington's preeminent environmental lobbyists, feels that "too many people take public officials for granted. One way not to is to go work in their next campaign."

Not all political favors require a political response and if your organization has 501(c)(3) tax status your political options will be somewhat limited. But nothing should stop you from publishing a public thank you in the pages of your newsletter, or from sending congratulatory letters to the editor of the local newspaper praising your public official. Testimonial dinners, trophies, and awards are also appropriate ways to honor officials who have made a difference to your river campaign, and one of the best expressions of thanks is a river trip.

Keep a Watchdog Organization on the Scene

It's not enough to manage the media, work the players, promote alternatives, generate letters, and shepherd an army of volunteers. It's not even enough to win the passage of Wild and Scenic bills, to enact land-use ordinances and river corridor management plans. All those things will dramatically reduce the nature and number of threats to a river, but as long as your river flows it will be at risk. If you want permanent protection, therefore, you need a permanent presence.

Thirty years after Marion Stoddart first began organizing the clean-up of the Nashua River, the Nashua River Watershed Association continues her work. And in all probability it will be doing her work 30 years from now.

The Westport River Watershed Alliance was started in 1975 and is busier today than ever. That's because it has assumed the role of permanent watchdog, monitoring town councils, opposing inappropriate development, looking for signs of pollution, testing water quality, and promoting sound land use planning.

On the other hand, after Citizens for Gauley River won Congressional protection in 1988, they pretty much packed up and went home. Major issues, like riparian land acquisition and management of heavy recreational use, went unaddressed. The West Virginia Rivers Coalition is beginning to fill the vacuum but the Gauley would have been better served by a continuous and permanent watchdog organization on site.

Indeed, as dam battles, Wild and Scenic campaigns, and hydropower fights play themselves out in the years ahead, the evolving model for river protection is going to emerge from the work of river guardian groups which commit themselves to a process of continual vigilance and comprehensive restoration. Guardian groups keep track of political decisions that impact rivers, they educate and lobby government and business on river-sensitive behavior, they inform and involve the public through on-river events and outreach, they promote comprehensive river basin management plans, and they organize the political power to oppose inappropriate development. Prime examples are the Mattole Restoration Council and the Clark Fork–Pend Oreille Coalition. For those groups and hundreds of others, river protection is an ongoing, daily, weekly, monthly task, and a permanent commitment.

Some guardian groups get directly involved in sampling water quality and measuring biological health. Two national organizations—River Watch Network and the Izaak Walton League—provide guidance and support for that kind of citizen action.

River Watch Network creates partnerships with local watchdog groups, teaching volunteers how to monitor water quality and what to do with the results. The organization focuses on scientifically credible water monitoring and works closely with local river watch groups, high schools, and colleges to develop sampling programs which can be translated into corrective action. By 1993, River Watch Network was working with 37 groups on 63 rivers in 13 states. RWN partnerships are available in targeted areas, which will change from year to year, but currently include New England, the Hudson River watershed, the Upper Mississippi, and the Rio Grande.

Partnership groups must meet some basic criteria before River Watch Network will establish a program. Those criteria include a local commitment to carrying out a water monitoring program, which often requires technical support from a local water agency; involvement of a local high school or college; a commitment to involve river users—including the polluters—in fashioning a solution; and adequate funding potential.

Local river groups meeting these criteria get a lot of hands-on support from River Watch Network, which helps interpret water quality data to turn it into an advocacy tool. While the River Watch movement has already benefited numerous rivers and is spreading rapidly across the country, Jack Byrne, RWN's executive director, warns that river monitoring is a slow process and that, typically, two years can pass between the time a program is set up and the time credible results are available for some form of action.

River Watch systems not only provide useful data on the health of a river, they represent an effective organizing tool for involving the public and penetrating the school system. They also provide periodic opportunities for media coverage as the results of monitoring activities are announced.

Of course, river monitoring need not be limited to water quality. Bank erosion, setback violations, illegal diversions, grazing damage, and timber harvesting are all activities which affect river health and need to be closely watched by guardian groups.

The Izaak Walton League's Save Our Streams program focuses less on chemical purity than on the biological health of rivers. The SOS program teaches people how to trap, identify, and record aquatic life, since the presence of macroinvertebrates—large aquatic organisms that live in rivers and streams—is a good indicator of water quality and the health of the aquatic food chain. Aquatic life is an important indicator because some rivers may be chemically "clean" but biologically dead.

Founded in 1922, The Izaak Walton League has been around longer than any other river conservation organization and has 400 local chapters around the country. Anyone can participate in the SOS program simply by requesting a copy of the Save Our Streams Water Quality Monitoring Video. The video provides a demonstration of stream monitoring techniques along with information on stream pollution problems, stream sampling, identification of stream organisms, use of the stream survey, and advice on how to adopt a stream.

Ultimately, the healthiest and best protected rivers in the country are going to be those with strong guardian groups who take the river as a personal responsibility and keep a watchful eye on its health.

Keep a Shopping List of Work for Volunteers

The campaign activities outlined above will exceed the resources of most river conservation groups. There will almost always be a shortage of qualified bodies to do the necessary work, which is why most river campaigns depend on volunteers.

Are volunteers important in a river campaign? "Totally," says Wendy Wilson, who built Friends of the Payette almost entirely with volunteers. "Absolutely," agrees Mandy Weltman, who coordinates Friends of the River's volunteer-run annual conference.

The effective use of volunteers may, in fact, be a good gauge of the health and strength of a river conservation organization. It suggests that you're in touch with your grassroots supporters and that your workload is distributed as widely as possible.

Despite the value of volunteers, some groups have trouble making creative use of them. That's partly because organizing volunteers requires time and some thoughtful planning. It's not uncommon to find up-and-down cycles of volunteer activity, depending on the energy available to organize it.

Because supervising volunteers takes time, Mandy Weltman, who also manages F.O.R.'s San Francisco office, says, "It's not worth it to take someone just for the sake of having volunteers. You have to make sure they have the skills you need. And they need to be available on an ongoing basis. If you're going to train them to do something, showing up once or twice isn't enough."

Weltman suggests using volunteers to create a volunteer program. "Have your volunteers train other volunteers to keep the process going," she says. "That saves you time and it gives the original volunteers a sense of responsibility and ownership."

Friends of the River's annual conference is a three-day affair which attracts more than a thousand participants, takes six months to plan and nets more than $20,000. While Weltman is the salaried coordinator, the entire conference is organized and staffed by volunteers and probably wouldn't be possible without them.

Wendy Wilson says the Payette campaign relied on volunteers—nearly 500 of them—for virtually every aspect of the effort, including raising and deciding where to spend money. She says volunteers tend to fall into four categories: "There are the young and the restless who come and go, there are the plodders, the potential leadership volunteers, and the folks who want to be involved in the big picture and end up being your board members."

Of course, you can't make use of volunteers if you don't have projects for them to work on. It's a good idea, therefore, to keep a list of work that needs to be done and to update it at least once a week. A little bit of energy put into volunteer organizing can go a long way.

If your campaign hasn't by now been besieged by volunteers looking for something useful to do, put notices up at local high schools, colleges, retirement centers, and civic groups. Run a classified ad or announce the need for volunteers in a press release.

Have Fun

River campaigns have an inexorable tendency to turn into black holes, gravity sinks that suck in every ounce of human energy along with the leisure life you once thought you owned. The former executive director of a California river group was accustomed to spending 20 or 30 days per year in his kayak. After he took the job his annual average dropped to about five.

Burn-out is particularly dangerous in nonprofit organizations where the pay is low and the stress is high, so it makes good sense to schedule time to play. Too many people work hard to save rivers without spending enough time on them.

The best and last word on this subject comes from beyond the grave, from the self-described "voice crying in the wilderness", the man to whom saving rivers was one of life's most sacred acts—Ed Abbey.

> Do not burn yourselves out. Be as I am, a reluctant enthusiast and part-time crusader. A half-hearted fanatic. Save the other half of yourselves for pleasure and adventure. It is not enough to fight for the West. It is even more important to enjoy it while you can, while it's still there. So get out there, hunt, fish, mess around with your friends, ramble out yonder and explore the forests, encounter the griz, climb a mountain, bag the peaks, run the rivers, breath deep of that yet sweet and elusive air. Sit quietly for a while and contemplate the precious stillness of the lovely, mysterious, and awesome space. Enjoy yourselves. Keep your brain attached to the body, the body active and alive. And I promise you this one sweet victory over our enemies, over those desk-bound people with their hearts in safe deposit boxes and their eyes hypnotized by their desk calendars. I promise you this: You will outlive the bastards.

Part Two
Tools

Picking the right tools to save a river is a lot like picking the right tools to build a house. If you've never done either you'll be bewildered by the variety available and confused about how and when to use them.

To help in the selection, the following inventory outlines the principal tools employed to protect rivers. Basic provisions and applications of each tool are described along with a summary of strengths and weaknesses. For some river campaigns, a single tool—like Wild and Scenic designation—will suffice. But for most rivers, a combination of tools will be called for and even Wild and Scenic designation is only one step toward comprehensive protection. As this discussion unfolds you should be able to discover which tools will work for your river, which won't, and why. You may also discover that some tools are missing, that there is a need for river-saving remedies which haven't yet been created.

Chapter 5
River Saving Tools

If they are to fulfill their potential . . . each purchase must be based on full knowledge of a tool's intended purposes and a careful judgment of its probable usefulness to you.
THE READER'S DIGEST COMPLETE DO-IT-YOURSELF MANUAL

The National Wild and Scenic Rivers Act

The Wild and Scenic Rivers Act, passed into law in 1968, was landmark legislation which, in its scope and application, is still unique in the world. It provided legislative recognition that "certain selected rivers" have "outstandingly remarkable" values and that they should be preserved for all time in their free-flowing condition.

Eight rivers (12 if you count tributaries) were inducted into the Wild and Scenic System with passage of the Act, and as of November 1992 the count had risen to 152 river segments totaling 10,516 miles. Counting tributaries, the Wild and Scenic roll call goes well above 300, although that constitutes considerably less than 1 percent of the nation's river miles.

What It Does

The Act provides blanket protection against federally licensed dams, diversions, and other on-river development on designated river segments. It also sets aside a quarter-mile-wide riparian corridor in which development, on public lands, is restricted. Private lands in Wild and Scenic corridors are generally open to development.

Wild and Scenic Rivers are assigned one of three different classifications—wild, scenic, or recreational—to correspond to the degree of preexisting development. Different segments of the same river may be assigned different classifications, again depending on the natural qualities and degree of human intrusion.

An important thing to remember here is that the Wild and Scenic Rivers Act applies to both whole rivers and to river segments, and not just to those that are wild and pristine. Reaches of river with road access, private

Sauk River, Washington, a National Wild and Senic River. (Photo courtesy of Tim Palmer.)

property holdings, and other significant development can qualify as scenic or recreational segments, as long as they are free flowing.

How to Use It

There are several ways to get a river designated Wild and Scenic. A candidate river can be proposed by a citizen's group (or, as on the Wildcat River, by local government) for study as a part of the Wild and Scenic System. That requires a friendly Representative to introduce a study bill and an act of Congress to pass it. Study rivers are protected from development for up to six years.

For a long time, new inclusions in the Wild and Scenic System were mostly the product of citizen campaigns focused on a single river. The Tuolumne and the Chama and the New are typical examples. But Section 5(d) of the Act also charges federal agencies with the responsibility of submitting candidate rivers for Congressional consideration. It took several years for any real agency initiative to occur, but in 1982 a Nationwide Rivers Inventory was produced by the National Park Service which identified 1524 eligible river segments totaling 61,700 miles. The inventory was conducted under the watchful eye of Interior Secretary James Watt who insured that it wasn't overly generous. In fact, thousands of logical candidates were overlooked or ignored (including the entire state of Montana) and a later inventory of "outstanding rivers," conducted by American Rivers, included 15,000 entries totaling some 300,000 miles.

Real movement under Section 5(d) began when federal agencies—the Forest Service, National Park Service, and Bureau of Land Management— responded to an executive mandate and pressure from American Rivers to evaluate rivers under their jurisdictions as they developed land and resource management plans. As a result, planners in national forests and BLM Resource Areas all over the country have been forced to assess the rivers and streams under their jurisdictions (not just those in the Nationwide Inventory) and make recommendations on their Wild and Scenic "suitability" to Congress.

That process, which allows considerable public input, involves studies of both eligibility (are there "outstandingly remarkable" values?) and suitability (is protection in the public interest?). The eligibility phase determines which rivers meet the criteria established by the Wild and Scenic Act, while the suitability phase examines the positive and negative impacts of designation.

Politics plays a significant role throughout this process; some rivers are overlooked for eligibility because of objections from development interests, and even more rivers are found eligible but unsuitable because designation would be controversial, some form of development is being planned, or public opinion strongly opposes it. Rivers found eligible are supposed to be managed so that their Wild and Scenic values are preserved until a designation decision is made.

The planning process undertaken by the Forest Service and BLM has provided a major opportunity for citizen involvement. Intervention by river groups during inventories and eligibility studies has significantly expanded the number of rivers recommended. Appeals of Forest Service and BLM land use plans, for instance, have resulted in the inclusion of numerous additional rivers in California.

State Designation

A second path to Wild and Scenic protection leads through state initiative. Section 2(a)(ii) of the Act allows state governors to nominate candidate rivers directly to the Secretary of the Interior, who has the authority to make a unilateral decision. The candidate rivers must already have some form of state protection with appropriate management plans, and they must pass through a National Park Service review and a public comment process. State designated rivers must be managed by state or local agencies at no cost to the federal government. There were 13 state-sponsored rivers in the federal system as of late 1993.

The state-administered Wild and Scenic designation is an underutilized feature of the Act, perhaps because state legislators are more vulnerable to pressure from special interest lobbyists than are members of Congress, who work farther from the scene of the crime. An excellent handbook for organizing state-sponsored Wild and Scenic campaigns is available from American Rivers.

Pros

Most importantly, the Wild and Scenic system recognizes the inherent value of preserving wild rivers and establishes a federal policy to do so. Wild and Scenic protection categorically prevents federally licensed dams and diversions, eliminating one of the most destructive threats to a river. It is the one form of protection which cannot be overridden by a FERC hydropower license.

Wild and Scenic Rivers are also supposed to be managed according to specific guidelines which require comprehensive management plans dictating the kind and quality of uses they are put to. A good management plan is a blueprint for the long-term use and protection of the river and is worked out in cooperation with local interests. Federal land Wild and Scenic watersheds can be protected from intrusive forestry practices to the extent dictated by preservation of outstandingly remarkable values.

Recreation and access are often enhanced and scenic values are protected on Wild and Scenic rivers. Logging and new mining claims are supposed to be prohibited along federally owned "wild" river segments. Some Wild and Scenic designations are accompanied by appropriations to buy property or conservation easements to add further protection and increase access.

One of the less tangible values of Wild and Scenic designation is the educational influence it has on agency managers who are forced for the first time to confront the challenge of protecting rivers for the public trust.

Cons

First and foremost, Wild and Scenic Rivers do not provide ecosystem protection. Destructive activities can occur up or downstream from designated segments, as well as in watersheds and floodplains. Development in the half mile-wide Wild and Scenic corridor is only limited on federal land. That translates into 1320 feet on either bank, not enough to reach the ridge-tops on a river of any significant size, and private land is largely unaffected. Washington's Wild and Scenic Skagit once had exceptional fishing and the largest number of wintering bald eagles in the lower 48 states, but much of the river flows through private land and great swaths of its old growth watershed have been defaced by clearcuts, which has caused a dramatic decline in the fishery.

While Wise Use alarmists stir up fears to the contrary, the Act provides very little jurisdiction over privately owned land, allowing landowners to cut, mine, build, or cultivate to their hearts' content. On rivers with a significant percentage of private land, property owners often raise vehement objections to Wild and Scenic designation out of fear that private property will be condemned. The Act does allow for condemnation if less than half the riparian corridor is privately owned, but there are strict limits on how much land can be taken and, in practice, condemnation has rarely been used.

The record for management plans required on Wild and Scenic Rivers has proven, in practice, to be a mixed bag. There is widespread sentiment among agency managers and conservation professionals that winning designation is the easy part of the Wild and Scenic battle. The hard part is developing a management plan and executing it. It takes a lot of time and money to put together an effective plan, and most resource agencies have little of either. Citizen participation is crucial to success and a river watchdog group needs to oversee both development and implementation of the plan.

State River Protection Programs

The Wild and Scenic Rivers Act was not the beginning of legislated river protection. Wisconsin created the first state system in 1965, and 33 states had enacted some form of state river protection by 1993.

There are so many different state programs that a simple summary isn't possible. Some states have ventured only timidly into the current of river protection with anemic programs that do little more than define lofty ideals. But others have enacted proactive legislation that has produced substantial results. Vermont has adopted what could become a national model with its Comprehensive State River Policy Act, which seeks to safeguard fisheries on all rivers with blanket protection for instream flows while allowing the legislature to designate "outstanding resource waters" on which dams are prohibited.

What They Do

Many state programs mimic the federal Wild and Scenic Act in general structure and function, but there are a variety of other models. Common to most state systems is a prohibition on dams and major instream disruption, although state systems lack jurisdiction over federal agencies and don't protect against FERC hydro licenses, Corps of Engineers Dams, or Bureau of Reclamation water diversions. In practical terms, however, state river protection is a significant political obstacle to federal instream river projects.

Typically, state systems aren't as strict as the federal Act, although they have one major advantage in that they have the capability of regulating private land use, which is the single most important tool for protecting private land rivers.

State systems have, on average, been less aggressive than the federal system in adding rivers. Some states have passed innovative programs and then left them to languish. California protected five rivers when it passed a Wild and Scenic Act in 1972, but didn't add another river until 1989.

A useful summary of state systems has been compiled in a book by Kevin Coyle, of American Rivers, and Chris Brown, of the National Park Service's Rivers, Trails, and Conservation Assistance Program. Titled "Conserving Rivers, A Handbook for State Action", the book outlines the universe of state river programs and offers much helpful advice in creating and utilizing them.

How to Use Them

Most state river programs with any teeth involve a legislative process not unlike the federal system, although at least one state makes designation of protected rivers an administrative procedure. Given the variety of state models, strategies for designating state rivers are numerous. Coyle and Brown have listed four approaches typically used to seek state river protection.

1. *River-by-river designation.* A piecemeal approach, adding a river or two at a time, the process varies from state to state but usually follows a series of steps similar to federal designation procedure, while leaning more heavily on public input and the creation of viable river management plans.

2. *Designation of groups of rivers.* Sometimes states address the protection of several rivers in a single package. State designations have been done both by legislative act and by statewide ballot initiative and, as with federal omnibus river bills, they either win big or they lose big.

3. *Watercourse-only designation.* Some states have chosen a more expedient form of river protection which caters to private property concerns by protecting the river only to the high water mark, without intruding into the riparian corridor. This kind of designation eliminates a source of controversy while still addressing serious threats like dams, diversions, channelization, and pollution.

4. *Protected-areas designation.* The Northwest Power Planning Council (NPPC) demonstrates how state governments sharing a common interest in preserving river resources can collaborate to extend protection over a broad area. Concerned about loss of salmon habitat, Idaho, Montana, Oregon, and Washington joined forces to identify critical spawning rivers and to deny access to the region's power grid for any hydropower developer proposing a project in the protected areas. While creation of the NPPC required an act of Congress, it is conceivable that a similar strategy could be applied by state water agencies to address such problems as polluted runoff and agricultural water conservation in multistate river basins like the Colorado, Columbia, Snake, and Mississippi.

Pros

The major advantage of using a state river program instead of the federal Act is that state protection allows for the regulation of private land use, like logging, mining, flood plain, and shoreline development. Zoning, water diversion, and streambank alteration can only be addressed at the state or local level.

Regulation or elimination of gravel mining, for instance, is a major conservation objective on many western rivers, but federal designation provides little regulatory relief on private land, where most of the mining takes place. Remedies have to come instead from state and local action. And when it comes to the legal quagmire of western water law, only states have jurisdiction.

The Mississippi Headwaters Board enforces a River Protection Ordinance on the Upper Mississippi which regulates development along a 400-mile corridor and prohibits commercial use within a quarter mile of the river. If that kind of regulation were imposed by the federal government the result would be civil war.

And while the federal system has tended to focus on the nation's most outstanding showcase rivers, state systems may begin to recognize the more pedestrian but no less deserving candidates, particularly in more urban areas where there are almost no federal designations.

Perhaps the most fundamentally important point about state river protection is that in the long run, as the Wild and Scenic process runs its course and the conservation focus shifts to a truly watershed-based agenda, the forum for action is likely to be local, not national. Wild and Scenic protection can't address polluted run-off, groundwater overdrafts, agricultural water waste, and urban development. Remedies for those problems must come, by and large, from the states.

Cons

Being closer to the problem is both a blessing and a curse. State legislatures are more vulnerable to pressure from special interests, and special interests flock to river issues like effluent to Boston Harbor. State river programs tend, therefore, to be less aggressive than the federal Act and more willing to compromise river values. And even rivers that are protected are more vulnerable to legislative reversals. After California's Eel River was included in the state system, but hadn't yet received federal protection, a Southern California water executive was heard to say, "When ever we need it, of course, we'll go take the Eel. We've got the votes."

While land use decisions which could protect river corridors are, by and large, the province of local government, local government is often the least likely entity to restrict riverside development. Restrictive flood plain zoning, for example, is supposed to be encouraged by the National Flood Insurance Program, but city councils and county supervisors all across the country keep on approving flood plain development.

Many state river programs lack management plans, and a majority of state programs have no funding. California has invested virtually no money in its system, which it assumes to be "self-administering" and there are no funds in the treasury to do so. Without a management budget, there is no staff looking out for the interests of state rivers, which means that other state agencies can run amok. Some of California's timber harvest plans have had to be challenged in court because they allowed intensive logging in the sensitive watersheds of protected rivers.

Statewide River Assessments

Joni Mitchell once sang, "Don't it always seem to go that you don't know what you got 'til its gone." That pretty much sums up the reason for statewide river assessments: you can't save what you don't know. If, back in 1956, there had been statewide river assessments in Utah and Arizona, Glen Canyon would not have been "the place no one knew." And if people had known Glen Canyon, if it's extraordinary values had been objectively assessed, the dam that buried it might not have been built.

Statewide river assessments, the slow outgrowth of the Wild and Scenic movement, are fundamental to a comprehensive state river protection program. While 33 states have some form of protected river system, by 1993 only 11 had conducted statewide assessments (seven had completed less complete state studies).

What They Do

While a number of states have assembled studies and inventories of one sort or another, a definitive model for statewide assessments didn't emerge until Maine collaborated with the National Park Service to produce a cooperative assessment in 1982. That assessment created a model that has become the standard for other states. It goes far beyond a simple river inventory by measuring both the values and the competing uses of each river. A successful assessment will always be unique, the Maine model can't be cloned for every state, but certain key features are necessary.

1. Rivers have to be assessed in terms of the full range of resources they provide. That includes water quality, fisheries, threatened and endangered species, urban and agricultural water supply, gravel mining, wildlife habitat, riparian land use, groundwater recharge, aesthetic, cultural and historic values, and recreation.
2. The assessment should include every river in the state exceeding a defined minimum size.
3. Assessments should involve the public in the assessment process (through technical and advisory committees), which increases credibility and public support.
4. An assessment should be conducted cooperatively by state and federal agencies along with citizen groups.

A statewide assessment is no simple job. Done properly it will typically take at least two years and it requires the active support and participation of state and federal agencies. But once you have one it will become one of your most valuable river-protection tools.

How to Use Them

If your state is among the majority without a river assessment, you could be instrumental in creating one. The initiative has to come from the state, but the National Park Service can provide encouragement and offer technical support, while a coordinated lobbying effort by river activists can move the process along. California, despite a state Wild and Scenic System, did nothing about an assessment until 1992. That meant that major resource decisions, in a state totally dependent on the flow of its rivers, were being made in an information vacuum. That changed when the California Resources Secretary, with prodding from American Rivers, among others, asked the National Park Service to coordinate an assessment which got underway in 1993.

Pros

States with comprehensive assessments have achieved enormous river conservation benefits. One result is that a body of objective information is gathered which, for the first time, presents a detailed picture of the condition of a state's river resources. And the process of compiling those data unites diverse constituencies in cooperation rather than confrontation.

Tangible benefits abound. After Vermont conducted its assessment, the state restricted gravel mining on all its rivers. And a Vermont landowner changed his plans for a small hydropower facility when he discovered the unique natural values of his brook.

After Maine conducted its assessment, the Governor issued an Executive Order making river conservation a state priority. The state then adopted fishery management plans for 10 rivers and enacted five pieces of legislation to protect outstanding rivers from dams, enhance fisheries, and limit shoreline development.

Cons

A bad assessment, if it fails to address competing uses and doesn't adequately measure the negative impact of development on rivers and riparian corridors, may be worse than no assessment, since it creates a false picture of river resources and conservation needs. One likely reason for the meager progress on statewide assessments more than 25 years after passage of the Wild and Scenic Act, is that many states are still hesitant to stir the hornet's nest of controversy they fear would erupt. The first phase of California's assessment, for instance, is skirting delicate issues like gravel mining and forestry practices.

And since it may be impossible to include every stretch of river or stream, a statewide assessment will invariably exclude segments that some people believe should be included.

The Clean Water Act

Thanks to an amalgam of legislation known as the Clean Water Act, America's rivers have grown measurably cleaner over the past 20 years, at least in terms of conventional organic pollutants like fecal coliform and other sewage-born, disease-bearing bacteria. Inspired by the obvious degradation of rivers like the Potomac, the Willamette, the Cuyahoga, and the Hudson, Congress passed a series of pollution control amendments in the 1970s and 1980s which provided legal leverage and financial resources to clean up the nation's rivers. Provisions of the Act are enforced by the Environmental Protection Agency, the Army Corps of Engineers, and by the states themselves, under federally approved water quality programs.

The Clean Water Act's stated goals were to make the nation's waterways "fishable and swimmable" by 1983, to ban toxic pollution and to eliminate the discharge of all pollution into the nation's "navigable waters" by 1985. The discharge goal is still far out of reach and toxics are still being released into the environment, but substantial progress has been made in many river basins toward the fishable and swimmable standards.

The clear focus of the Act's early provisions was municipal and industrial pollution and it poured more than $50 billion into municipal sewage treatment plants, until federal grants for the program were phased out in 1987. But while municipal and industrial pollution was significantly reduced, polluted runoff steadily increased. Congress only partially addressed that problem in 1987 with amendments specifically addressing stormwater runoff. But there is still no real regulatory authority over the nation's biggest pollution problem—runoff from farm fields, forest clearcuts, and small construction sites.

Although the Clean Water Act has enormous potential for river protection, much of that potential has yet to be realized. That's partly because adequate monitoring and enforcement resources aren't available, and partly because the Act doesn't adequately address the issue of polluted runoff. Still, the Act is a powerful weapon against pollution discharge and key provisions give activists useful tools to take legal action against polluters, challenge the dredging and filling of rivers, and to seek state designation of "Outstanding National Resource Waters." The Act can also be used to challenge hydropower dams which would impact established water quality standards.

What It Does

The Clean Water Act requires that each state assign designated uses to its rivers—such as fishing, swimming, or water supply—and then establish and enforce water quality standards to meet those uses. Originally, the EPA also required states to develop areawide and statewide water quality management plans, with public input and participation. But that program has long since died, leaving a variety of finished and unfinished plans with no implementing mechanism.

The Act requires any company discharging pollutants into a waterway to apply for a National Pollution Discharge Elimination System permit. State agencies then review the application and a certificate of compliance is either issued or denied based on the applicant's ability to meet the established water quality standards. The Environmental Protection Agency is responsible for enforcing the Act, but Section 505 gives the public an opportunity to intervene with citizen lawsuits when violations are missed or ignored.

The Clean Water Act covers a variety of water quality issues because the term "discharge" doesn't just apply to municipal or industrial waste, it includes changes in water temperature, dissolved oxygen, turbidity and, depending on which legal opinion you listen to, even stream flow. Fisheries and whitewater boating have also been treated in some legal decisions as values falling within the reach of Section 401 of the Act, which establishes the state water quality certification process.

How far the Act can be stretched to protect instream flow, fisheries, and boating is a point of legal contention and there were, at this writing, two cases before the U.S. Supreme Court that were expected to decide whether states can veto FERC permits based on degradation of aesthetic or recreational values. Conflicting legal opinions also leave open the question of the Act's applicability to instream flow. Much clearer is the definition of "navigable waters" which has come to mean almost any stream you can float a boat on, and some interpretations include seasonal streams that dry up during part of the year.

While areas of confusion exist about application of the Clean Water Act to discharge activities affecting biological, aesthetic, and recreational values, this much is clear: if someone wants to build a FERC-permitted hydropower dam or diversion, he or she has to get a 401 certificate to show that the project won't violate state water quality standards. That requirement has been a useful tool in some river campaigns and, depending on upcoming Supreme Court decisions, it could become an even more effective tool in the future.

A recent example of the effective use of the 401 certification process is the proposed Salt Caves hydro project on the Upper Klamath River in Oregon. Even though the Upper Klamath is protected by the Oregon Scenic Rivers System, the Federal Energy Regulatory Commission was set to approve a license for a major hydropower diversion project, subject only to the granting of a 401 certificate from the Oregon Department of Environmental Quality. Oregon denied the certification on the grounds that the discharge from the dam would raise the river's water temperature by one degree. That ruling was appealed all the way to the Oregon Supreme Court where a decision was pending as this book went to press (and while Interior Secretary Bruce Babbitt was considering a request from Oregon to include the Upper Klamath in the Federal Wild and Scenic System). Without the 401 roadblock, the license would have been granted before Babbitt appeared on the scene and it would have been too late for consideration of Wild and Scenic designation.

Having said that, it should also be understood that the court challenge to Oregon's denial of 401 certification underscores continuing controversy over whether states can legally apply the Act to protect the nonchemical, biological values of a river.

Section 404 of the Act, although it is usually associated with wetlands protection, provides another potentially useful tool to protect rivers. Section 404 gives the Army Corps of Engineers authority to regulate the discharge of dredged or fill material into rivers and wetlands, which covers most kinds of stream developments, including dredging and dam construction. Any dam on a navigable river, therefore, must also receive a Section 404 permit from the Army Corps.

This may sound at first blush like the water quality equivalent of letting Bonnie and Clyde supervise bank deposits, and to some degree the analogy fits. But the Corps is embarked on what it insists is a "new environmental ethic" and it has demonstrated a surprising aggressiveness in carrying out its Section 404 mandate to protect wetlands. Also, the EPA has veto power over Corps dredge and fill permits, and both the National Marine Fisheries Service and the U.S. Fish and Wildlife Service can participate in the review of 404 applications. And the Corps has exhibited at least some willingness to deny dam permits which would pose a threat to endangered species.

In reviewing a 404 permit, the Corps is required to consider, among other things: the public or private need for the proposed activity; the availability of alternative sites or methods to achieve the desired objective; and the cumulative impact of the proposed activity in combination with other existing or proposed activities. The Corps must also weigh the projected impact of the proposed activity on fish and wildlife, water quality, flood damage prevention, recreation, aesthetics, and land use. EPA guidelines dictate that a 404 permit can't be granted "if there is a practicable alternative to the proposed discharge that would have less impact on the aquatic ecosystem."

But that's not all the Clean Water Act does. An "antidegradation" provision of the 1987 amendments could evolve into a major river protection tool, if the states ever exercise sufficient initiative and if the EPA applies enough pressure. The Act has, since 1972, stated that the nation's water quality should be "maintained". The EPA has interpreted that language, generally, to mean that existing in-stream water uses, and the water quality "necessary to protect the existing uses," must be maintained and protected. In the 1987 amendments to the Act, this interpretation is explicitly addressed as an "antidegradation" policy, the implications of which could be far reaching if agreement is ever reached on the meaning of "existing use." Controversy has arisen over whether the term applies to anthropocentric as well as natural activities.

The EPA's antidegradation policy outlines three increments of protection. The first level requires states to work to ensure that "all existing in-stream water uses" and attendant water quality be maintained. The second level adds extra emphasis for protection of rivers with water quality high enough "to support propagation of fish, shellfish, and wildlife and recreation. . . ." Rivers in these first two categories may experience some pollution but their uses must not be compromised or impaired, and there must be a public process for determining that a compelling economic need justifies the degradation. There is, of course, a gaping loophole in this policy because the definition of "degradation" is open to a wide range of interpretation.

The third antidegradation level goes much further and applies to rivers which constitute an "outstanding national resource" and for which no degradation of water quality is to be allowed. This third category has given rise to the term National Resource Waters and has raised hopes it will be broadly applied to rivers flowing through national forests, BLM lands, National Parks, and wildlife refuges. But it can't be applied until states make the necessary designations.

The antidegradation policy outlined here could become an important river protection tool. Virtually any activity that threatens a river could be interpreted as changing existing instream uses. But it may be some time before an appropriate interpretation of the term, and aggressive action by the states, fulfills the promise of the policy.

How to Use It

The Clean Water Act is an open invitation for private citizens to get involved in river protection. Because of the regulatory teeth the Act provides, citizens can take action against polluters and river trashers with real hope of obtaining relief. Here are some of the things citizens can do:

1. Monitor the water quality of rivers at discharge sites to measure compliance with water quality standards. Clandestine dumping is a not uncommon industrial practice and some citizen groups have been successful, through surveillance and water monitoring, in nailing the bad guys. This is a particularly good activity for boaters who can access wastewater outfalls not accessible by land. Doing this requires training and access to a chemical laboratory. River Watch Network is a good place to seek advice.

2. Monitor rivers for overall biological health (not just chemical purity), trace evidence of degradation to logical sources, publicize the results, and call on state agencies and the EPA to respond. This, too, is a highly technical undertaking but citizen monitors have been trained all over the country, and the Izaak Walton League's Save Our Streams program is a good way to learn the process.

3. Obtain copies of monthly pollution discharge reports from suspect companies and review them for compliance. All companies with NPDES permits must report discharge violations, but the overburdened regulators don't always review the reports or take prompt action.

4. Sue. Section 505 of the Clean Water Act gives citizens the opportunity to sue both polluters and the government agencies responsible for regulating them, provided that citizens can establish legal standing. Standing is established when a plaintiff demonstrates that his or her current and ongoing use of the affected resource (the river) would be affected, at the site of that use, by the activity that would impact the river. In simpler terms, if you can demonstrate that you fish, swim, boat, or otherwise regularly and currently use the river at the affected site, you probably have standing to sue.

Besides standing, citizen suits must fulfill one other requirement: 60 days before a suit is filed both the EPA and the appropriate state water quality agency must be informed of the intended legal action. The violator in question must also be notified, and if a civil or criminal action to correct the problem is initiated by the EPA or the state during the 60-day period, a citizen suit is preempted.

5. Lobby state regulatory agencies and your legislature to regulate toxic discharges into waterways according to their actual impact on the biological health of the river, not just on EPA-mandated standards.
6. Review hydropower license and relicensing applications for opportunities to apply Section 401 requirements.
7. Pressure state agencies to implement aggressive antidegradation policies as required by the EPA, and to adopt "no degradation" standards for "Outstanding National Resource Waters."

Pros

The Clean Water Act has had an enormous impact on the health of rivers and it could become an even more effective tool if polluted runoff and antidegradation provisions are more aggressively employed. It is by far the most effective tool for protecting wetlands and, in the 401 certification requirement, offers one of the few legal roadblocks to a FERC hydropower permit.

The Act has provided more opportunities for citizen lawsuits than any other piece of environmental legislation short of the EIS process, and it empowers citizen activists with a clear legislative mandate to take independent legal action when regulatory agencies don't do the job.

Cons

Application of the Clean Water Act, especially the provisions addressing polluted runoff, watershed protection, and antidegradation policy, has been inconsistently applied by the states. State water quality standards vary widely, some states haven't designated specific uses for their rivers, and many states provide so many variances that loopholes for powerful nonpoint polluters are plentiful.

Too much emphasis is still given to chemical purity without reference to the biological health of rivers, although that is supposed to change in 1995. States are often reluctant to employ narrative descriptions and biological criteria in their water quality assessments because they know that the more comprehensive biological data often paint a bleaker picture of water quality.

It is virtually impossible to measure the water quality of every river in every state, and in fact only about a third of the nation's rivers are monitored in any two-year period. And while there is at least a nascent effort to identify and designate National Resource Waters, in which no pollution will be allowed, the thrust of water quality efforts to date has been to mitigate rather than eliminate, and mitigation simply slows the rate of degradation; it doesn't stop it.

The Endangered Species Act

The federal Endangered Species Act is both the most powerful and the most controversial piece of environmental legislation ever enacted by Congress. It has provided for the legal (if not actual) protection of more than 800 threatened and endangered species and of at least portions of the critical ecosystems they depend on.

The Endangered Species Act, under fire and up for Congressional reauthorization as this book went to press, provides important opportunities for river activists. It is a powerful weapon but, because of the political backlash it creates, sometimes a dangerous one to use.

In addition to the federal ESA, most states have their own versions of the Act and it is not unusual for there to be discrepancies between state and federal listings. California activists, for instance, won an "endangered" listing under the state Act for the Sacramento winter run chinook salmon before the fish was granted "threatened" status under the federal Act.

What It Does

The purpose of the Endangered Species Act of 1973 is elegantly simple: It provides both a legal means for conserving the ecosystems upon which endangered and threatened species depend, and it creates a program for the conservation of those species. To qualify, species must be "listed," following an exhaustive review process. Listing for terrestrial species is done by the U.S. Fish and Wildlife Service, while marine and anadromous species are listed by the National Marine Fisheries Service. Listing can be a contentious and tortured process, as the snail darter and spotted owl illustrate.

The Act creates two categories of listing: An *endangered* species is "in danger of extinction throughout all or a significant portion of its range," while a *threatened* species is "likely to become an endangered species within the foreseeable future."

Part of what gives the Endangered Species Act its teeth (and stirs so much controversy) is a provision that decisions on listing species must be made independent of financial or social consequences (although economic impact plays a major role in other provisions of the Act). The listing process is supposed to be guided by science, not politics. It is, of course, obvious that this isn't always the case. Politics does, in fact, play a major role in species protection (the Reagan Administration delayed a decision on the Northern spotted owl for nine years), but several tough listings have nevertheless been made in the face of major opposition.

Once a species is listed, some remarkably stringent rules take effect. Listed species are protected from any action authorized, funded, or taken by a federal or state agency that would threaten their existence. Additionally, listed species cannot be "taken" (an all-purpose word which includes killing, hurting, removing, uprooting, and other nasty actions) by anyone, without a special permit, regardless of where they are found.

There are, of course, exceptions to every rule, and in the case of the ESA, members of a listed species can be taken "incidental" to other activities (like urban development or construction of a dam), if an approved Habitat Conservation Plan is developed to offset any damage to the species.

The Act requires the U.S. Fish and Wildlife Service and the National Marine Fisheries Service to develop and administer recovery plans for the protection of all plant and animal species listed as threatened or endangered. But both agencies are overwhelmed by the work required and at this writing only 60 percent of listed species had approved recovery plans.

How to Use It

Aquatic ecosystems have the greatest variety of nonoceanic species on the planet and the highest rate of extinction. It is impossible, therefore, for the Fish and Wildlife Service, the National Marine Fisheries Service, or any other agency of government, to monitor the species health of all the plants and animals inhabiting river environments. That's where river activists come in. Endangered species experts at the U.S. Fish and Wildlife Service will tell you that both the listing process and the formulation of recovery plans are deeply affected by public input.

Here are some of the ways you can use the Act to protect your river.

1. If you have evidence that a listed species occupies your river's ecosystem, find a competent biologist to confirm and document its presence. That evidence can than be presented to the Fish and Wildlife Service or your state's Fish and Game department, along with an explanation of the development activity threatening both the river and the species' habitat. If, for instance, that activity were a water diversion, the ESA could be used to mandate more water for your river, assuming that existing or increased instream flow could be shown to be necessary for the protection or creation of critical habitat.

2. If you think an endangered species in your river ecosystem isn't being properly protected, you can join the parade of litigants who have filed citizen suits under the Endangered Species Act to ensure that the Act is fully implemented and enforced.

3. If you feel there is insufficient critical habitat to protect a listed species in your river system, you can petition the Fish and Wildlife Service under the Administrative Procedures Act for an administrative modification to expand critical habitat.

4. If you suspect there is a threatened or endangered species in your river which hasn't been listed, you can propose a new listing by submitting a petition to the Secretary of Interior, along with descriptions of the species' taxonomic status, its biology, and an explanation of why it is endangered. Your case will be bolstered if you provide sufficient reference information to make life easier for USFWS staff reviewing your petition. The more information the better.

The species you propose for listing need not be in danger of overall extinction; listing can be granted to a distinct population of a species in danger of disappearing from even a portion of its range. Once you submit a petition, it will be reviewed for accuracy and, if accepted, the species will be considered a "proposed species." At that point, the Fish and Wildlife Service initiates intense research to determine the true status of the species and the nature of "critical habitat" necessary for its survival and recovery. A lengthy public review process is also initiated, during which organized opposition may emerge.

The Service is supposed to decide, within 12 months of receiving your petition, whether or not to list the species. (During this time the species receives some very limited protection in the form of increased consideration by federal agencies about the effects of their activities.)

Sometimes the Service may decide a species should be listed, but that other listings are of greater priority given limited resources. Or the Service may decide that not enough information is currently available to make a listing decision. Those species, commonly referred to as "candidate species," have historically been left in limbo awaiting listing decisions, and receive virtually no protection under the ESA. Over the years, a backlog of more than 3500 candidate species awaiting listing proposals has built up. However, thanks to a recent lawsuit filed by environmentalists, the Fish and Wildlife Service has agreed to eliminate the backlog by 1996.

Because of the sheer volume of new petitions and backlogged candidate species, and because a listing decision may have a profound impact on development and therefore be subject to heavy political pressure, it can sometimes take years to get a species listed.

5. You can participate in the development of recovery plans for listed species, thereby influencing important decisions about the preservation of critical habitat in your river system.

Pros

Listing a species as threatened or endangered is one of the surest ways of stopping a river-threatening activity or forcing the restoration of an aquatic ecosystem.

Restoration efforts on the Sacramento River lagged until a series of listings under both the state and federal Endangered Species Acts—including the Winter run chinook salmon—gave state and federal agencies a strong incentive to act. Those listings didn't happen spontaneously; citizen pressure helped make them happen.

The ESA can also be used as a carrot or a whip to inspire public agencies toward actions they might otherwise be reluctant to take. It is cheaper and faster, some agency officials believe, to take preemptive actions to protect a species before the heavy hand of the ESA is imposed from above.

Cons

Use of the Endangered Species Act provokes an almost religious backlash from the Wise Use movement and stirs up paranoia in the hearts of those Americans who fear any government control of private property.

Aquatic organisms include the most rapidly growing numbers of endangered species, creatures crucial to the food chain but largely anonymous and unseen. It's hard to build a constituency for these species since the public usually lacks sympathy for salamanders, mussels, and obscure fish. Listing of the tiny Delta Smelt in California forced the State to reserve additional water for the Sacramento–San Joaquin Delta, which benefited numerous species but enraged Central Valley growers who wanted the water. A contractor from the Central Valley voiced a common sentiment when he complained to the *San Francisco Chronicle*, "You're taking our water to protect a one-inch, transparent fish that smells like a cucumber?"

While economic impact is not supposed to be a factor in the listing process, it *is* supposed to be a factor in the determination of critical habitat and recovery plans. That means that the economic value of water diversions, for example, would be weighed against the value of enhanced stream flows for the preservation of endangered fish.

Beyond the issues of public backlash and economic impact is the question of effectiveness. None of the fish listed since the Act took effect have reached the state of recovery and at least four listed fish have vanished from the face of the earth.

Finally, the time required for a listing to be approved is often so long that use of the Act usually isn't an effective short-term strategy for protecting your river.

State and National Environmental Policy Acts

The Mother of federal environmental legislation is the National Environmental Policy Act, which Richard Nixon signed into law on the first day of 1970. NEPA was passed eight years after the publication of *Silent Spring* and two years after the Wild and Scenic Rivers Act in a climate of growing environmental awareness. But Congress surely could not have grasped the true nature of the creature it had created and the impact it would have on America.

The major provisions of NEPA included: a lofty declaration of environmental policy, the creation of a Council on Environmental Quality to oversee the Act and advise the president on the state of the environment, and a legal mechanism, known as the Environmental Impact Statement, to provide a means for enforcing the new policies.

It seems clear now that Congress never imagined the role Environmental Impact Statements would begin to play in the nation's life. Environmental activists, who would stage the first Earth Day that April, took to the EIS process like endangered salmon to a clear mountain stream. Finally there was a tool capable of challenging the twisted logic of pork barrel public works projects, finally there was a way of focusing public attention on the environmental impacts of dams and diversions and other river-killing activities. The world hasn't been the same since.

State environmental policy acts (SEPAs), and state environmental protection acts (sometimes called "little NEPAs"), provide for a similar process at the state level, requiring environmental assessments for any activity performed, permitted, or funded by state or local government. In some states, private development is covered as well. SEPAS merely require analysis of environmental impacts, while little NEPAs employ regulatory tools to limit destructive impacts. Some states refer to their assessments as Environmental Impact Reports, to distinguish them from the federal "statements." Where little NEPAs exist, the vast majority of river conservation issues will involve state rather than federal environmental impact review.

What They Do

The key provision of the National Environmental Policy Act requires that an Environmental Impact Statement be prepared for any "major federal action," and for any activity assisted, permitted, regulated, approved, or partially financed by the federal government, which is "major" in scope and could have a "significant" effect on the environment. The EIS must review all environmental consequences of the project or activity, including air and water quality, presence of rare or endangered species, noise, aesthetics, infrastructure impacts, and traffic congestion. And perhaps most significantly, an EIS must also review alternatives to the proposed project or activity which would have a less damaging environmental impact.

When it isn't clear whether an EIS is required, a less detailed Environmental Assessment (EA) must be conducted. If the EA concludes that an EIS is not required, a "finding of no significant impact" (FONSI) is issued.

Parts of the EIS process are open to the public, which is invited to attend hearings and present testimony. Public testimony is taken at "scoping" sessions to frame the scope of the study. A Draft Environmental Impact Statement is then prepared and is reviewed by the public in a round of hearings before a final EIS is prepared. Findings of significant impact do not necessarily mean the project or activity will be abandoned; more often than not they aren't and, unless it would violate another law, agencies can rule that some value—usually economic necessity—overrules the question of environmental damage, or, more likely, plans will be developed to mitigate the damage. Of great significance to river guardians is the fact that river-threatening projects cannot proceed while an EIS is being prepared.

How to Use Them

The preparation of Environmental Impact Statements and Reports offers important opportunities for activists to influence decisions affecting rivers and streams. First, of course, you have to know about the activities or projects in question. Public notice is required for any EIS process, followed by open scoping sessions which seek to define the issues to be studied. There is then a public comment period, during which hearings are held and testimony is taken.

This process provides for a wide range of citizen actions. Among the most important are these:

1. Analysis of an Environmental Assessment resulting in a finding of no significant impact. If you believe an EA is mistaken and that a FONSI should not have been issued, you can sue the offending agency under the Administrative Procedures Act, alleging specific injury to a recognized interest, such as damage to a fishery or degradation of water quality.
2. Presentation and submission of testimony during scoping sessions and EIS hearings. Present as much expert testimony as you can muster.
3. Analysis of the Draft EIS and submission of comments. Read the draft EIS carefully and submit comments on its inadequacies. Emphasize constructive and credible alternatives to the proposed project.
4. Seek allies in government agencies, like the EPA or the U.S. Fish and Wildlife Service or your state Department of Fish and Game, to submit testimony and comments supporting your position. Finding sympathetic voices in agencies with jurisdiction over your river will bolster your credibility.
5. Review the Final EIS for adequacy in addressing the issues raised by public and agency comments. Pay particular attention to discussion of al-

ternatives, a subject often shortchanged in EIS preparation. If the EIS fails to adequately address alternatives, you have grounds for a legal challenge.

Pros

Like no other piece of legislation, NEPA has empowered the public and given it a place at the decisionmaking table. The arcane and mysterious world of project planning and cost–benefit analysis was exposed to the light of day and recourse was provided for challenging bad projects.

Numerous activities damaging to rivers have been stopped or modified by citizen participation in the EIS process. And an entire culture of government, which depended on inaccessibility and unaccountability to perpetuate gargantuan waste and ecological havoc, has been at least partially purged.

And while NEPA doesn't always provide the intervention you seek to protect a river, the lengthy EIS process can buy valuable time while you get organized politically.

Cons

A remarkable number of bad projects, like Gillham Dam on the Cassatot and New Melones on the Stanislaus and Tellico Dam on the Little Tennessee, have been built in spite of the National Environmental Protection Act. Revealing the danger of an environmental atrocity does not in itself preclude approval of a river-threatening project. Federally supported projects have broad authority to proceed once the NEPA process has been properly completed, even when the EIS makes clear a project will harm the environment.

The first river-related court test of NEPA came in its first year of application when the Environmental Defense Fund and other groups used the new tool to challenge construction of an unneeded flood control dam on the Cassatot River in Arkansas. A federal district court judge ruled that NEPA did, in fact, require a review of alternatives to the dam project and added the scathing observation that, "The most glaring deficiency in this respect is the failure to set forth and fully describe the alternative of leaving the Cassatot alone. . . ." Happily, the Corps was forced to prepare a comprehensive EIS. Unhappily, a federal court approved the subsequent document and the dam was built.

Relicensing, Recontracting, and Mitigation

In the early decades of this century, when many of America's dams were being built, there were no environmental laws, no environmental movement, and very little concern about the harm being done to the nation's rivers. Hundreds of those dams were hydro projects which dewatered rivers and damaged fisheries. They were erected with permits from the Federal Power Commission (which became FERC) and are now expiring.

During the same period, the great reclamation works in the West were being constructed, and irrigation contracts were being let by the Bureau of Reclamation, usually for 40 years. Those contracts, many of which are also now expiring, allowed for the diversion from rivers of massive amounts of impounded water and they created enormous environmental damage.

The expiration of hydro permits and irrigation contracts presents river activists with a rare and brief opportunity to correct some of the abuses heaped on rivers. Intervention by river guardians in the relicensing and recontracting process has the potential for changing permit and contract terms and, in some rare instances, of actually removing dams.

What It Does

Hydropower relicensing is conducted by the same folks who license new hydro projects, the Federal Energy Regulatory Commission. By the end of the century several hundred hydropower permits will expire (including the ones for more than 230 dams that ran out in 1993), and river activists around the country have mobilized to intervene.

Whenever an original license expires, FERC must completely evaluate all aspects of the project, including its very existence, and it must do so in light of today's environmental values. Happily, the public can play a role in that process. FERC intervention procedures give the public an opportunity to, in effect, take back their rivers by insisting on a complete evaluation of the licensed project and even challenging its continued right to exist.

Relicensing can be used to impose mitigation measures that reduce the harmful impacts of hydropower projects. Among the mitigation actions that could be required of a hydro plant operator as a condition of relicensing are:

- Increased stream flows to sustain fish and wildlife
- Modified release schedules to insure sufficient water for fish spawns and migrations
- Structural modifications to provide cooler downstream temperatures for fishery enhancement, and to reduce danger from nitrogen supersaturation at the base of dams
- Reduced fluctuation of reservoir levels to improve shoreline ecosystems
- Installation of effective fish ladders
- Restoration of spawning gravels, wildlife habitat, and riparian vegetation
- Improved public access for river recreation

- Improved water release schedules to enhance whitewater boating
- Removal of obsolete and destructive dams

In addition, the relicensing procedure can lead to creative settlements among utilities, conservationists, and government agencies which cut years off the process, reduce the contentious nature of the experience, and result in innovative license agreements with profound environmental benefits. Recent settlements have led to such things as the establishment of trust funds for watershed land acquisition, fisheries habitat improvement, modified flows to protect fisheries, improved recreational amenities, and recreational water releases.

The opportunity for reform isn't so clear when it comes to revising the terms of expiring irrigation contracts. Because there isn't an administrative process for challenging the long-term agreements between western growers and the Bureau of Reclamation, river guardians have had to go to court. Prior to the election of President Clinton and the appointment of Bruce Babbitt to head the Interior Department, the Bureau had insisted that renewal of 40-year water contracts, which have devastated California's San Joaquin River and the delta it feeds, did not require Environmental Impact Statements. The Natural Resources Defense Council and seventeen other plaintiffs went to court to protest that decision, hoping for a court ruling that would force the Bureau to measure the real impacts of these massive water diversions. As this book went to press the matter was still in court.

While changing the conditions of expiring water contracts may be more difficult politically than hydropower relicensing, it nevertheless offers an important opportunity for legal challenges to the status quo use of public water.

How to Use It

The FERC intervention process follows a set of clear procedural steps, and an excellent popular reference to that process is *Rivers at Risk,* the Echeverria, Barrow, and Roos-Collins book produced by American Rivers, which guides citizens expertly through the FERC regulatory maze. Be warned, however, that some FERC regulations have changed since the book's publication, so you'd be wise to check with FERC or American Rivers to learn about new rules and procedures.

In a large nutshell, relicensing is supposed to go like this: Five years before their licenses expire, hydropower operators are required to tell FERC whether they intend to file for a renewal. FERC then issues a public notice of the applicant's intention.

Formal filing of a relicensing application must then be made no later than two years before expiration of the existing license. After FERC reviews and accepts a relicensing application, it publishes a public notice announcing a comment date, which is also the deadline for filing a motion to intervene. The elaborate foreplay preceding the comment date is important to give interested parties time to prepare. So if you intend to intervene in a relicensing application, your preparation should ideally begin one or two years before the comment date, which means three or four years before the license expires.

While an intervention is the best way to seek mitigation conditions to reduce the harmful impact of a hydro project, it's also possible to pursue a "nonpower" license, which allows for either the reoperation of a facility for some other purpose, like recreation, or the restoration of a project site to its original condition, which would suggest removal of the offending dam.

The "nonpower" option may smack of environmental fantasy, but part of its appeal is that the Federal Power Act allows anyone to apply and thus opens the door for a well-orchestrated citizen grab of an undesirable dam. In truth, nonpower applications are rare and none that we know of have yet been successful. However, efforts to oppose relicensing and promote removal of Edwards Dam on Maine's Kennebec River hold promise, and the two dam's on Washington's Elwha River will likely be removed by the end of this decade.

Several successful hydropower relicensing campaigns have been organized in New England, New York, Michigan, Minnesota, Wisconsin, and the Pacific Northwest. These diverse efforts were brought together to form a National Hydropower Relicensing Campaign, organized principally by American Rivers.

In New England, the Conservation Law Foundation and Appalachian Mountain Club, among others, have introduced the idea of leveraging the protection of significant watershed land as a condition for the granting of a lucrative, long-term hydro license. Massachusetts environmental groups and the Massachusetts Department of Environmental Management have proposed establishing a "river enhancement fund" from hydropower project revenues. In Michigan, a coalition of environmental and fisheries groups assembled a powerful team of more than a dozen *pro-bono* lawyers to handle relicensing cases. The coalition has worked closely with the state resources agency to reach a settlement affecting 11 relicensings on three of Michigan's finest rivers. The settlement has been valued at $30 million, and contains numerous innovative provisions, including:

• Modified project flows that will help make projects "environmentally neutral"

- An estimated $800,000 in recreation developments and the upgrading of existing recreation sites
- Funds for installation of devices to prevent the entrainment and death of fish through project turbines, along with payments to the state for fish habitat restoration
- Water quality enhancement funds, and other measures

Another successful hydropower relicensing campaign was organized by New York Rivers United, which in 1993 was intervening in at least 10 hydro projects, some with as many as 10 dams each. NYRU has unleashed some innovative strategies in its campaign, among them the idea of hydropower projects paying "water rent" fees to finance a "natural resource restoration fund."

The idea is to use the relicensing process to impose a kind of user fee on hydro projects which divert and impound rivers, and to invest the collected revenues to both mitigate and compensate for the damage caused by the projects. New York Rivers United is also gearing up a team of "hydro rangers" to monitor hydro sites and prepare dossiers on compliance with permit conditions. "When we find violations, we'll notify FERC," promises NYRU board member Pete Skinner. "There's nothing worse than a FERC compliance audit. Companies are terrified of them."

For the alteration and mitigation of water contracts there is no pat formula. Most federal water contracts are held by the Bureau of Reclamation, which until 1993 has had a historic aversion to changes in the status quo. Expiring contracts for water taken from rivers at some significant environmental price would be appropriate targets for court challenges, utilizing the Endangered Species Act, the Clean Water Act, and NEPA.

Pros

Hydropower relicensing is the only opportunity available for influencing the operational terms of hundreds of nonfederal dams now blocking and degrading the nation's rivers. And it is one of the few tools that can be used for the ultimate mitigation—dam removal.

Cons

This isn't a job for dilettantes. Intervening in hydro relicensing requires expertise, time, and patience. FERC regulations are complex and deciphering them is best left to those with experience. An enormous amount of time (and money) can be invested in an intervention with little or no result, and negotiating creative settlements that avoid long-term legal battles is necessarily the province of professionals.

Water Rights and Instream Flow

Instream flow is one of the central issues in river conservation, and one of the most difficult to address. The appropriation of streamflow is both a well-protected legal right and a major cause of river degradation. Both the Colorado and the Rio Grande are sucked virtually dry before they reach the sea, Arizona has lost 90 percent of its riparian habitat largely as a result of water diversions, and rivers all over America suffer from insufficient flow.

But reducing diversions, putting more water back in rivers, is a complicated process because water rights are jealously guarded and defined by laws which have historically protected users but not rivers. Numerous books, law firms, and careers have been devoted to water rights law, and anything more than a cursory review is beyond the scope of this chapter. But it's important for river activists to understand the subject because the laws that allow diversions from rivers can also be used to put water back in them. What follows are a few of the basic facts.

1. East Is East and West Is West

Water rights law has evolved very differently in the East and West, following separate doctrinal paths. Western water law evolved in a climate of water scarcity and is based on the doctrine of prior appropriation which allocates water rights according to seniority—thus "first in time, first in right." When the supply runs low the oldest, most "senior" rights have first dibs on the water. A prior appropriation right allows the diversion of a specific amount of water, at a specific point, for a specific use, on specific lands, over a specific period of time.

Under Western water law, rights can be granted to any qualified applicant capable of putting the water to "beneficial use," not just to people with property along the river. Those rights are freely transferable, which means they can be bought and sold. It is common, therefore, for the holders of western water rights to divert a river's flow completely out of its basin to a point hundreds of miles away.

Besides the "beneficial use" requirement, western water rights come with a few other conditions. Appropriated water must be taken out of the river, it must be used on the land designated by the right, and it must be completely used or the surplus will be considered abandoned and the right can be lost.

Eastern water law is based on the doctrine of riparian use, which allows a "reasonable" amount of water to be diverted by every stream-side property owner. The law doesn't set specific allocations, largely because eastern rivers, fed by abundant rain, were historically thought to contain sufficient water for all uses. But that reality is changing as eastern population growth generates more demand for river water.

The meaning of "reasonable" is determined by the courts on a case-by-case basis, although it has been clearly established that upstream users can't deprive downstream users of the entire flow of the river, nor can they "unreasonably" pollute it.

Some states east of the Rockies have developed permit systems to regulate riparian diversions. Unlike rights, the permits don't recognize seniority, they may be granted only for specific "priority uses," and they may be altered to meet changing water supplies and demands.

2. Consumption Is Protected, Instream Flow Is Not

From an environmental perspective, the single, overwhelming reality of water law—East and West—is that it protects consumptive, out-of-stream users, not rivers. Until recently, water law simply ignored the rights of rivers to have any guaranteed flow. The "beneficial" use historically mandated by western water law included human consumption, irrigation, and hydropower, but it did not include preservation of fisheries and riparian corridors.

The legal disenfranchisement of rivers has begun to change as states take measures to protect streamflow. More and more states are moving to increase permitting and water allocation intervention, and eastern states are relying less on use of common-law riparian rights. Some western states have modified water laws to provide for minimum streamflows that will protect fish, wildlife, and recreation. Eastern states are beginning to modify riparian rights doctrine with minimum streamflow requirements and varieties of appropriative rights.

But passing laws permitting establishment of minimum streamflows is one thing, putting them into practice is something else. Establishing minimum flows requires lengthy and often expensive instream flow studies to determine the volume of water required to protect aquatic or recreational resources. Most states with programs for protecting instream flow are far behind schedule in completing their studies.

How to Use It

Water rights laws offer two basic strategies for putting water back in rivers: establish minimum flows or acquire water rights. What follows is a summary list of those options.

1. Application for Instream Flow Rights

In states where instream flow rights have been established, state agencies—and in some cases organizations or individuals—can apply to acquire them. Once an instream right is secured, it gets a priority date and takes its place in line behind senior rights holders but ahead of any newer rights.

Applying for water rights is a nice idea in theory, but in practice there are severe limitations. In most states, only state agencies can apply for instream rights and laws limit the amount of flow that can be protected. Further, on streams with lots of prior appropriations—the kinds of streams which usually need instream protection—a new instream right will be very junior and thus last in line for water. But on wild and pristine rivers where there aren't hordes of permitees standing in line, applying for instream rights can help preserve streamflow and prevent future degradation.

2. Intervention in the Permit Process

In those states which regulate water diversions with a permitting process, river guardians can intervene to protest the renewal or granting of a permit, or to ask for reductions in the diversion to protect instream flow. State water resource agencies have a certain amount of discretionary authority (which is seldom used) to attach conditions to water permits in order to protect public values like water quality and fisheries. This strategy applies mainly to Washington, Oregon, and California, but expanded use of discretionary authority is an important river conservation goal and activists should consider campaigning for it wherever rivers are clearly suffering from diminished flow.

3. Requesting Stream Closures and the Withdrawal of Appropriation Rights

When a river or stream is oversubscribed and is clearly suffering from diversion distress, citizens can sometimes petition the state to close the stream to further withdrawals. Usually that's only possible, however, when there has already been a streamflow assessment to determine a minimum flow. Washington state allows for stream closures when water withdrawals would threaten fish populations. Temporary closure can be granted during studies for a river basin management plan, and a stream can be permanently closed under the terms of a final management plan or instream flow study.

4. Requesting Condemnation and Reallocation

This is an extreme tactic which can only be used in those western states which reserve the authority to condemn and reallocate water rights. It is highly controversial, invites litigation, and would only apply to a stream so degraded by diversion that public values like water quality or an important fishery are at grave risk and outweigh consumptive benefits.

But if you can persuade a state agency to pursue this course of action, perhaps by threatening a Public Trust lawsuit (see below), the state will condemn the consumptive right and convert it to an instream right held in public trust. A court then determines a fair value to be paid to the holder of the condemned right.

5. Requesting Adjudication of Water Rights

Adjudication is the process whereby a court-appointed judge reviews water diversions, usually in an entire river basin, to determine whether the diverters have legal rights and whether they're following the terms of those rights. Adjudication can reveal illegal diversions, incomplete diversions, and abandoned water rights. The adjudication process allows the state to reappropriate unused water and return it to the stream. In some states, adjudication can be used to mandate greater water use efficiencies.

The process for initiating an adjudication varies from state to state, but is usually started by either a state agency or by water rights holders.

6. Finding Water through Cancellations or Abandonment of Water Rights

To be valid, water rights have to be continuously used, and when they're not, activists can step in to acquire them. In most states, that even applies to partial abandonment, which allows for the unused portion of a water right to be acquired.

This tool is not widely used, however, because finding abandoned water rights is no mean feat and there is no guarantee that found water will be protected unless it is acquired by an instream water right with the necessary seniority. In Oregon, for instance, when a water right is abandoned, the water returns to the river to be used by the next appropriator in line. Instream interests can't capture the water unless they hold a senior instream right.

Monitoring and measuring diversions is a time-intensive process for which most states lack the staff and budget. It is, however, a goal being pursued by Water Watch of Oregon, which is lobbying the state to require new water rights holders (and eventually existing ones) to measure and report their consumption. At present, most states lack even a reporting process that would allow regulatory oversight and enforcement of diversion requirements by water rights holders.

7. Purchase and Lease of Water Rights

In the western U.S., water rights, like development rights, can be purchased, leased, or even donated. State agencies, which are usually not predisposed to do so, can acquire such rights, but so can private individuals and organizations. The process is both simple and complex. Finding a willing seller just requires money (or the willingness to make a charitable donation) and a search along the river in question. But conveying the right to an appropriate agency and converting the right to instream use will usually require a lengthy administrative process, which includes the provision for protests to be heard.

In 1987, The Nature Conservancy secured a 29-mile-long conditional water right for 300 cfs flowing through the Black Canyon of the Gunnison River and conveyed it to the Colorado Water Conservation Board. The Water Board applied to the Colorado Water Court for permission to commit the water to instream use. In late 1993 the application was still under review and a decision wasn't expected for at least two more years.

The Nature Conservancy has taken the lead nationally on the purchase of water rights for instream flow, with other acquisitions in Colorado, Arizona, and elsewhere. Their expertise should probably be called upon by any river guardians seeking to use this tool.

The Oregon Water Heritage Trust is also involved in the search for water rights which can be purchased or leased to enhance instream flow. And the Water Heritage Trust, founded by Huey Johnson in San Francisco, is promoting the idea around the nation.

Pros

The opportunities for citizen efforts to enhance instream flow are growing as states begin to address the issue. River guardians can play an important role in pressuring state agencies to conduct instream flow assessments, to target possible water rights for purchase or lease, and to seek minimum streamflows. Water rights law provides some useful tools to pursue this process, and acquisition of water rights, while a limited and complex tool, has been used successfully to protect several western streams.

Cons

The administrative and legislative process for obtaining minimum stream flows moves at a glacial pace. Even when minimum stream flows are established, they may be set too low to fully preserve a river or stream, and instream rights will usually be junior to older consumptive rights. Acquisition of instream rights is also very slow—The Nature Conservancy's acquisition of three instream flow rights in Arizona took four to eight years to secure.

Public Trust Doctrine

If there is a secret weapon in the arsenal of river activists, a tool for freeing instream flow from the death grip of water contractors, it may well be the Public Trust Doctrine.

The Public Trust Doctrine is an evolving body of law which defines the state's responsibility towards the navigable waters and the lands beneath them which it holds in trust for the public. Originally applied strictly to navigation, commerce, and fishing, the doctrine has been expanded through a growing body of case law to include the environment fish depend on, other wildlife and natural resource values, and recreation.

While the reach of the Public Trust Doctrine is limited to "navigable waters," the term has been defined in various states to include tributaries of navigable rivers, a definition which covers most boatable rivers and streams. But because the doctrine is largely the product of state-level legal decisions and legislation, interpretations of "navigable" and applications of the doctrine vary from state to state.

What It Does

The Public Trust Doctrine gives activists a tool to challenge legislative and administrative decisions harmful to rivers. And it can force state decisionmaking into a more careful consideration of public trust values.

The application of a public trust standard to projects and activities affecting rivers immediately raises the environmental ante and forces states to apply a higher standard of judgment. It also places on public agencies the burden of proving that their actions are not environmentally harmful.

The single most important feature of Public Trust law is that it can override prior legal rights. Thus, water rights which are demonstrably harmful to a river can be set aside by application of the doctrine, regardless of how old they are. For that reason, Public Trust Doctrine has important applications to streamflow issues all over the country.

How to Use It

The Public Trust Doctrine has a number of practical applications for protection of rivers and streams. It can be used to educate and persuade decisionmakers about natural values that should be preserved. And as a lobbying tool, the Doctrine can be injected into policy deliberations, and Public Trust demands can be made during scoping sessions and other public hearings.

If public officials fail to respond to what you believe are their Public Trust responsibilities, you can threaten them with a Public Trust lawsuit. And if the threat fails to leverage a more environmentally friendly response, you can then sue them.

Public Trust case law has established some impressive precedents. California's Mono Lake was rapidly shrinking as a result of water diversions by the City of Los Angeles from tributaries that fed the lake. But then a Public Trust suit brought by the Audubon Society established the public's right to challenge the diversions and to propose an environmentally sustainable lake level. The California Supreme Court ruled that the state must "take the public trust into account in the planning and allocation of water resources. . . ." A subsequent court decision significantly reduced the Los Angeles diversions, despite a long standing appropriative water right.

The Doctrine may be particularly useful in states where there are no programs or policies to protect instream flow or where no environmental conditions are placed on water diversions. While a few states have adopted public trust legislation, it is principally a judicial doctrine subject to interpretation by courts from state to state. So before you launch a Public Trust suit for your river, research case law to discover how it has been applied in your state, and seek the advice of a knowledgeable environmental or water attorney.

Pros

Public Trust Doctrine has the potential of being the most sweeping and comprehensive river protection tool available. Its application overrides other considerations, like prior water rights, and its coverage includes the full range of natural values river activists seek to protect and restore. Because the doctrine is applied largely by the courts it is removed from the political arena and the reach of special interests.

Cons

There is still no precise definition of the public interest that is protected by public trust doctrine, and that leaves room for a lot of interpretation. Because its application is driven by case law, the Public Trust Doctrine may receive very different interpretations from one state to the next.

Because the doctrine is largely dependent on judicial process, resolution of Public Trust issues may be both expensive and long in coming as appeals wind through the courts. And relying on a judicial process for making public policy is slow and inefficient.

Flood Plain Management

Flood plain development is a little like smoking. Common sense says that eventually it could kill you, but it's just too hard to quit. Twenty-five years ago Congress recognized the dangers of flood plain development and understood that more public works plumbing wasn't going to stop floods. So they passed the National Flood Insurance Program, intending to provide a carrot and a stick to move development out of harms way.

What It Does (or Doesn't Do)

The National Flood Insurance Program, adopted in 1968, offers subsidized flood insurance (the carrot) in communities willing to develop regulations that limit flood plain development (the stick). The carrot worked, the stick didn't. Instead of restricting development, the insurance subsidies encouraged it. While thousands of communities adopted the required flood control plans providing a 100-year level of protection, they simultaneously opened the door to a flood of development made possible by federally backed insurance.

The unintended result of the federal insurance program is that developers build housing tracts and office buildings in high-risk floodplains, shielded by the fictional security of flood control plans theoretically capable of providing protection from a 100-year flood. New flood plain residents aren't usually aware of the risks, and banks are happy to lend money because their investments are protected by the federal government.

Increased development creates increased runoff, and when the inevitable floods come, not only do residents suffer danger, damage, and loss, but taxpayers get stuck with billions of dollars in relief expenses. The National Flood Insurance Program was supposed to be partially self-financing, but because of the level of liability it has helped create, it is now all but broke.

How to Use It

So, in light of this flood control policy debacle, what kind of tool does flood plain management offer river activists?

As this book went to press, Congress was reconsidering reform legislation that, depending on its final configuration, might add tougher restrictions on development in 100-year flood plains. Powerful opposition from the National Association of Realtors and the National Association of Homebuilders thwarted a previous attempt to pass a reform bill. If, by the time you read this, that legislation has not passed, the river conservation community should rise up with one voice and demand reform.

While passage of federal reform legislation is important, there is much activists can do at home without waiting for help from Washington. Zoning is the province of local government and zoning decisions affecting flood plains are made routinely, and often quietly, all over the country all the time. Whether or not your community is participating in the National Flood Insurance Program, you and your river organization should be closely monitoring all zoning decisions affecting flood plains and organizing any necessary opposition. And if your community has a local flood control agency, you can seek to influence its planning processes and guide it toward enlightened flood plain management decisions.

That's what Friends of the River tried to do in California as the City of Sacramento prepared a zoning plan for one of the most flood-imperiled metropolitan areas in America. The Natomas region of that city, referred to earlier in this book, is a 55,000-acre flood plain, most of which would be buried beneath a blanket of water 8 to 23 feet deep if a 100-year flood breached its levees. Natomas is also a gold mine for real estate development and more than 31,000 people have already moved in. Perhaps 200,000 more will follow if city and county zoning intentions prevail.

To try to inject some common sense into the city's deliberations, Friends of the River distributed to City Council members a computer-generated inundation map showing the depths flood waters would reach throughout the basin. They backed up their graphic display with pages of expert testimony and the dire warning that Sacramento would be sewing the seeds for disaster by allowing more urban development in the flood plain.

Similar efforts should be undertaken by all river groups dealing with flood plain issues. The importance of citizen involvement in flood plain protection is so great, that even the Tennessee Valley Authority, which buried one of the South's finest flood plain valleys behind Tellico Dam, has published a "guide for concerned citizens" on conserving flood plains. (This paradox may be explained in part by the TVA's growing commitment to environmental protection.)

Steps suggested in the TVA guide include (1) studying existing local flood plain management programs, (2) influencing flood plain decisionmaking by lobbying local officials and participating in public hearings and citizen advisory groups, (3) helping to identify, document, and publicize the resource values provided by the undeveloped flood plain, (4) fund raising for the acquisition of undeveloped flood plain land, and (5) seeking new legislation or authority for local flood plain protection.

One tactic not suggested in the TVA guide, but worthy of consideration, is the rental of billboards to post warnings in flood plains slated for development. An appropriate message might read, "If you buy a house here, buy a boat too. You'll need it."

Pros

Flood plain management is a fundamental part of river conservation. It benefits both the flood plain environment and the river itself, which may subsequently be freed from the threat of a flood control dam. The urgent need for flood plain management grows daily as development continues to expand in the nation's river basins.

Cons

Until there is reform of the National Flood Insurance Program, and until tougher restrictions on flood plain development are adopted, flood danger will continue to grow and river corridors will continue to shrink.

Water Efficiency and Conservation

Water waste is one of the more worrisome excesses of our consumer-obsessed society. The solution to the problem of wasted water—conservation programs and water-efficiency technology—offers river activists both a high moral platform to stand on and a variety of practical river-protection tools.

What It Does

Water conservation is a motherhood and apple pie issue that has been embraced with religious fervor. But while the gospel is being preached all over the country by born-again water managers, salvation is a long way off and the water efficiency and conservation potential of the United States has barely been tapped.

That may be, in part, because of public confusion over the meaning of those terms. Speak the words "water conservation" and most people immediately imagine sacrifice, doing without, letting the lawn die, and showering with friends. But efficient water planning and technology can conserve vast quantities of water with no sacrifice in lifestyle or standard of living.

The importance of water conservation goes far beyond its value as an alternative to water development projects. Groundwater pumping has lowered water tables all over America and it is rare to find a stream today with anything approaching its historic levels of flow. So any effort aimed at stream restoration and flow enhancement should automatically include a campaign to reduce consumption and increase efficient use of water.

That means, among other things, making sure your local water agency has a real conservation program, not just some cute brochures and a few thousand showerhead flow restrictors. A real conservation campaign includes a program for leak detection, universal water metering, water pipe pressure reduction, rebates for use of water efficient technologies, efficiency requirements for new plumbing, increasing block rate pricing to discourage waste, water-efficient municipal landscaping, protection of recharge areas through open-space zoning, and, ultimately, an aggressive commitment to both wastewater reclamation and dual water systems to reuse grey water in new construction.

Examples abound showing the remarkable results of these strategies. Boston reduced its average daily water consumption by 26 percent over the last decade through a conservation program which included, among other things, aggressive leak detection and repair. In the wake of the Two Forks Dam defeat, the Denver Water Board has adopted conservation measures that have already reduced average consumer use by nine percent. And even rainwashed Seattle has decided to meet all its new water needs through the nineties from increased efficiency instead of new supply. The city plans to save more than four billion gallons per year by the beginning of the next century.

According to a research institute at Ohio State University, accurate water metering results in a reduction of water use ranging from 13 to 45 percent. Lowering water pressure in pipes reduces flow at the tap and saves three to 10 percent of typical household use.

While Congress has adopted water-efficient standards for plumbing in new construction, the nation's infrastructure remains highly water-inefficient. Replacing high-volume toilets with high-efficiency 1.5 gallon models has proven to be a cost-effective alternative all over the country, but retrofit programs are still relatively rare. The Los Angeles Department of Water and Power initiated a toilet rebate program that, in two years, resulted in the installation of 227,000 low-volume toilets and a savings of 10,000 acre feet of water. Now the Department is expanding the program to include more of the city. An added bonus to toilet retrofit programs has been discovered by at least one California city which used crushed toilet bowls as road-building material.

How to Use It

The potential for water conservation should be applied as a test to any proposed water development project which could harm a river or stream, and all water development projects should be forced to demonstrate that conservation is not a cheaper and less damaging alternative. To effectively promote that policy for the benefit of your river, you may have to (1) conduct an assessment of the true need for the water being developed, (2) assess the possibilities for reducing demand and, (3) propose technologies and policy changes that will provide greater efficiencies.

For that kind of work you need expert help, and the Rocky Mountain Institute has some of the best research on water conservation and efficiency in the nation. RMI, you will recall, prepared a water conservation analysis which helped persuade the EPA to kill the proposed Two Forks Dam on the South Platte River. They also helped the Cahaba River Society prepare a technical broadside to dissuade the Birmingham Water Board from damming Alabama's Locust Fork River.

Other excellent work on agricultural water conservation has been developed by Inform, a nonprofit research and education organization based in New York, and by the Natural Resources Defense Council in San Francisco. Both organizations have promoted gypsum block soil moisture monitors, subsurface drip, computerized weather station data services to guide irrigation, and other simple technologies capable of producing dramatic reductions in agricultural water consumption. And RMI has developed case studies showing a range of options for increasing both agricultural and urban water efficiency.

If water conservation and efficiency isn't being adequately addressed in your community, you may want to promote it as part of your river organization's agenda. That would mean, among other things, an education and public information campaign, and lobbying water agency officials and local government.

On a grander scale, you may want to follow the lead of the Environmental Water Leadership Coalition, a group of California environmental groups who negotiated a set of Best Management Practices with managers from most of the state's major urban water agencies. The agreement established a baseline of water conservation actions the water agencies all agreed to pursue.

Pros

Water efficiency is a valuable tool that benefits virtually any river or stream campaign. It provides an alternative to more supplyside water projects, reduces the need for diversions, reduces outflow and thereby lessens the need for wastewater discharge, saves energy needed to heat and pump water, and promotes an ethic of responsibility toward the planet's most limited and essential natural resource.

Cons

There is a major obstacle and a dangerous downside to agricultural water conservation. The obstacle, in much of the West, is the "use it or lose it" rule which requires that people who hold appropriative water rights use all their allocation, or lose it. The threat of losing part of a water right is not an inducement to conserve. This legal dilemma is being addressed in a variety of states in a variety of ways, but until it is universally resolved it will remain a major obstacle to the achievement of true irrigation efficiency.

The downside of conservation is that it makes available substantial amounts of new water, which can be used to fuel substantial amounts of new development, which can then put substantial new pressures on rivers and streams. For that reason, comprehensive water conservation programs should include provisions for returning a percentage of conserved water back to rivers to enhance instream flow.

One other caveat: In some places, excess irrigation water—sometimes called tail water—drains off fields to recharge shallow aquifers, support riparian vegetation, and augment streamflow. This is particularly true during dry periods in late summer. It is possible, therefore, that as irrigators become more efficient in their use of water, the result could include reduction of streamflows and impact on riparian vegetation. The beneficial effects of irrigation tail water are hard to assess without knowledge of the soils, topography, and hydrology of the area in question.

Economic Analysis

While conservationists sometimes cringe at the thought of putting a dollar value on rivers and watersheds, the fact remains that economic analysis is an essential tool in river protection. You may not be able to reduce a stretch of whitewater or a scenic river canyon to figures on a balance sheet, but you can certainly quantify its recreational value, estimate the worth of its fishery, and assess its importance as a clean water supply.

What It Does

Economic analysis, as we discussed in Chapter 3, really has two components: one involves dissecting the economic rationale put forth by proponents of river-threatening projects, and the other involves a valuation of the natural resources being threatened. Both are important.

Federal dam projects require the preparation of cost–benefit analyses, which must demonstrate a return on investment better than 1:1 over the amortized life of the project. Analyzed objectively, federal dam projects routinely fail the cost–benefit test, but the benefit figures are often fattened by inflated recreation estimates and other economic sleight-of-hand to produce a positive equation. Similarly, river-threatening projects routinely underreport the value of environmental resources degraded or lost, and inflate the value of mitigation measures proposed.

How to Use It

Among the river issues for which economic analysis is a valuable tool, are these.

1. *Hydropower proposals.*   As noted earlier, when energy conservation can be demonstrated as a feasible alternative to a hydropower plant, the Energy Consumers Protection Act requires that the Federal Energy Regulatory Commission give serious consideration to the conservation alternative. But neither FERC nor the applicant is likely to promote the alternative; that's up to you.

2. *Water storage projects.*   There is no similar regulatory mandate affecting water projects, although projects governed by NEPA are required to review alternatives in their Environmental Impact Statements. If you can demonstrate the economic advantage of water conservation, as at Two Forks, you may be able to steer decisionmakers away from a storage dam.

3. *Pollution.*   When the complete cost of pollution is calculated, it is clearly cheaper to keep rivers clean than to clean them up after they've been fouled. Calculating that cost advantage provides a convincing campaign tool.

4. *Loss of fishery habitat.*   Compare the cost of restoring anadromous fish runs to the cost of preserving the habitat they need to survive and you have a strong economic argument for preserving rivers and streams.

5. *Loss of whitewater and scenic boating.*   As the Gauley campaign proved, recreational boating is a fast growing sport with enormous economic value.

6. *Degradation of riparian corridors.*   When rivers are degraded, diverted, and polluted, they bring down the value of riparian land. Restored river corridors dramatically increase land values.

7. *Flood plain development.*   Compare the cost of catastrophic flooding to the revenue lost from limiting flood plain development and you have a powerful economic argument for keeping houses and businesses out of flood plains.

Pros

Economic analysis helps expose the inadequacies of questionable water and energy development projects and dramatizes the true cost of pollution and flood plain development. It is a powerful tool for demonstrating that environmental protection benefits business and that free flowing rivers are important economic assets.

Cons

Reducing river conservation to a financial equation can obscure the legitimate and essential biological and spiritual value of wilderness and wild rivers. Public trust values aren't measured in dollars.

Citizen Environmental Lawsuits

It has been suggested that the battle cry of the environmental movement should be, "Sue the bastards!" There's more than a little truth wrapped up in that sentiment.

What They Do

The great advances in environmental legislation over the past 25 years have not been matched with corresponding regulatory vigor. Indeed, during the Reagan Administration, some regulatory agencies with responsibility for environmental protection worked actively against their congressional mandates. What has kept the environmental movement on track, and the river conservation movement alive, has been the provision in almost all federal environmental legislation for citizens to sue.

The Clean Water Act has been a major stimulus of citizen suits, since the Act establishes discharge standards, a permitting process, and daily monitoring reports which can be reviewed by citizens. Illegal discharges can be monitored at outfalls and chemical evidence is often easy to collect.

But citizen suits to protect rivers can also be brought under the Safe Drinking Water Act, the Resource Conservation and Recovery Act, The Comprehensive Environmental Response, Compensation and Liability Act (which establishes the Superfund program), the Toxic Substances Control Act, the Surface Mining Control and Reclamation Act of 1977, and the Endangered Species Act. And, of course, state and federal environmental protection acts allow lawsuits over the necessity and adequacy of environmental impact statements.

How to Use Them

In cases involving corporate violation of environmental laws, the filing of a citizen's suit first requires that a letter of intent be sent to the offending company and to the relevant state and federal regulatory agencies. The company then has 60 days to correct the violation, and the regulatory agencies have the same time to take action. If there is no redress during that period, the suit can proceed. A similar "exhaustion of remedies" rule applies to litigation covering the inadequacy of environmental impact statements; plaintiffs must first pursue standard administrative remedies before a lawsuit is allowed.

Because litigation is such an integral part of the river conservation movement, virtually any river campaign will benefit from the presence of a lawyer, either as a board member, an active volunteer, or simply to provide legal counsel on a *pro bono* basis. But even if you have access to experienced legal help, if you're contemplating a citizen suit it's wise to consult with some of the established experts in environmental law. That means contacting the Sierra Club Legal Defense Fund, the Environmental Defense Fund, the Natural Resources Defense Council, the National Environmental Law Center, the Conservation Law Foundation, or the Southern Environmental Law Center, among others.

While citizen suits are the most common form of legal relief for environmental issues, complaints can also be submitted to grand juries, which are convened annually in each county or township. Grand juries routinely investigate and report on the performance of local government agencies, and they can sometimes be effective in exposing governmental action which endangers or fails to protect rivers. Access to a grand jury is usually handled through a complaint form which should be accompanied by substantial documentation. If the grand jury is interested in your complaint, you may be called on to testify about the problem.

Pros

Environmental legislation has given citizens both the standing and the legal tools to achieve unprecedented protection for rivers. Because the full potential and Congressional intent of environmental legislation is often not achieved by regulatory agencies responsible for implementing it, citizen suits are a necessary and highly effective recourse.

Cons

Lawsuits are expensive and time consuming. And you can lose. Successful litigation increasingly requires attorneys with expertise in environmental law. Look carefully before you leap.

Greenways and Comprehensive River Management Plans

Up to now we've been talking about tools you can use to keep bad things from happening to rivers. Now we want to talk about tools that can make good things happen to rivers.

In 1962, when Marion Stoddart looked out over the scum-coated, pollution-filled, all-but-dead Nashua River, some strange synaptic miracle occurred in her brain: she saw a living river flowing through a corridor of green. Thirty years later the miracle is manifest. Eighty-four miles of pristine and protected shoreline, 7400 acres of riparian land, a wildlife refuge, special wildlife management areas, and a three-mile long urban river park where canoeists can paddle through the center of town, are all part of the Nashua River Greenway.

What has happened on the Nashua River is happening all over the country. After ignoring rivers and streams for more than a century, communities from coast to coast are waking up to the riparian treasures in their midst and are responding with efforts to create greenways. In so doing, they are also creating one of the best ways to stimulate public interest and investment in their rivers and their communities.

A typical greenway protects just the riparian corridor of the river, which is a worthy achievement in itself. But, increasingly, river activists are expanding their focus even further by developing comprehensive river management plans, aimed at restoring and protecting the whole system—watershed, flood plain, riparian corridor, riverbed, and the water flowing through it. River management plans, or river corridor plans, or watershed restoration plans—the names vary—all to one degree or another attempt to assess the full range of resource values and issues relevant to a complete river system in order to create a management model that will best serve both the river and the public.

What They Do

In a real sense, the most important thing greenways do is be green. They are corridors of nature where some semblance of the natural order is allowed to survive and even thrive. Typically, river greenways are pieced together through scenic easements and land purchases to create a protected corridor along both banks of the river. Land use is controlled by local zoning ordinances, setback regulations, and the creation of public parks. Greenways often, but not always, extend into or through urban areas.

The benefits of greenways are both environmental and economic. A healthy greenway provides improved flood protection, enhances wildlife habitat, prevents soil erosion, and filters polluted runoff. And because greenways enhance scenic values they also raise land values and stimulate local economies.

River management plans are a little less easy to characterize because there are so many models with such a span of focus. They range from the massive multiagency, two-state Merrimack River Initiative in Massachusetts and New Hampshire to the Mattole River Watershed Alliance and its efforts to restore the whole watershed of that remote Northern California river.

What characterizes river management plans and distinguishes them from greenways is their focus on rivers as whole systems and their emphasis on creation of a reliable database with which to develop comprehensive planning tools. River management plans incorporate in-depth studies which look at such things as water quality, hydrology, geomorphology, wildlife, riparian plant habitat, land ownership, zoning, recreation and access, fisheries, spawning habitat, tributary health, mining, natural beauty, economics, and flood plain development. Not all river management plans pay adequate attention to the health and influence of surrounding watersheds, but the trend is in that direction. Greenways, which focus on isolated sections of a river, are sometimes first steps toward a more comprehensive river planning process.

How to Use Them

Many, if not most, greenways and river management plans originate with citizen action. They are often the product of a local river organization which has taken the initiative to articulate a vision for the river and to organize the resources required to bring the vision to life.

But while the vision may come from a river group, the creation is a collaborative effort. It doesn't happen without the participation of various government agencies, local businesses, and lots of ordinary citizens. Greenways are typically launched with a study funded by grants from foundations or resource agencies and with the support of local government. The objective is a plan which can then be reviewed by the public and sold to business and government as a blueprint for restoring and protecting the river corridor.

One of the best places to shop for support in launching a greenway is the National Parks Service Rivers and Trails Conservation Program. This innovative program is headed by a veteran river activist and a major part of its agenda is providing technical support for the creation of greenways and river corridor plans. We've touched on this program earlier in the book, but the details bear repeating here. If you want to tap into the program, you have to find a local government partner committed to supporting your effort. That could be a water agency, park district, city council, resources agency, or any other government entity willing to sponsor your plan. You also have to be able to demonstrate proof of public support and financial assistance from public and private agencies.

The NPS then provides services ranging from one-time consultations to complete studies. They often provide extensive organizing support by conducting workshops and helping in the development of conservation agendas and river management plans.

The Environmental Protection Agency also has money available for water quality planning grants, and the U.S. Fish and Wildlife Service has programs and funds to support restoration of fisheries and habitat.

In any given state there is likely to be an agency with interest in helping you develop your plan. When the Mattole Restoration Committee embarked on the novel idea of investing local citizens with the responsibility of restoring their own watershed, they were given a $50,000 grant by the California Department of Fish and Game to get the project started.

Pros

Ultimately, this is what river protection is all about: taking responsibility for the river and its watershed. Creating greenways and river management plans presents a prime opportunity for citizens of the watershed to get to know and understand their river. And once they begin to see the results of cleaner water, restored fisheries, healthier riparian habitat, they will have a permanent investment in the river's health.

Cons

River management plans and greenways take a long time. They offer no short-term solutions. The Nashua River Greenway began with two miles of riverfront and 500 acres of land. It took more than 20 years to reach its present state. The conceptual plan for a parkway on the San Joaquin River, prepared by the San Joaquin Parkway and Conservation Trust, envisions a series of steps stretched out over more than 20 years.

Greenways require money for the purchase of land and conservation easements. River corridor plans require the cooperation of such a diverse variety of interests that consensus is often difficult and compromise of environmental values a frequent concern.

Land Acquisition and Conservation Easements

Look at a map of the Wild and Scenic System and you'll see that most of the designations cover upper watersheds and remote rivers. That's because most Wild and Scenic Rivers are on public land, far from the entangling issues of land use zoning, construction setbacks, design review, and perc tests. To a lot of people in the activist community, Wild and Scenic Rivers are the easy ones to save. The tough ones are downstream, where rivers flow through private land.

In a nationwide survey of river activists, River Network discovered that land development was their biggest concern. Clearly that's because land development continues to encroach into river corridors with little legal restraint and there is no simple tool available to stop it. Public land rivers have a multitude of agencies, from the Forest Service to the BLM to the National Park Service to the U.S. Fish and Wildlife Service, to look after their welfare and protect them from abuse. If some of these agencies have also been among the abusers, they are nevertheless charged with the responsibility of managing river resources, and legal recourse is available when they shirk their duties. There are no such agencies responsible for rivers flowing through most reaches of private land.

Dealing with abuses to private land rivers often calls into play a variety of river-saving tools to address a variety of different problems. But when all else fails and you don't know what else to do for your river, it's time to think about buying it.

Now, not many of us are going to be capable of writing a check for a river, although as we'll see in a moment it has been done. But we may be able to talk interested landowners into selling their property to a land trust which will convey it to a public agency for permanent protection. Or, barring that, we may be able to convince riparian property owners to sell conservation easements to their land, while continuing to own and enjoy them.

What It Does

Land acquisitions and conservation easements both eliminate the possibility of future development for a parcel of land. Acquisition is generally the most preferred and most expensive option. Generally it involves an agreement between a willing seller and a buyer capable of disposing of the land in a way that provides permanent protection. Typically, the buyer will be a public agency with funds available for the purchase of riparian land. Purchase may also be made or brokered by a land trust. River Network has preserved several threatened riparian parcels through its Riverlands Conservancy program and can provide expert advice on the process.

A case in point is Greer Spring, one of the natural wonders of the Missouri Ozarks and a tributary to the Wild and Scenic Eleven Point River. Greer Spring, along with 6900 acres of surrounding woodland, was bought in 1988 by Leo Drey, a leading Missouri conservationist who simply wanted to see the resource protected. In 1990 Drey gave River Network an option on the land and offered to sell it at a $500,000 loss if the Anheuser-Busch Foundation would donate the same amount toward its purchase. River Network ultimately brokered the transaction and the land is now protected in the Eleven Point Wild and Scenic River corridor and in a newly created Greer Spring Special Management Area managed by the Forest Service.

Conservation easements often have a wider application than outright purchase because they allow property owners, many of whom don't want more development around them anyway, to stay on their land. In exchange for tax benefits and cash payments, they give up future development of their property. Usually the land can even be sold, but the easement remains in place.

If you can't buy a piece of property or purchase a development right for it, an alternative to consider is the process called "limited development." Promoted by land use expert Andrew Johnson, limited development offers a menu of development options which preserve both a maximum amount of open space and a maximum amount of owner profit. As outlined by Johnson, options for a property on which open space is to be preserved but where some degree of development is inevitable include:

- Donation of part of the property to a land trust as an open space parcel
- Creation of a homeowners' association to provide perpetual management of the open space, in cooperation with a land trust
- Retention of a homestead lot for landowners wishing to remain in their homes, while selling off other lots adjacent to the open space lands

How to Use It

Unless you have experience brokering land buys or conservation easements, this is not something to try by yourself. Your first step should be to contact a local land trust or River Network for advice. Finding a willing buyer requires personal contact and positive relationships with riparian landowners. It also means responding quickly when you know important pieces of property are on the market.

The necessary ingredients for a transaction include the seller and a buyer or buyers with enough money to make the purchase. Numerous local, state, and federal agencies have budgets for land acquisition. Both the Forest Service and the BLM are prospective land buyers, as are state resources agencies. Counties frequently establish open space districts which fund land purchases with sales taxes or other levies. When no single agency can afford the purchase price of a piece of land, several buyers—including private land trusts—can sometimes be brought together.

Given the complexities of tax benefits and the variety of purchase options available, negotiating either a land purchase or a conservation easement is best left to someone with experience. But although you may not swing the deal yourself, you will still play a key role in the transaction if you can establish a positive, personal relationship with the seller and provide convincing arguments for the need to protect the river it adjoins.

Pros

Land acquisition and conservation easements eliminate uncertainty about the fate of riverside property, providing protection in perpetuity, removing any threat of development and helping to preserve the riparian corridor. Willing sellers are often large landholders like timber companies, and buying the land takes it out of production, allowing part of the watershed to heal. Ironically, while development opportunity is eliminated, land values may actually increase.

Cons

The most important ingredient for these tools to work is also one of the scarcest ingredients available—money. Buying the land or development rights won't stop dams or other river development up- or downstream, and finding a willing seller in some of the most critically endangered river corridors is difficult to impossible.

River Restoration

Sooner or later it comes down to this. Behind the glamour of the big dam fights and the development battles and the Superfund pollution problems, is the complex and mundane job of nursing an injured river system back to health. Restoration is where much river conservation ends up, putting the pieces back together.

Putting the pieces back together involves many different activities, and the use of many of the tools already described here. That includes enhancing streamflow, improving water quality, restoring fishery habitat, restoring the riparian environment, protecting the flood plain from further development, restoring damaged watersheds, counting fish, taking water samples, and stabilizing banks.

What It Does

In a narrow sense, river and stream restoration entails the structural and biological healing of a river, but in fact most river restoration projects focus on a specific segment. That is a noble and worthy objective, but ultimately, river restoration must address the entire system, from the forested slopes of the watershed, to the flood plain and the riparian corridor, to the banks and bottom of the river itself.

There is no single model for river restoration and there is no single legislative tool to support it. There is, in fact, a bewildering array of technical assistance programs and financial grants available from federal agencies for river restoration, but the legal and administrative tools at the public's disposal are scattered randomly through the bureaucracy; there is no coordinated and coherent river restoration policy, no statute law to guide the work.

Among the federal agencies providing varying kinds of support for river restoration efforts are these:

1. The Rivers and Trails Conservation Assistance Program. Mentioned several times throughout this book, the Rivers and Trails Conservation Assistance Program of the National Park Service has one of the best support programs for river restoration work. NPS staff are available to consult with river conservation groups and help develop greenway and comprehensive river management plans.

2. The Rural Clean Water Program. This program helps protect water quality in rural areas by assisting in efforts to control polluted runoff and soil erosion. Grants are available for specific local pollution control efforts. One river benefiting from assistance provided by this program has been the Westport River in Massachusetts.

3. The Small Watershed Program of the Soil Conservation Service. Intended to help planning and implementation of watershed management, this program provides grants and technical assistance to state agencies, local government, and nonprofits working to reduce erosion and flooding, improve fish and wildlife resources, and recharge groundwater reservoirs.

4. Resource Conservation and Development program of the Soil Conservation Service. This SCS program provides grants from $10,000 to $500,000 for projects which conserve and improve conditions for fish, wildlife, recreation, riparian restoration, wetlands, water quality, and other natural values.

5. Watershed Protection and Flood Prevention Loans from the Farmers Home Administration. These loans are intended for local nonprofit agencies, and the private landowners who may apply through them, to develop projects for flood prevention, water quality management, fish and wildlife development, water recreation, and other purposes.

6. The Wetland Restoration program of the U.S. Fish and Wildlife Service. Designed specifically to support the creation and restoration of wetlands, fish passage and fish habitat on private land, this program provides direct financial assistance and cost-sharing grants.

7. The National Estuary Program. Administered by the EPA, the National Estuary Program is designed to help both state and private agencies develop comprehensive conservation and management plans for specific estuaries.

8. The Fish and Wildlife Management Assistance program of the U.S. Fish and Wildlife Service. This is an important program aimed specifically at conservation and restoration of fish and wildlife resources, including fishery studies and river basin restoration programs. Available to federal agencies, states, and Indian tribes.

9. The Environmental Contaminants program of the U.S. Fish and Wildlife Service. Established to address the problem of fish and wildlife contam-

ination from toxic substances, this program provides technical assistance to public and private interests.

10. The Dingell-Johnson Federal Aid in Sport Fishing Restoration Program. As the name suggests, this program distributes federal aid for restoration of sport fishing. Matching grants are available to state resource and wildlife agencies for fish and wildlife protection, streamside enhancement, recreation, and education.

How to Use It

The most straightforward river and stream restoration projects are usually those engineered by fishing groups like Trout Unlimited, which select degraded trout streams and structurally restore them to viable fish habitat. Other outstanding restoration projects have been done by members of various state conservation corps. But restoring entire river systems, to achieve healthy watersheds and flood plains, is a far more complex and challenging task. Throughout the country efforts are underway to tackle the bigger picture, but it is a daunting challenge made more difficult by the absence of clear federal policies and coordinated agency support.

The best single reference work on river restoration is a book published in 1992 by the National Research Council called "Restoration of Aquatic Ecosystems." Researched, written, and reviewed by eminent professionals, the book is a bible of information on river issues and restoration techniques. It concludes with a set of 17 recommendations for a national restoration strategy. They include:

- Establishment of a National Aquatic Ecosystem Assessment Process
- Creation of an intergovernmental and interagency process to develop a unified national strategy for Aquatic Ecosystem restoration
- Assignment of leadership for a national restoration strategy to a single governmental agency
- Creation of a National Aquatic Ecosystem Restoration Trust Fund
- Allowance for states and local governments to trade federal funds intended for construction and repair of water projects for money to be invested instead in aquatic restoration projects
- State and federal encouragement for the trading of water rights to promote aquatic ecosystem restoration

River restoration is by definition a collaborative process requiring coordination and cooperation among numerous private and public interests. If the goals outlined above were implemented, the necessary coordination would be substantially simplified and empowered.

The Oregon-based Pacific Rivers Council is promoting a similar agenda through a proposed National Riverine and Riparian Conservation Act, which would set national standards for the preservation of riparian and riverine habitat, and which would also encourage establishment of state Riparian and Riverine Ecosystem Recovery Programs.

Their plan envisions a National Watershed Registry for private land rivers, not unlike the National Registry of Historic Places. Registered rivers would qualify for federal grants and assistance in the implementation of restoration plans.

Pros

River restoration, aided by tools like the Public Trust Doctrine, is the real promise and challenge to the river-saving community. It is the most important work we will do.

Cons

Current river restoration efforts can't meet the real need before them. Historically, river restoration has been largely piecemeal and limited to narrow corridors. America's rivers won't truly be protected until we treat whole systems, from source to mouth, from ridge-top to ridge-top, up and down tributaries and across the flood plains. To do that there needs to be a degree of state and federal coordination and policy simplification that does not now exist.

The Big Picture Tool: Reform

The river protection tools outlined in this chapter would be far more effective if they were coupled with the reform, elimination, or creation of a diverse variety of federal legislation.

The National Flood Insurance Program is in urgent need of overhaul, which shows some promise of happening as this book goes to press. Far from reducing the danger of floods by guiding development out of flood-prone areas, the current Program has so corrupted the intent of Congress it actually encourages development in flood plains. The result is not only ever-increasing flood damage but ongoing degradation of flood plains, wetlands, and river corridors.

There is no excuse for the continued existence of the 1872 Mining Act. It is a national disgrace that antiquated policy, set in law more than 115 years ago, should still guide the extraction of minerals from the public lands of the United States. All over America, thousands of mineral mines are leaching steady streams of poison into our rivers and streams. Mining companies pay next to nothing for mineral leases and then walk away from the mess they create with no obligation to clean it up.

Even though Congress made a half-hearted attempt in 1987 to reform FERC's penchant for disregarding the environmental impacts of hydropower projects with passage of the Electric Consumers Protection Act, that agency still operates with indifference to prevailing environmental values. Congress should either toughen further the environmental mandate it gives to FERC, or take hydropower licensing completely out of the agency's hands.

The Central Valley Project Improvement Act is a healthy start toward redressing the imbalance in western water allocation. For once, fish and wildlife have a place at the table. The CVPIA should be used, therefore, as the inspiration, if not the model, for similar reforms of other federal water projects, with the objective of improving guarantees for instream flows and enhancing fish and other aquatic species to self-sustaining levels.

As this book went to press, Congress was confronting the future of the Clean Water Act. Far from backing away from its original commitment, Congress should strengthen the Act to give it the regulatory teeth it needs to seriously address the problem of polluted runoff.

Congress should give the Wild and Scenic Rivers Act some new life by mandating the timely completion of river assessments for each listing in the Nationwide Rivers Inventory. The Inventory should also be aggressively expanded to more realistically reflect the nation's true river heritage, and candidate rivers should be spared further development until assessments are completed.

Congress should follow the advice of the National Research Council by creating a unified national strategy for aquatic ecosystem restoration.

And new legislative initiatives should be explored to promote the restoration and protection of whole river systems so that conservation efforts are organized along watershed lines and by the people who live there.

Reforms like these would profoundly empower the efforts of citizen activists and increase their chances for success. An important part of a river campaign's agenda, therefore, is the support of any legislation leading toward these kinds of reform.

Part Three
An Overview of Issues

Previous chapters have explored at length the techniques and tools for saving rivers, but we haven't focused directly on the values which make river ecosystems so important to save, and we haven't reviewed the complete inventory of issues which put them at risk. That's the focus for the third part of this book.

Chapter 6
Values of Free-Flowing Rivers

There has always been a conflict between those who feel their values are eternal and those who feel they are relative.

R. KOSTELANETZ

People who love rivers don't usually need technical explanations or elaborate inventories to explain or defend their value. A river is worth saving for what it manifestly is: a corridor of water, rock and land, a zone of life, a place of inexpressible beauty constantly reshaping itself. But the value of rivers exceeds anything most of us can imagine—it encompasses the very essence of planetary life. Healthy rivers are so important they define, in many respects, the health of the planet.

What follows is an inventory of the basic values rivers provide, most of them obvious upon examination and most of them systematically ignored as rivers all across the country have been degraded and destroyed.

Riparian Ecosystems and Biodiversity

Poets and biologists share a vision of rivers and streams as the arteries and capillaries of Earth. That romantic metaphor is grounded in scientific fact. Riparian ecosystems nourish and sustain the most complex and important food chains in nature, distributing nutrients, carrying off waste, pulsing with life. They are the breeding grounds, the nurseries, and the habitat for a bewildering variety of species, and they are the natural systems most vulnerable to the destructive impacts of human development.

River ecosystems are defined not just by channels of moving water and vegetated streambanks, but by the flood plains, watersheds, wetlands, and estuaries which constitute complex and interrelated hydrological systems. They are further defined by the substratum of the river bed, which scientists call the "hyporheic zone," a critically important region extending for hundreds, even thousands, of yards underground beyond the stream channel. This subterranean space supports as many as 100 species—including worms, shrimp, insects, and microscopic organisms—that serve as the base for the aquatic food chain.

The food chain woven through this interconnected environment ranges in size and complexity from the tiny microorganisms inhabiting the interstices between riverbed gravels in the hyporheic zone, to invertebrates like stone flies to crustaceans like crayfish, to frogs and salamanders and turtles, to minnows and larger predatory fish, to ducks and geese, to mink and otter, beaver, bear, osprey, and eagle, and all the other terrestrial species and birds of prey which depend on fish for food.

Crucial to the integrity of this food chain is the riparian vegetation which stabilizes watershed slopes and stream banks, filters pollution, shades the water and cools it for heat-sensitive fish. It also supplies nutrients, habitat and food, and provides the transition from bank, to flood plain, to watershed slope.

The health of the flood plain is integral to the health of the river and to the mix of species it supports. Flood plains absorb and meter out water, providing essential regulation for volume and velocity so that stream and riverbeds aren't scoured and stream banks don't erode.

Riparian ecosystems are complex, integrated environments. Impact on one component of the ecosystem affects every other component. Mussels, for example, play an important role in preserving water quality by filtering out bacteria and suspended particles. Mussels filter water through their gills, an anatomical amenity missing in mussel larvae. So the larvae attach themselves to fish gills which breath for them until they mature. For each species of mussel, there is a specific host fish, and when that fish disappears so does the mussel.

Despite their value, river systems have been devastated by human development. A 1990 study by The Nature Conservancy reported that, in North America, 34 percent of fishes, 28 percent of amphibian species, 65 percent of crayfish, and 73 percent of mussels were in danger, their status ranging from "rare to imperiled." And the rate of extinction appears to be accelerating much faster for aquatic species than for their terrestrial counterparts.

More than one biologist has described the effect of this species decline on the health of ecosystems as being analogous to the removal of rivets from an airplane wing—pull enough of them out, the wing falls off and the plane crashes.

Fisheries

Fish are the most obvious and often the most important index of the health of a waterway. Dead and disappearing fish alert us, in ways few other species can, to the decline of our rivers. Fish have the greatest economic, recreational, and, perhaps, spiritual value of all riverine species. A river may be dying in a thousand little increments, but we tend to ignore the problem until the fish disappear.

The anadromous fisheries of North America—Atlantic and Pacific salmon, steelhead, shad, alewives, and striped bass—are all under siege. As noted earlier, Atlantic salmon stocks are just now being nursed back from the edge of extinction while Pacific salmon are fighting to survive. Winter run chinook salmon in the Sacramento River dropped below 200 fish in 1991, and the Snake River Fall chinook run dropped to 78 fish in 1990. These are mere fragments of the original runs. And in 1993, the Pacific Rivers Council filed a petition under the Endangered Species Act for listing of the coho salmon.

In this century, 40 species of North American fish are believed to have become extinct; 19 of those species have vanished since 1964 and 10 have disappeared since 1979. The Lower Colorado River, below Lake Mojave, has no native fish left at all. In the Sierra Nevada, 69 percent of the native fish are in serious decline or endangered. Arizona has 30 species of native fish and 25 are listed as threatened or endangered.

These fish are an essential part of the food chain, but not just for the raptors and carnivores that eat them—they are essential to humans as well. The Pacific Northwest salmon fishery contributes 60,000 jobs and $1 billion to the regional economy, and those figures come from a fishery that has declined more than 90 percent from historic levels.

A federal study of the economic impact of the Glines Canyon Dam on Washington's Elwha River concluded that the dam is costing $500,000 per year in lost revenue from salmon and tourism. The Elwha is one of only a few rivers that once supported all five species of Pacific salmon.

A 1988 report on the status of California's salmon and steelhead fisheries concluded that doubling of statewide production could generate 8000 new jobs and increase business revenues by $150 million per year.

Since the majority of America's rivers don't have commercial salmon runs, however, it should also be noted that sport fisheries all over the country are put at risk when rivers are degraded. Native trout are usually the species most vulnerable to habitat destruction, pollution, and increases in water temperature. Fishing groups active in stream restoration can testify to the enhanced value of a healthy fishery. And usually, if you have healthy, self-sustaining populations of native fish, you have a healthy river.

Cultural Resources

Like the Merrimack in Massachusetts and the Stanislaus in California, rivers everywhere are the focal point for human society. Most of the world's great cities are situated on rivers, and early human settlements great and small were scattered along river corridors. Throughout history rivers have been places of culture and commerce and they dictated the distribution of civilization.

The Merrimack River in Lowell, Massachusetts flows through a red brick corridor of commerce, its banks lined with mile after mile of mills dating back past the turn of the century. Those mills were part of America's industrial revolution and the pollution they produced contributed to the biological death of the Merrimack. Now the river has been revived and many of the mills are restored as historic artifacts in the Lowell Heritage Park, the first urban national park of its kind.

At the other end of the country, the Stanislaus River flows through a different kind of history as it passes rusting mining debris from the California Gold Rush and the village sites, grinding holes, and petroglyphs of ancient Miwok people. But while important artifacts of our national heritage are preserved and displayed in Lowell, no such effort has been expended for the artifacts of Miwok life in the Stanislaus Canyon, perhaps suggesting something about cultural priorities and national values. In the Stanislaus, the Miwok heritage is now largely buried beneath a reservoir.

Some of the richest cultural traditions in America are river centered or river dependent. Wild rivers have been avenues for exploration, adventure, and escape from early times, and the nation has taken river legends—both real (Lewis and Clark) and imagined (Huckleberry Finn)—to its cultural heart. On rivers, commerce and culture mix. Paddlewheel steamers created an industry and a lifestyle. Picturesque fishing fleets at the mouths of rivers in California, Oregon, Washington, Alaska, and New England bespeak both an enterprise dependent on the health of rivers and a culture struggling to survive.

River corridors are rich in history because that's where much of our early history was made. From the Hudson to the Wabash to the Mississippi to the Sacramento, rivers trace the unfolding story of the United States. Every riverside community has its own unique relationship with a river and every river has its own unique story to tell. By and large we have ignored those stories, but the cultural history they contain is still ours to discover and preserve.

Recreation

The special value of river recreation is that it can be enjoyed in harmony with nature, rather than at nature's expense. Recreational use of a river requires little or no intervention by engineers and is often improved, in fact, by the absence of human "enhancements." Reservoirs, on the other hand, exact an enormous price from the environment. That price is then compounded by the impact of ubiquitous motor boats and their consumption of fossil fuels.

This is not to suggest that reservoirs are implicitly bad. In fact, the exploding popularity of whitewater sports owes something to the reliable and extended flows supplied by storage dams. But for decades the agenda for public investment in water recreation has been driven by a cultural addiction to the internal combustion engine. What we got from government, therefore, was strictly reservoirs; the multiple values of river recreation were largely ignored.

But statistics from the National Park Service indicate that free-flowing rivers are rapidly growing in popularity as one of the nation's leading recreation resources. That popularity corresponds, in part, to the growth of the river conservation movement and the exposure it has given to the wonders of wild rivers. It may reflect as well the human need to stay in touch with the natural world and the unique magic of moving water.

River-oriented activities include canoeing, kayaking, rafting, swimming, picnicking, camping, hiking, hunting, bird watching, photography, and simply lolling about. Not to mention fishing, which is one of the two or three most popular recreation activities in the U.S., enjoyed by nearly 60 million people in 1985. Not all fishing is done on rivers, but fly fishing,

Atchafalaya River, Louisiana. (Photo courtesy of Tim Palmer.)

West Branch of the Penobscot River, Maine. (Photo courtesy of Tim Palmer.)

which is more often associated with trout and free-flowing streams, continues to grow in popularity.

One of the most important recreational values rivers provide is hard to measure because surveys aren't taken on the number of people who visit rivers just to look at them, to stand beside them in silent wonder, to take pause from life's pressures in the presence of moving water. This intangible value separates rivers and river corridors from the noise and congestion and preoccupation with speed typical of reservoirs, and offers a recreational experience closer to the true meaning of the word. But the growing popularity of river greenways suggests that the restorative value of rivers is gaining wider recognition.

Urban Amenities

Many of America's cities—both great and small—are located on and defined by rivers. Portland and Albuquerque and New York and New Orleans and St. Louis and Cincinnati and Washington and Philadelphia and Minneapolis and Richmond and Birmingham and Sacramento and Pittsburgh are a few of the obvious examples.

Beyond the value of commerce rivers bring to cities is the value of ambience, of amenity, of aesthetic presence they provide. Rivers offer fluid, free-flowing counterpoint to the rigid structures and predictable order of cities. They introduce a corridor of nature between corridors of asphalt and they remind city dwellers of the natural world beyond the urban boundary.

Where cities once exploited, abused, and then ignored rivers in their midst, they are now coming to recognize, restore, and appreciate them. The National Heritage Park along the Merrimack in Lowell, Massachusetts has transformed a depressed downtown area into a thriving business and tourism center and has given local residents a resource of historic interest and great aesthetic value.

The American River Parkway flows through the heart of Sacramento, draws upwards of six million visitors each year, and provides residents of Sacramento and its suburbs with an opportunity to swim, paddle, bike, birdwatch, fish, picnic, and just relax within minutes of the state capital.

Boulder Creek, which flows through the heart of Boulder, Colorado, has been transformed into one of the finest urban river parks in the nation. A whitewater slalom course, restored trout fishery, pedestrian paths, a five-mile greenway, wetlands, open space, flood plain protection, and clustered development have been combined in a model of what can be achieved when river management is committed to preserving a natural system.

Two of the most important urban amenities in Washington, D.C. are the Potomac River and Rock Creek Park. Twenty-five years ago the Potomac was a scenic cesspool, full of sewage scum as it floated past the Lincoln Memorial. Today the Potomac runs almost clean, if not always clear, and it offers one of the finest urban whitewater runs in the world.

Rock Creek, meanwhile, traces a circuitous path through the capitol city, providing a green, wooded oasis with riding trails, picnic areas, and the National Zoo. Residents insist it is the only place to be on a July afternoon when both the temperature and the humidity are in the nineties.

These examples, and others like them in Missoula and Cincinnati and Chattanooga and Richmond and Boise, demonstrate how important the presence of a healthy river is in the life of a city or town. But communities across the country are also discovering that creating a river greenway can be an expensive challenge. In Santa Rosa, California a citizens advisory committee has created a plan to reverse decades of damage to the town's namesake creek. They plan to develop a greenway with bike paths and picnic areas, but it's a difficult job. Not just because urban development crowds the stream, or because portions of it have been straightened and channelized, but because for three blocks the whole creek is funneled through a tunnel beneath City Hall.

Like Santa Rosa, cities and towns all over the country are belatedly (and expensively) discovering the value of a free-flowing river or stream in the heart of an urban environment. The lesson, learned on river after river, is

that it's easier and cheaper to protect a river before the fact than to restore
it after the damage has been done.

Water, Power, and Sewage Disposal

For nearly 300 years, America's rivers have been developed to provide
water, power, and sewage disposal. While those uses seem at times to be
mutually exclusive, many rivers around the country have been called upon
to provide all three. The frequent result has been rivers alternately
dammed, diverted, drained, and polluted. These human uses have produced enormous economic value, but they have also exacted an enormous
ecological (and economic) cost through massive impacts on fish and wildlife, loss of biodiversity, and the destruction of natural beauty.

Accurate statistics on the resource value of rivers are hard to come by,
perhaps in part because river resources have long been taken for granted.
There does not seem to be a reliable accounting of the amount of drinking
water taken from the nation's rivers and streams, and such an accounting
would be wildly inaccurate unless it managed to somehow measure as well
the amount of groundwater taken from river-fed aquifers. Still, the figure
is enormous, and most major cities—from Los Angeles to New York—
depend heavily on rivers for water. In California, fully 60 percent of developed water is estimated to come from rivers and streams flowing out of
the Sierra, and more is taken from other mountain ranges.

The amount of river water available for human consumption varies radically depending on point of view. Most fisheries biologists would agree
that the nation's rivers are already oversubscribed and that, rather than
take more water out of our rivers, we should leave more water in them.
Clearly, as human consumption grows, so will the value of water and the
conflict between instream and consumptive use.

Computing the wastewater carrying capacity of the nation's rivers is
even more difficult to estimate, not only because national figures haven't
been compiled, but because so many unregulated discharges occur that
reliable estimates would be almost impossible, and storm-drain run-off
would skew the figure even further. Suffice it to say that for centuries rivers
have been the primary sewage disposal sites for most of humanity.

The impact of all that wastewater and industrial discharge has changed
significantly in the past 25 years as a whole generation of state and federal
clean water legislation has triggered the investment of billions of dollars in
wastewater treatment facilities. But as our effluent gets cleaner, we still—
by and large—dispose of it in rivers and streams and we will into the for-
seeable future.

This isn't always a bad thing. In some parts of the country, treated wastewater is beginning to have considerable secondary value in maintaining streamflow. The Los Angeles River is alive today, if still profoundly ill, thanks to massive infusions of treated wastewater. But river activists remain rightfully suspicious about the risks from heavy metals and biological pathogens not removed from treated sewage.

Hydroelectricity is one river resource for which accurate figures exist. While the amount varies from year to year depending on weather and hydrological conditions, on average the nation gets 10 percent of its annual energy fix from hydropower plants. There are enormous pressures from utilities and energy speculators to increase that percentage, and the Federal Energy Regulatory Commission has been busy authorizing about 250 new (although mostly small) hydro projects each year. The energy industry believes America's rivers have enormous undeveloped hydro potential. The environmental community believes rivers are already abused and overworked.

Suffice it to say that America's rivers work hard. And given our dependence on rivers for water, power, and waste disposal—not to mention transportation and recreation—it probably would not be an exaggeration to rate rivers as the nation's single most important natural resource.

Water Quality

Cynics point out that both rats and humans have a tendency to foul their nests. That observation is supported by our historic treatment of rivers. Given the higher intelligence of humans, it is curious that we have tended to dump our sewage, our trash, and our toxins in the same water we use for drinking and recreation.

The alarming and frequently dramatic degradation of water quality in America's rivers and streams helped launch the environmental movement and provided one of its first clear objectives. Fish kills, nauseating odors, and rivers catching fire were symptoms of a systemic illness too obvious to ignore. The result was a package of legislation that has come to be called the Clean Water Act—and clean water has been a national priority ever since.

Although the nation's rivers are now chemically cleaner than they have been in almost a century, this new priority is still ignored almost as often as it is honored, and the U.S. is nearly a decade behind its original deadline of eliminating all pollutants into navigable waters by 1985. And while industrial and municipal waste has been cleaned up substantially, polluted runoff from farm fields and storm drains has become the leading cause of river pollution.

Water quality is a complex issue, and the definition of pollution used by the Environmental Protection Agency encompasses not just chemical and biological contamination, but temperature, turbidity, dissolved oxygen, and even stream flow. A river can be chemically clean while suffering from thermal pollution, eutrophication, sedimentation, and inadequate flow. The bad news is that little is being done to improve the biological health of rivers, and the EPA won't require states to use biological criteria in its water quality reporting until 1995.

The problems of pollution are obvious, but often the evidence isn't. When a river is so dirty that it smells and looks bad, or isn't safe to drink, we tend to take action to clean it up. But when a river looks clean, or when the less visible and tangible indices of water quality decline, we tend to ignore them until there is a dramatic impact on the biological health of the river, or on the people who use it. By then, river-dependent species may be endangered or dead, and the cost of restoration soars.

So despite more than two decades of legislative remedy, clean water is a river value still very much in need of improvement and protection. While industrial and residential pollution is being gradually eliminated, agricultural and urban runoff, along with grazing, logging, dam building, diversions, and toxic mine debris, continue to take a heavy toll on the quality of flowing water.

Soil and Bank Stability

Of all the natural values of rivers and streams, the most ignored and one of the most at risk is the stability of stream banks and watershed slopes, the physical structures which shape and define rivers.

Watershed and streambank stability have a profound influence on the health of rivers and streams; you can't protect a river without protecting the soil around it. We have been slow to address the relationship between watersheds damaged by logging, or streambanks trampled by cattle, and the loss of healthy fisheries and spawning habitat. We are only now beginning to treat rivers as complete systems, connected hydrologically and biologically to the surrounding land. Which means that land use decisions affecting the health and stability of watersheds, flood plains, riparian corridors, and streambanks are also, by definition, river-use decisions.

Preserving watersheds, flood plains, and streambanks is doubly difficult precisely because land that is up and away from the bed of a river is normally viewed as disconnected and separate. So protecting those vital river values requires intruding into the realm of private property and commercial development where public resistance is high.

Flood Protection

One of the most fundamental, and fundamentally overlooked, values of rivers is the natural flood control they provide when left with at least some of their natural environment intact. It's a value seldom computed in cost–benefit studies and all too rarely utilized as a method of flood control. Instead, rivers are dammed, channelized, and leveed, development covers the flood plain, and while modest and frequent floods are curtailed, when flooding does occur it is magnified in scope by the river system's reduced capacity to store water, and by the unfortunate presence of so much more human investment.

The Mississippi River flood of 1993 makes clear on a vast and tragic scale the limits of structural flood control. Left in something approaching their natural state, provided with room to expand and wander, given enough forest and wetland and flood plain, rivers have a remarkable capacity to absorb rainfall and runoff.

But, stripped of their meanders and wetlands, squeezed between levees, their watersheds logged and their flood plains developed, rivers must inevitably flood. That's true no matter how many dams and levees are built to control them.

And it is almost always cheaper—usually orders of magnitude cheaper—to preserve the river's natural course, to give it room to move, to provide it with wetlands and forests to slow and absorb flood waters, than to build huge, expensive monuments to protect what cannot be protected, and to then pay for the astronomical damage caused by the inevitable flood. Dams and levees don't stop floods, they just make floods less frequent and more devastating.

Economics

Without going too far out on an ecological limb, it's safe to say that rivers are among the earth's most valuable and vulnerable resources and that they, perhaps more than any other single feature on the planet, are essential for the health and prosperity of human civilization.

The elements of any equation designed to calculate the economic value of rivers would have to include the value of water for drinking, irrigation, industrial use and hydroelectric production, the value of fish and wildlife dependent on rivers and wetlands, the value of river-based recreation, the value of pollution dispersal, the value of river-based transportation, and the enhanced property value of riparian lands.

With that said, it's clear that the cumulative economic value of rivers is beyond calculation. But tangible economic values can and should be calculated for the whole range of uses of any given river, in part to counter the prevailing assumption that only extractive and consumptive uses provide economic benefit to society. As communities around the country begin developing proactive management plans for their rivers, the economic value of instream uses will be more clearly defined. And when that happens society will better understand that clean water and healthy fisheries are just two of a host of economic values rivers provide, and that it is cheaper to protect a river than to restore it.

Above and beyond the quantifiable economic value of a healthy river is the intangible economic benefit a river bestows on the land it flows through. The quality of life in Sacramento, California is immeasurably enhanced by the presence of a federally protected Wild and Scenic reach of the American River, flowing through a linear park in the middle of a vital city.

We need healthy rivers for many reasons and economic considerations may not be high on everyone's scale of values. But when our rivers are allowed to decline and die, the economic cost can be enormous.

Natural Beauty

Natural beauty, many people would argue, is reason enough to save rivers. And many people, therefore, find it hard to understand the mentality capable of drowning Glen Canyon, burying the Missouri, drying up the Everglades, or paving the Los Angeles River. The last few people to float through Glen Canyon were unanimous in their disbelief that a place of such breathtaking and tranquil beauty could be destroyed. It sits beneath Lake Powell now, gathering silt and bearing mute testimony to a value in desperate need of defense.

We glorify natural beauty even as we destroy it, its value is universally acknowledged even as it slips away.Because rivers are among nature's most beautiful works, the damage we do to them is painfully apparent. And yet our culture has sanctioned that damage on an epic scale and a majority of us have acquiesced.

Natural beauty can never be computed in a cost–benefit ratio. The beauty of rivers should be defended because its loss diminishes us all. It is worth protecting just because it's there.

Chapter 7
Problems

Many of the problems the world faces today are the eventual result of short-term measures taken last century.

JAY W. FORRESTER

While this is a book devoted to solutions, it is implicitly about problems—the universe of issues river conservation needs to confront. And although most of the issues addressed below have been discussed anecdotally in preceding chapters, river activists may find it useful to review them in more detail. Keep in mind that while some rivers face a single threat (like a dam), more often the problem is compound, a layering of abuses which do not respond to single solutions. And even if the first order of business on your river is stopping a dam, it's likely there are other less urgent, more chronic problems you will eventually have to confront.

Dams

No human development presents as singular and visible a threat to a river as a dam. Dams have the unique capacity to utterly disrupt an entire river ecosystem with one act of construction. And while a dam may not be forever, its monumental presence promises to outlast several human generations and the animal species whose habitat it destroys.

There are so many dams on America's rivers that no one seems to know the precise number, although estimates range from 60,000 to 80,000 and the Environmental Protection Agency suggests the figure of 68,000 major impoundments. When farm ponds are added to the equation, the National Research Council reports a total of "well over" 2.5 million dams in the United States.

Those dams have buried 17 percent of the nation's river miles beneath reservoirs, and they have adversely affected an even larger percentage of river habitat by interrupting flows, altering water temperature, blocking wildlife migration corridors, and imposing numerous other changes on natural systems. By contrast, less than 1 percent of the nation's river miles are protected in their natural state.

Abandoned dam on a tributary of the Price River, Utah. (Photo courtesy of Tim Palmer.)

While dams have created ecological havoc, it's important for us to acknowledge the good dams have done. We all depend on the power and water produced by dams, as well as on the navigation and flood protection they provide. But far too many dams have been built, many for no justifiable reason. Between 1962 and 1968 more than 200 major dams were completed in North America *each year* and, during the same period, smaller dams were being constructed at the rate of more than 2000 per year. More than 6000 major new dams have been proposed in the U.S. during the last ten years. The numbers may be difficult to grasp, but it's not difficult to imagine the negative impact all those dams have had on rivers and streams.

Dams serve a variety of different functions and, although many dams are built with multiple purposes, we will better understand dams and the problems they create if we divide them into three categories.

Storage Dams

Major storage dams—which are almost always multipurpose projects also offering flood protection, recreation, and often hydropower—represent the archetypal river threat. Their construction imposes a massive environmental trauma on river canyons, their reservoirs bury vast reaches of free-flowing river, and their regulation of downstream flow frequently upsets dynamic hydrologic cycles upon which plants and animals depend.

With dams in the way, sediment transport is blocked, which eliminates a source of replenishment for riparian farmland and leads to subsidence and erosion of delta lands. Coastal beaches are eroded away when replacement sediment is not available from rivers blocked by dams.

Because most multipurpose storage dams release clear, cold, sediment-free water, the discharge radically effects every aspect of the downstream ecosystem. Cold, deoxygenated water released from the bottom of reservoirs negatively impacts native stream organisms used to warmer, aerated water. Clear water, deprived of dam-trapped sediment (called "hungry water" by hydrologists) seeks to reestablish equilibrium by scouring up new sediment from streambed and banks, accelerating erosion, and downcutting the riverbed. As the riverbed is downcut, the mouths of tributary streams slump, causing further erosion up into tributaries, which degrades key spawning habitat.

The driving force behind storage dams is the need—or the perceived need—for more water. Until very recently, water development policy (like energy development policy) has been the product of supply-side thinking. Water has traditionally been viewed as a limitless resource, and whenever more supply was needed new dams and reservoirs were built. Little attention was paid to the demand side of the equation and the possibility of

Ross Dam, Skagit River, Washington. (Photo courtesy of Tim Palmer.)

stretching supplies by reducing consumption and increasing efficiency of use. The result was, and is, extravagant waste.

Take, for example, the proposed multipurpose version (as opposed to the flood control-only version) of Auburn Dam, which would—if it's ever built—cost something in excess of $2 billion. The water storage component of that cost was estimated in 1990 at about $400 million, for which a maximum of 270,000 acre-feet of new water would be stored each year.

With those figures tucked in the back of your mind, consider the question of irrigated cotton in California, of which there are some 1.1 million acres. Cotton uses vast amounts of water—three to four feet, or more, per acre each year. But experiments with subsurface drip irrigation have demonstrated that this simple technology can reduce the water requirements of cotton fields by more than 50 percent, with the added benefit of an increase in productivity.

Subsurface drip is expensive to install, costing something on the order of $1000 per acre. But if, for the sake of argument, we were able to take the $400 million earmarked for water storage at Auburn Dam, and invest it instead in subsurface drip irrigation, we could efficiently irrigate 400,000 acres of cotton. If the results of the extensive experiments done to date are an accurate guide, four hundred thousand acres of subsurface drip would save, perhaps, 800,000 acre-feet of water, year after year, or about three times the most optimistic firm annual yield of Auburn Dam.

These figures are rough estimates and there is as yet no funding mechanism for investing water storage money in irrigation technology. But that simply underscores the problem: an inadequate commitment to irrigation efficiency and agricultural water conservation. In the Western U.S., irrigated agriculture uses about 85 percent of all developed water, and the General Accounting Office has estimated that 50 percent of the nation's irrigation water is wasted.

It would be wrong, of course, to single out irrigated agriculture as the only example of inefficient water use. Some of the nation's major cities—like Sacramento—still don't use residential water meters, and all over the country leaking water pipes waste water. But more importantly, we have yet to adopt any comprehensive national program to mandate urban water efficiency and to require that water rate structures encourage conservation instead of waste.

More than 20 years ago the National Water Commission called for pricing reform, penalties for excessive water consumption, leak control programs, universal water metering, and plumbing codes requiring installation of water efficient fixtures. With the exception of federal codes for new plumbing, those suggestions have only been implemented randomly around the country, and usually only in response to local water crises.

The single most effective way to protect rivers from more storage dams is to require more efficient use of the water already developed.

Flood Control Dams

Water storage and flood control are usually companion purposes for large dam projects, even though the objective of one contradicts the other. The purpose of a water storage dam is to hold a maximum pool of water for as long as possible. The purpose of a flood control dam is to keep a minimum pool of water for as long as possible. These twin purposes usually result in construction of a larger dam than is needed for either single objective, and they often lead to a conflict in the management of the dam. (Glen Canyon Dam on the Colorado River was almost over-topped in 1983—the dam height was raised with marine plywood to contain rising flood waters—and Folsom Dam was almost lost in 1986, because in both cases reservoirs were kept too full).

The impacts of flood control dams are the same as for storage dams, with one added problem: When a dam is used for flood control the level of the reservoir behind it must be periodically lowered to accommodate incoming flood waters, which then raise the level again. This periodic and sudden fluctuation of reservoir level can destabilize sensitive canyon slopes creating landslides into the reservoir, further degrading the remaining watershed habitat. And of course, all reservoirs used for water storage, flood control, or hydropower invariably exhibit so-called "bathtub rings" of naked mud and dead trees as the water level drops over a season of use.

But these negative impacts are minor when compared to the real problems with flood control dams; they don't stop floods, they encourage floodplain development, and their construction often leads to more disastrous flooding than would occur without them.

Take, for example, Warm Springs Dam, built in the 1970s and 1980s on Dry Creek, a tributary of California's Russian River. The lower reaches of the Russian River are populated with summer resorts and small towns built directly on the flood plain, and after heavy winter rains the river routinely tops its banks. Over the years, local residents had become resigned to periodic flooding.

The Army Corps of Engineers, which built Warm Springs Dam, promised the project would relieve flooding in the lower river, taking at least three feet off future flood crests. The project was completed and fully operational by the winter of 1985–86, which is when it met its first real test. On Valentine's Day, Northern California was engulfed in a rain storm of epic proportions and the Russian River rose to record heights. The town of Guerneville, where several citizens, reassured by the presence of the dam, had canceled their flood insurance, was completely inundated and isolated by water. Baffled residents, who thought the dam would provide security, had to be evacuated from their submerged homes in National Guard helicopters.

Warm Springs Dam did not actually fail this hydrologic test. The dam did what it was supposed to do. What failed was the *concept* that dams are the solution to floods. It's a mistake to think that dams stop floods; more accurately, they delay floods, make them less frequent. It's true that the nation's hundreds of flood control dams have contributed to the safety of human populations along river corridors. But that safety is never absolute and it contributes to a false sense of security, which itself encourages more people to live in the path of inevitable flood waters.

Despite the billions of dollars invested in flood control in this century, the annual cost of flood damage continues to rise, largely because of the proliferation of development in flood plains. The Army Corps of Engineers claims that its flood control projects have returned $3.50 in value for each dollar spent, but Corps figures are notoriously suspect. They do not, for instance, include the true cost of environmental destruction created by flood control projects, they wildly exaggerate recreational benefits, and they often claim value for as-yet unbuilt development which Corps projects will allow and encourage in the flood plain. Author Tim Palmer cites a study done by a resource economist at the University of Wisconsin who examined the cost–benefit ratios of 100 Army Corps projects. He concluded that only about 25 percent would "survive rigorous analysis" writes Palmer, "and that half of these would not be cost-effective if environmental damages were counted."

The Great Mississippi Flood of 1993 makes tragically clear the false security of flood control projects. No amount of dams and levees and sandbags will stop the Mississippi from periodically asserting its awesome power. And it will never be practical or even possible to build adequate levees around every town and village along its banks. In fact levees, by constricting the river into an unnaturally narrow channel, actually raise the level and speed of flood waters, making them more destructive.

There is no mystery to all this. Years ago both the Task Force on Federal Flood Control Policy and the now-defunct National Water Commission supported flood plain management as the best way to solve the problem of floods. The National Flood Insurance Program was enacted to discourage flood plain development. But zoning decisions in flood plains all over the country suggest the message still hasn't been heard.

Hydropower Dams

While news of the death of big dams may be somewhat exaggerated, the species is clearly in decline, wounded by budget deficits and pummeled by

Holtwood Hydroelectric Dam, Susquehanna River, Pennsylvania. (Photo courtesy of Tim Palmer.)

environmentalists. The Bureau of Reclamation has even announced it is getting out of the dam business altogether. But the same prognosis can't be made for hydro dams, especially the small versions of less than 80 megawatts which have proliferated like mushrooms since Congress enacted legislation to promote alternative energy. Passed in 1978, the Public Utility Regulatory Policies Act, popularly called PURPA, did for hydropower what the 21st Amendment did for the sale of beer.

In 1976 the Federal Energy Regulatory Commission received 13 applications for preliminary permits to build hydropower projects. In 1981 the number of applications soared to 1859. The frenzy, which environmentalists have dubbed "hydromania," was triggered by PURPA provisions requiring utilities to both buy power from independent energy producers and to pay "avoided cost," which meant the cost utilities would have to pay to generate the power or acquire it from other conventional sources. These provisions virtually guaranteed that anyone who could bring a small hydroplant on line could then settle back and count the profits.

Hydromania was exacerbated by the predisposition of the Federal Energy Regulatory Commission to ignore environmental impacts when considering hydro permit applications. And even after reform legislation was passed in 1986 requiring that environmental impact be given "equal consideration" with power development, the Commission's decisions suggested continued indifference to the environmental consequences of hydroprojects. At this writing it remains to be seen whether new appointments by President Clinton will alter the FERC status quo.

Above and beyond FERC's predisposition to value hydropower permits over protection of free-flowing rivers is the problem of its jurisdictional autonomy. Thanks to a provision of the Federal Power Act, FERC lives in a regulatory world of its own and, while it can not intrude on Federal Wild and Scenic Rivers, its licensing prerogative extends almost everywhere else, and it can and does override decisions by state agencies and the EPA. Thus, even while the Upper Klamath was being protected in Oregon's Scenic River System, FERC was proceeding with licensing steps for the Salt Caves hydropower project that would dewater the river's historic canyon.

The proliferation of hydropower projects is one problem; their operation is another. We've already discussed the impact of fluctuating hydropower releases from Glen Canyon Dam, which have wrecked the Grand Canyon's delicate riparian ecosystem. Elsewhere around the country the operation of hydropower dams causes similar problems as rivers are turned on and off like faucets. Adequate instream flow is a condition of a power plant permit, but many hydro projects built early this century escaped any licensing requirements. For many others the permit requirements are inadequate to protect fisheries and recreation, and still others are simply operated in violation of their permits.

Hydropower projects pose two separate threats to rivers. One is caused by impoundment, about which we have already written, and the other is caused by diversion of water. Some hydro diversions are brief, as short as the width of a dam, but others go for miles through tunnels and penstocks before water is returned to the stream.

Another problem created by hydropower projects can best be illustrated by a statement quoted in Portland's *The Oregonian* by the chairman of a Montana power company. "I happen to be one of those people," he said, "who thinks the aesthetics of a place are improved by putting a nice transmission line through it." Thousands of miles of wilderness have been "improved" by hydroelectric power lines, although most people wouldn't describe the results as beautiful.

Diversions

If rivers are the arteries of earth, then diversions, to torture the analogy a bit, are the hemorrhages that bleed rivers dry.

Of course, we couldn't sustain civilization without diverting water from rivers, so the issue is really a question of degree. And the degree to which we have been diverting rivers has wreaked ecological havoc.

The Colorado River flows for 1450 miles from high in the Rocky Mountains, but by the time it reaches the Gulf of California it is a feeble, polluted trickle, oversubscribed by the seven states that divide its water. The Kern River, which drains the longest watershed in the Sierra Nevada, is pumped completely dry in mid-summer before it exits Bakersfield. Excess diversions have contributed to the drastic decline and extirpation of salmon runs throughout coastal California. Some 95 percent of Arizona's riparian habitat is gone, largely because of water diversions.

The problem isn't limited to the arid West. In Massachusetts, the Merrimack River has been targeted for increased municipal diversions ever since a massive clean-up made its water acceptable for human consumption. River guardians there now worry that more diversions will pose new danger to a river being nursed back to health.

Diversions would be less of a problem if widespread protections existed for instream flows, but only a handful of states have initiated minimum streamflow programs. And as we discussed earlier, surveying rivers to establish the minimum flows necessary for fish and other aquatic life is so time-consuming most states are reluctant or unable to do it.

Efforts to protect streamflow are compounded by the complex tangle of water rights law detailed in Chapter 5. In most states consumptive uses are given a higher priority than instream uses and water rights law reflects that value system. The process of acquiring water rights for instream use is also difficult and slow.

In the West, the problem has been magnified by federal reclamation policies which diverted vast amounts of water and made it available for irrigation through long-term, low-price contracts which encouraged overconsumption and inefficient use.

There have been some genuine reforms, like the 1992 Central Valley Project Improvement Act which made more water available for fish and wildlife in California's Central Valley. But that legislation is an exception to the rule and excessive diversion remains a problem without a comprehensive and practical solution.

Groundwater Development

While we're on the subject of water diversion we need to touch briefly on the problem of groundwater development. A quarter of the nation's water supply comes from underground aquifers—in Arizona groundwater

Canal for the State Water Project below Oroville Reservoir, Feather River, California. (Photo courtesy of Tim Palmer.)

provides more than 60 percent of the supply—and many of those aquifers have a symbiotic relationship with rivers.

But the importance of groundwater is belied by the way it is haphazardly developed. In many parts of the country groundwater pumping is totally unregulated, which often leads to overdrafting of aquifers and the steady lowering of water tables. That in turn leads to diminished stream flow, land subsidence, and a reduction in water storage capacity as the emptying aquifer is compacted.

In some parts of California's San Joaquin Valley, farmers are pumping water from more than half a mile deep, and so much groundwater has been removed that vast tracts of land have dropped more than 20 feet. The Ogallala aquifer, grandaddy of subsurface bathtubs, was being overdrawn by some 14 million acre-feet in the 1970s. All over the West, streamflow has been reduced or eliminated by groundwater pumping. Arizona is one of the few states with any comprehensive groundwater regulation, but many of its streams are already siphoned dry and for years Tucson was pumping groundwater at five times the rate of recharge.

Without the kind of groundwater regulation that now exists in Arizona and was recently imposed on the Edwards Aquifer in Texas, underground basins throughout the West will inevitably be drained. To avoid that fate, and to avoid the consequent impact on streamflow, groundwater needs to be both regulated and scientifically developed. Properly managed underground aquifers can be artificially recharged with injection wells and infiltration ponds. Computer programs now exist which model groundwater basins and provide optimal drawdown scenarios. One program developed by the Water Resources Institute in Grand Rapids, Michigan, has been used to identify areas of vulnerability in groundwater supplies and to direct urban development toward healthy, understressed aquifers.

Monitoring, regulation, and state-of-the-art technology can all help guide more intelligent groundwater development which will, in turn, benefit rivers.

Channelization and Dredging

Hard figures are elusive but estimates of channelized river miles in the U.S. start at 200,000 and move up. In Illinois, for example, one report estimates that about a third of the state's river miles have been channelized. Of the original 121 million acres of riparian habitat (defined as land within the 100 year flood plain) that once existed in this country, about 23 million acres remain. A substantial percentage of the loss—no one knows how much—is associated with channelization.

The ecological effects of channelization range from brutal to devastating. A channelized river is cut off from its ecosystem and the impacts, as itemized by the National Research Council, include: "removal or subsequent loss of riparian vegetation, loss of instream cover (snags), altered riffle pool sequence, decreased stream sinuosity, altered substrate composition, increased stream velocity, increased bank erosion and bed scour, increased suspended sediment, and increased water temperature."

Channelization usually follows the encroachment of urban or agricultural development into a riparian corridor and flood plain. As trees are cut and wetlands disappear, and as homes or cultivated fields push closer to the edge of a stream, its freedom to move and store water is severely constrained and its potential for flooding increases. When flooding inevitably occurs, the usual solution is an engineering one: the streambed is deepened and straightened and stripped of vegetation that would slow the passage of water. The goal is hydrological efficiency—move the water downstream as fast as possible.

Because channelized streams are asked to control larger and larger volumes of water as runoff increases from urbanization and the destruction of riparian habitat, they tend to flood anyway but with more serious consequences. Which leads to proposals for deeper and steeper channels, as the Army Corps now wants to do with the Los Angeles River.

Dredging sometimes accompanies channelization, and it is also done to open rivers for the passage of boats. Thus some 26,000 river miles have been dredged for barge traffic and to create inland ports. Dredging is a favorite activity of the Corps of Engineers, which tried to bisect the state of Florida with a barge canal. That project was finally stopped after the Oklawaha River was destroyed, but it paled in comparison to the Tennessee–Tombigbee Waterway. The Tenn–Tom, as it came to be called, was a $4 billion dredging project which chewed up 217 miles of the Tombigbee River in Alabama, all to duplicate the shipping function of the Mississippi River system.

There will probably never be another Tenn-Tom or Cross Florida Barge Canal, but dredging remains a threat on many of the nation's rivers and channelization seems to be a permanent part of U.S. flood control strategy.

Municipal and Industrial Pollution

Since 1972, tens of billions of dollars in state and federal money has been spent to clean up the billions of gallons of municipal and industrial waste that for generations had been dumped raw into the rivers of America. It has been money well spent, and the pressure exerted by state and federal clean water laws has reversed the unconscionable practice of using rivers and streams as sewers.

But while great progress has been made in the elimination of municipal waste, huge quantities of toxins continue to pour into rivers from industries violating clean water regulations. The lower Mississippi between Baton Rouge and New Orleans, for example, has become a dumping ground for industrial poison discharged by the hundreds of chemical plants congregated along the river. That stretch has come to be called—for good epidemiological reasons—"Cancer Alley."

The violations persist because there aren't nearly enough human and financial resources available to monitor industrial discharges, or even to review the daily discharge reports which thousands of industries file on a daily basis. Those reports openly reveal illegal discharges of toxic waste, but state and federal agencies can often do little more than a cursory audit, and fines are typically so modest that many polluters prefer to pay rather than invest in expensive treatment technology. Some of the most dramatic examples of illegal dumping have been brought to light not by regulatory agencies but by environmental organizations and state Public Interest Research Groups.

And while great progress has been made, discharges of raw or inadequately treated municipal sewage are still occurring in rivers around the country. As late as 1993 there were discharges of untreated and inadequately treated wastewater into the Merrimack River. Santa Rosa, California, has state-of-the-art treatment facilities, but it has been struggling for a solution to an overburdened sewage plant since a 1985 spill released 750 million gallons of raw wastewater into the Russian River. The Rio Grande, as it passes through Brownsville, Texas and Matamoros, Mexico has been described as "a virtual cesspool" by American Rivers, which put that stretch of the river at the top of its 10 most endangered rivers list for 1993.

The crux of the municipal sewage problem is that the federal government ran out of Clean Water Act money to build new treatment plants before the need was filled. Now the grant program is dead and states are having an increasingly hard time finding the necessary funding. A partial solution being promoted by river activists and municipal managers alike is a reduction of wastewater into the system and increased reliance on wastewater reclamation. Less input means less output and less damage to rivers and streams.

But even as we reduce the load of toxics flowing into our rivers, we are still dealing with the legacy left by decades of unrestrained chemical pollution: PCBs, dioxin, and a potpourri of heavy metals mixed through the mud of our riverbeds and passed up the food chain. The impact of some metals, even in very small concentrations, can be devastating on

Industrial discharge into the Monongahela River, Pennsylvania. (Photo courtesy of Tim Palmer.)

aquatic life. And the layers of PCBs left in numerous riverbeds may be impossible to remove.

Toxic chemicals aren't the only problem. Between 1988 and 1993 there were 76 outbreaks of epidemic disease in the U.S. caused by waterborne pathogens—bacteria, viruses, and protozoa. The Centers for Disease Control and Prevention estimates 940,000 cases of waterborne disease annually, with 900 deaths. The real extent of contamination from waterborne pathogens is impossible to measure because the symptoms can't always be traced to a source and because milder cases go unreported.

Disturbing as these pollution problems are, they are relatively mild compared to the impact of polluted runoff.

Polluted Runoff

In academic and scientific circles the official term is "nonpoint source pollution." The environmental community, in an attempt to demystify the language, is promoting the term "polluted runoff." Whatever you call it, we're talking about the leading water quality problem in the nation.

Polluted runoff is, among other things, the drainage from farm fields, which is often a concentrated soup of herbicides, pesticides, fertilizer, animal manure, and salts leached from the soil. It is also the overflow from storm drains which gather the accumulated debris washed off rooftops, parking lots, streets, and highways. Polluted runoff is all the chemical and organic garbage our society leaves in the path of moving and percolating water, and it is stuff that eventually ends up in our rivers and streams. That includes heavy metals, motor oil, gasoline, airborne acids, pet wastes, lawn care chemicals, tire residue, and road salt.

Polluted runoff accounts for almost 70 percent of the pollution entering our rivers, and no amount of investment in sewage treatment plants will solve it. And because levels of pollution are partly the product of streamflow volume, river diversions exacerbate the problem.

In Massachusetts, 65 percent of the river miles measured by the EPA as of 1993 failed to meet federal water quality standards, primarily because of polluted runoff.

Chesapeake Bay, one of the richest and most ecologically important estuaries in the world, is overwhelmed with polluted runoff. Catches of herring, shad, and striped bass have plummeted. Once the most productive oyster bed in the world, the Bay now produces about one percent of its original shellfish bounty. All this because of an assault by waterborne nutrients and chemicals carried downstream by the Susquehanna, the Patuxent, the Potomac, the Rappahannock, the Nanticoke, and numerous other rivers and streams draining a vast region of agricultural and urban development.

The Susquehanna River is the major tributary of Chesapeake Bay, and it delivers some 40 percent of the nitrogen and 21 percent of the phosphorus fouling the Bay as it winds through dairy farms in Pennsylvania and Maryland, picking up polluted runoff along the way. Tens of thousands of acres of aquatic plants, vital to ducks, geese, fish, and crabs, have been wiped out in the Bay because of nutrient-spawned algal blooms which choke off sunlight and suck up oxygen.

A study done in 1984 by the Association of State and Interstate Water Pollution Control Administrators offers some statistical perspective on polluted runoff, albeit almost a decade old and of perhaps questionable accuracy given the huge gaps in national water quality monitoring. Nevertheless, according to the Association's data, 11 percent of total river miles in the U.S. were ranked as being moderately to severely impaired because of nonpoint sources of pollution. Sixty-four percent of the impact came from agriculture, 9 percent came from mining, and 5 percent came from urban runoff. The biggest single runoff problem was soil sediment, which accounted for 47 percent of nonpoint pollution in affected rivers.

All this suggests two important conclusions: First, that simply increasing investment in waste water technology isn't going to save our rivers. Second, that difficult land use decisions, affecting urban and agriculture development and design, forestry practices, and mining policies will have to be made if we want to reverse the damage.

And while the 1984 study indicated that negative impacts were significantly affecting only 11 percent of total river miles, the river miles affected are the most important ones in the country. They nourish Chesapeake Bay and the Sacramento–San Joaquin Delta, they include much of the Mississippi and the rivers feeding the Everglades, they encompass some of the most precious river miles we have.

Hazardous Wastes

The problem of hazardous wastes may be implicit in the preceding discussion of polluted runoff, but it deserves a category all its own.

Rivers and wetlands are our most vulnerable ecosystems and the impact of industrial poisons is magnified both by the biological sensitivity of water systems to toxic elements, and by the fact that moving water rapidly distributes waste. Thus when a Southern Pacific Railroad tank car fell into California's Upper Sacramento River in 1991, dumping almost 20,000 gallons of a potent biocide, 40 miles of a nationally renowned blue-ribbon trout stream were sterilized within hours. More than 200,000 fish were killed along with every living organism in the river.

That was not a unique event. Thirty years ago a chemical plant in Austin, Texas flushed pesticides into that state's Lower Colorado River, killing every fish for 140 miles. Of course, nature is remarkably resilient and rivers poisoned by pesticides can eventually recover. But what about rivers doused with radiation?

While the plight of its plummeting salmon stocks gets most of the attention, the Columbia River faces another, more ominous threat as it winds through the Hanford Nuclear Reservation north of Richland, Washington. Spent reactor fuel rods, along with radioactive wastewater, are stored in septic tank-like trenches placed 60 feet above groundwater and 1000 feet from the river. Radioactive waste percolating through the soil was supposed to be filtered clean, but today scientists say strontium-90 enters the Columbia at levels 500 to 1000 times the federal standard. The Department of Energy has estimated that about 500,000 gallons of radioactive waste has seeped into the Columbia in the last 40 years. And a local conservation group claims that billions of gallons of radioactive waste are gradually percolating down to the groundwater basin.

Mining

If you want a good idea of the impact mining can have on a river, go visit the Clark Fork between Butte and Missoula, Montana. Nearly a century of mining and smelting, some of it produced by the famous Anaconda copper mine, has littered the watershed with toxic tailings and created the nation's largest Superfund site. Silver Bow Creek, a Clark Fork tributary, is coated with copper, zinc, cadmium, iron, manganese, lead, and arsenic. It is now a sterile stream. Water quality and ecological health in the main stem have been severely impacted, and while impressive efforts have been made to clean up the Clark Fork, the toxic legacy of all that mining remains a monumental challenge. Just a few miles upstream from Missoula, for instance, is an aging and unstable dam holding back more than five million cubic yards of contaminated sediments full of heavy metals.

The most common and dangerous consequence of mining in river watersheds is the production of acid mine tailings. When mining debris containing iron pyrite, a sulfide, is exposed to air and water it generates sulfuric acid. The acid in turn leaches heavy metals out of the surrounding rock. When this doubly toxic mix enters rivers and streams it is fatal to fish and other aquatic life.

Mining experts consider this phenomenon, called Acid Mine Drainage (AMD), the most serious environmental challenge facing the mining industry which, according to the U.S. Bureau of Mines, spends a million dollars a day trying to treat it. Worldwatch Institute has estimated it will take $1 billion to clean up or control the acid mine drainage problem around Butte, in the watershed of the Clark Fork. It has been estimated that the U.S. has accumulated nearly 50 billion tons of mining and mineral processing waste and that more than 12,000 miles of rivers and streams are adversely affected.

While AMD impact has been reduced somewhat by mitigation efforts, another mining menace is growing in the Gold Rush range of the Sierra Nevada. There, countless abandoned mines are leaking mercury, once used to extract gold from ore. The mercury ends up in rivers and streams where it poses a growing danger not only to fish and wildlife but to the human populations who drink the water and eat the fish. You get an idea of the magnitude of the problem when you learn that a single creek flowing into the North Yuba River contains 95 abandoned mines. No one knows how many of those mines are contaminated, but fish taken from the Yuba River had mercury levels higher than the FDA standard for human safety.

State and federal laws simply don't address many of the problems caused by mining, as was dramatically demonstrated by a recent mishap at the Summitville mine on Colorado's Alamosa River, at the headwaters of the Rio Grande.

Summitville, licensed by the state of Colorado in 1984, was owned by Galactic Resources, Ltd., a Canadian company which went bankrupt without posting a bond big enough to cover the cleanup costs for its mine. Summitville has leaked acid discharge into the Alamosa, killing tens of thousands of fish and the EPA ended up having to hire a work crew, at $33,000 per day, to prevent 160 million gallons of cyanide solution from spilling into the river.

Problems like the Summitville debacle will recur until Congress reforms the Mining Law of 1872, a legal anachronism giving mining companies virtually free access to the nation's mineral wealth without the responsibility of cleaning up the mess mining creates.

An entirely different kind of mining activity is threatening many rivers in the West, which are being stripped of their gravel deposits by companies selling aggregate. River gravel is the most popular and valuable base for cement and asphalt, and riverbed mining has been a way of life on western rivers for generations.

As a result, spawning beds are destroyed, erosion is accelerated, riverbeds are downcut, and riparian vegetation is stripped away. The bed along one stretch of the Russian River has dropped 20 feet, which has in turn caused erosion of tributary streams and a significant lowering of the local water table.

Since riverbed gravel mining is regulated by local government and regional water quality control boards, citizen intervention has potential for stopping the practice. But acid mine drainage is largely the legacy of past mining practices and it can only be addressed through long-term and expensive clean-ups initiated by states and the federal government.

Agriculture

Study the causes of river degradation and you reach one inescapable conclusion: of all human activities, agriculture has had the greatest negative impact on the health of rivers. Dams may be more dramatic and municipal and industrial pollution may be more obvious, but nothing has so reworked the landscape (and therefore the riverscape) of the nation, and nothing has so clearly dictated the policies which have degraded rivers, as agriculture.

Saying that is not meant to suggest that we all become Breatharians. We have to eat and agriculture is what feeds us. But it is to suggest that many of the primary, as well as secondary, problems visited upon the nation's rivers are the result of agricultural policies which have created needless damage and abuse.

Agricultural activities which harm rivers include the draining of wetlands, the destruction of riparian habitat with cultivated fields and orchards, the damming and dewatering of rivers for irrigation water, the overdrafting of groundwater basins, the poisoning of rivers and streams with polluted runoff, the trampling and pollution of streambanks with livestock, the rip rapping of streambanks, the creation of levees to eliminate floods, and the siltation of spawning grounds with topsoil eroded from cultivated land.

Impacts of Erosion

Of all the impacts of agriculture on rivers and streams, erosion may be the most subtle and insidious. Erosion is the inevitable result of cultivated soil and is enhanced by disruption of the riparian corridor by farming or cattle grazing. Erosion produces fine sediments, which constitute 47 percent of the content of polluted runoff nationwide. To call sediment pollution may be confusing, but not when you discover what it does. Fine sediment particles remain suspended in rivers for some time, causing cloudy, turbid water and depriving aquatic plants of the light they need for growth.

Denuded riverbank due to overgrazing and degrading riverbed, near Marsing, Idaho. (Photo courtesy of Tim Palmer.)

When plants disappear, turbidity may increase even further because plant roots are no longer available to anchor streambed sediments.

When aquatic plants are eliminated, so are the associated snails and aquatic insects which eat the plants and are in turn eaten by young fish. Larger fish are affected because there is less food for them and because they can't see as well to hunt in cloudy water. Thus the food chain is broken and the biological health of the river declines.

By plugging and coating river gravels, high levels of sediment can also have a devastating impact on spawning habitat since many fish species need clean gravel to deposit their eggs. Sediment also threatens the viability of freshwater mussels and it fills up the interstices in the hyporheic zone which harbors the base of the aquatic food chain.

Beef versus Fish and Wildfowl

Most of the activities of agriculture are necessary to a degree, but there has been a profound absence of balance between agricultural production and protection of river systems. In its hunger to cultivate every available acre, agriculture has crowded rivers and streams, eliminating riparian habitat, meanders, and flood plains. In its insistence on irrigating hundreds of thousands of acres of marginal land, agriculture has drained the water from countless stream channels.

Solutions to this problem are imbedded in the need for a variety of reforms aimed at irrigation practices, irrigation efficiencies, agricultural water pricing, and water use priorities. Irrigated agriculture is often heavily subsidized and seldom pays the true price for its water. That's particularly true when you factor in the environmental costs of water development.

Some of agriculture's demands become difficult to defend when you learn that it uses 70 to 80 percent of all developed water in the U.S., and nearly half of that water goes to grow feed for cattle and other livestock. This means that de facto priorities have been established which, among other things, arbitrarily make cattle more important than salmon and striped bass and ducks and geese. For decades we have been committing our fluid resources to the production of beef at the expense of fish and waterfowl.

This observation isn't intended as beef bashing; rather it's meant to illustrate the need for better and fairer allocation of water and the need to protect the rivers from which we take it. The solution is not, of course, to eliminate agriculture. Rather it is to require that agriculture become more sensitive to its impacts on rivers and streams, that it make better and fairer use of the water available, and that some of that water be reallocated for instream use. Until we recognize and correct the enormous disparity between extractive use by agriculture and instream use for fish and wildlife, our rivers can not be protected or restored to health.

Forestry

On Deer Creek, a tributary of the North Fork Stillaquamish in Washington, a timber cut destabilized the watershed slopes, triggering a landslide which sent mud and rock and trees tumbling into the creek. The result: a world class steelhead stream was destroyed.

On Last Chance Creek, in California's Plumas National Forest, a Forest Service-approved timber sale in a fire-scarred watershed, resulted in wholesale leveling of the trees. Following the harvest, a summer storm dumped five inches of rain on the region and, without timber to hold it in place, the watershed collapsed in an avalanche of mud. The mud fouled the creek and flowed on into larger creeks compounding the damage downstream. A quarter of a million tons of soil was gone in a flash and the subsequent, ongoing erosion is irreparable. One geologist described the damage as "destruction of the soil for future use. I mean, it's gone . . ."

Deer Creek and Last Chance Creek are not isolated examples. Thirty percent of the water draining the Plumas National Forest is so full of eroded sediment it no longer meets California water quality objectives.

Clearcuts on mountainsides above the Sauk River, Washington. (Photo courtesy of Tim Palmer.)

And this is happening in the Sierra Nevada, a region considered among the most beautiful in the world.

A healthy forest, it has been said, is a river's best friend. But contrary to conventional wisdom and good science, forest harvest plans have routinely permitted logging on unstable watershed slopes, destroying healthy forests and the rivers they once protected. Part of the problem has been unceasing pressure by the Forest Service to cut trees. Another part of the problem has been a relative absence of technical personnel with expertise in hydrology. The forest service is full of timber harvest planners but has very few hydrologists.

And still another part of the problem is the absence of cumulative impact studies. Certainly, if you were to add up the cumulative effects of myriad unrelated timber harvest plans on the health of a forest's rivers and streams, you would discover a pattern of destruction that would beg for remedy. But that seldom happens, and so forests are carved up piecemeal, watersheds erode, and rivers suffer and die.

The forestry problem is no mystery; those who study it understand what must be done. The National Research Council laid out the solution quite simply in a 1990 report which states, "It is essential to design harvesting practices and systems that do not reduce long-term productivity, add unwanted sediment and debris to streams, reduce desirable wildlife habitat, or destroy beautiful forest vistas." It's good advice, but we're a long way from heeding it.

Land Development

In 1969 an earthquake rocked Santa Rosa, California forcing the city to begin an urban renewal project in its damaged business district. A master plan was drawn up and eventually a giant mall was planned at one end of the commercial corridor. The mall was sited adjacent to Santa Rosa Creek, the stream mentioned in Chapter 6 that had been routed under City Hall. Several old creekside buildings were to be moved or demolished in the process, leaving a strip of land open to the creek that would have served perfectly as a small park for mall shoppers.

Working with a clean slate for its downtown district, the City Council could have restored that reach of natural creekbank by replacing cement rip rap with wire gabions and new riparian vegetation, incorporating the creek into the plans for the mall, creating a complimentary greenway where shoppers could relax and picnic. Instead the city approved plans to site commercial buildings on the land, with their backs to the edge of the creek, blocking off public access and a chance for the park. Now, almost 20 years later, as the city completes plans to restore the creek, that lost opportunity is a haunting reminder of the short-sighted planning that has typified our treatment of rivers and streams.

The prevailing philosophy of urban planning has treated waterways as nuisances instead of amenities. And it suggests a historic unwillingness to design human development in harmony with nature. More than a million acres of undeveloped land is converted to urban use each year, and a lot of that land borders rivers and streams. We have the planning tools, but too often we lack the vision to shape urban development harmoniously to the waterways it encounters.

Thus we push houses up to the banks of rivers and streams, and then channelize the streambeds when they begin to flood. And we allow development to mushroom on flood plains and then punish the rivers for flooding by adding dams and levees to control them. And while we're doing all this, we also log the watersheds and destabilize their slopes so that runoff and erosion increases.

These are patterns of development which have evolved through a largely *laissez-faire* process, guided more by economic expediency than by resource-driven logic. Human development—both urban and agricultural—has had a devastating effect on the health of rivers because land use planners don't take into account their biological and hydrological needs.

In 1969, the pioneering urban planner and landscape architect, Ian McHarg, wrote *Design With Nature* to describe the possibility, and the need, to incorporate, rather than exclude, nature in our planning processes. McHarg was one of the first to develop sophisticated computer models to guide land use decisionmaking and to incorporate the values of nature into human development. That approach, which is finding favor now in the guise of "bioregional planning," has been largely absent from the decisionmaking processes which have guided the development and use of rivers.

River guardians can influence land use planning and its impact on rivers to the degree that they participate in the planning process. That means religious attendance at planning commission meetings, it means organizing political support for planning commissioners who value river and watershed protection, and it means promoting the vision of healthy rivers and streams at all public hearings. The local planning arena is often the source of both the problem and the solution of river degradation.

Chapter 8
Building Relationships with Rivers

*In the years we have been here I have trained myself to listen to
the river, not in the belief that I could understand what it said,
but only from one day to the next know its fate.*

BARRY LOPEZ, RIVER NOTES

If you've read this far, your head is now full of facts and figures, techniques and tools, problems and solutions. You have an abstract understanding of what it takes to save a river, you know something about developing an organization, launching a campaign, building popular support.
Of course, you can never really learn to save a river by reading a book.
You've got to go out and do it, adapting what you've learned here to the
realities of your river.

And the most important message of this book has nothing to do with
techniques and tools, it has to do with the knowledge that river protection
isn't ultimately about litigation and legislation, it's about assuming a relationship with, and a sense of responsibility for, a river.

The plight of our rivers reflects a curious paradox. While Americans
worship wilderness as a concept, we collaborate in its demise. We've developed a culture which puts so much value in the development of natural
resources that it reserves little real respect for free-flowing rivers and wild
places. Perhaps that's also because, as Roderick Nash suggests, we have
emerged from a history in which wilderness was viewed as something to
be "conquered," "subdued," and "vanquished."

We have managed, therefore, to distance ourselves from rivers. We have
built our homes and factories and shopping malls hard up against our
rivers and creeks and brooks, but instead of incorporating those waterways
into our lives, we have turned our backs on them, dumped our trash in
them, kept them at arms length and out of sight.

Most of us know more about programming our VCRs (which admittedly isn't much) than we know about how a living river works, about what
hurts it and what makes it healthy. And so our abuse of rivers has not
been, for the most part, intentional, it has proceeded from ignorance and
indifference and distance.

It is important to understand, therefore, that transcending even the need for citizen action against dams and diversions and pollution, is the need for all of us to establish relationships with our rivers, to become involved with them, aware of them, committed to their health and safety.

To a remarkable degree that is beginning to happen. There are more than 2000 citizen groups scattered all over the country organized to protect rivers and watersheds. There may be more than 100,000 people actively working on behalf of their rivers. That constitutes a movement, and it is growing. Now, that movement needs to expand to embrace every river and stream, to protect every watershed and riparian corridor.

What we need is a nationwide network of individuals and organizations willing to align themselves permanently with the fate of their watersheds and free-flowing rivers. We need people who understand that not to act is to act, who will follow Teddy Roosevelt's advice to "do what you can, with what you have, where you are." Ultimately, as River Network activist Pete Lavigne points out, "environmental protection means accumulating power." When enough people decide to get involved with their rivers, enough power will be accumulated to save them.

And if that happens, perhaps we will begin to learn how to live in harmony with the rest of the natural world. Freeman House, the bioregional thinker who cofounded the Mattole Watershed Salmon Support Group, has written that restoration efforts on the Mattole River "might be the very means by which we learned what we needed to know in order to live integrated lives in living places."

The people inhabiting watersheds, says House, are the necessary participants in their protection and recovery. "The residents will remain in place after the government has come and gone. If the restoration program has been structured so that problems are defined and decisions made by inhabitants with the counsel of technicians, and if much of the work has been performed by local people, especially young people, then a population will remain whose identity has been extended to include their habitat . . . They will have the will to defend the place against further violations."

We are not inclined to destroy that which we know and love. The ultimate protection of rivers will come when enough people have attained that knowledge and developed that love.

Sources

Introduction

Palmer, Tim. *Endangered Rivers and the Conservation Movement.* Berkeley: University of California Press, 1986.

Chapter 1   Getting Organized

Alinsky, Saul D. *Rules for Radicals,* New York: Vintage Books, 1971.

Being A Player: A Guide to the IRS Lobbying Regulations for Advocacy Charities. Harmon, Ladd and Evans. Washington, D.C.: The Advocacy Forum, 1991.

Cohen, Gary, and John O'Connor, eds. *Fighting Toxics: A Manual for Protecting Your Family, Community and Workplace.* National Toxics Campaign. Covelo, CA: Island Press, 1990. Includes an excellent chapter on "Organizing to Win."

Cook, Christine M. C(3) or C(4)? *Choosing a Tax-Exempt Status.* Portland: River Network, 1991.

Coyne, Alasdair, ed. *Sespe Wild.* Ojai, CA: Keep the Sespe Wild Committee. Newsletter of the organization.

Hummel, Joan. *Starting and Running a Non-Profit Organization.* Minneapolis: University of Minnesota Press, 1980.

Johnson, Kenny, and Walsh, Lindy. *River Wealth.* Portland: River Network, 1991. A compilation of fund-raising activities used by river groups.

Klein, Kim. *Fundraising For Social Change,* Inverness, CA: Chardon Press, 2nd Edition, 1988. One of the best grassroots fund-raising books available . . . written by one of the best consultants.

The Land Trust Alliance. *Starting a Land Trust: A Guide to Forming a Land Conservation Organization.* Washington, D.C.: Land Trust Alliance, 1990

Lynch, Richard. *LEAD! How Public and Nonprofit Managers Can Bring Out the Best in Themselves and Their Organizations.* San Francisco: Jossey-Bass Publishers, 1993.

Mancuso, Anthony. *How to Form a Nonprofit Corporation.* Berkeley: Nolo Press, 1990.

Morgan, Arthur E. *Observations.* Yellow Springs, OH: The Antioch Press, 1968.

Non Profit Organizations, Public Policy, and the Political Process: A Guide to the Internal Revenue Code and Federal Election Campaign Act. Citizens Vote Inc., New York. Prepared by Perkins Coie with Harmon, Curran and Tousley, Washington, D.C., revised edition, 1990.

Palmer, Tim. *Stanislaus: The Struggle for a River.* Berkeley: University of California Press, 1982.

Partnership for Democracy. *Handbook on Tax Rules for Voter Participation Work By Section 501 (c) (3) Organizations.* Washington, D.C., 1990.

Pierce, Gregory F. *Activism That Makes Sense.* New York: Paulist Press, 1984.

Schaef, Anne Wilson, and Fassel, Diane. *The Addictive Organization.* New York: Harper and Row, 1988. "This book finally names the irrational behavior in organizations ... A dynamic and welcome addition to ... the lives of all those who have come to believe that somehow they, themselves, were the crazy ones." "A powerful book ... leaders and consultants should ... use it as a continuing reference."

Setterberg, Fred, and Schulman, Kary. *Beyond Profit: The Complete Guide to Managing the Nonprofit Organization.* New York: Harper and Row, 1985.

Wolf, Kevin, and Elliott, Rob. *Outfitter and Guest Fund Raising: The Pass-Through Contribution Model.* Portland: River Network, revised edition, 1993.

Wolf, Thomas. *The Nonprofit Organization: An Operating Manual.* New York: Prentice-Hall, 1987.

Chapter 2   Planning a Campaign

Barger, John. *Restoring the Earth: How Americans Are Working to Renew Our Damaged Environment.* New York: Knopf, 1985.

Deal, Carl. *The Greenpeace Guide To Anti-Environmental Organizations*. Berkeley: Odonian Press, 1993.

Elder, Don. *Comments on the Need For Alternatives to, and Impact of The Birmingham Water Works' Proposed Construction of a Water Supply Reservoir on the Locust Fork of the Warrior River, Alabama*. Birmingham: Cahaba River Society, 1992.

Florida Defenders of the Environment. *Restoring the Oklawaha River Ecosystem*. Gainesville: Florida Defenders of the Environment, Inc., 1989.

Fred Woods Productions. *The Town and the River*. National Park Service North Atlantic Region. Video.

House, Freeman. *To Learn The Things We Need To Know: Engaging the Particulars of the Planet's Recovery*. Sausalito, CA: Whole Earth Review, Spring 1990.

Mattole Restoration Council. *Elements of Recovery: An Inventory of Upslope Sources of Sedimentation in the Mattole River Watershed*. Petrolia, CA: Mattole Restoration Council, 1989.

National Park Service, Mid-Atlantic Regional Office. *River Work Book*. Washington, D.C.: Department of the Interior, 1988.

Palmer, Tim. *The Kings River: A Report on its Qualities and its Future*. Fresno: Committee To Save The Kings River, 1987.

Palmer, Tim. *The Snake River*. Washington, D.C.: Island Press, 1991.

Wallin, Philip, and Haberman, Rita. *People Protecting Rivers: A Collection of Lessons from Successful Grassroots Activists*. Portland: River Network, 1992.

Woodwell, John C. *Supplying Denver with Water Efficiency: An Alternative to Two Forks Dam*. Snowmass, CO: Rocky Mountain Institute, 1989.

Chapter 3   Building Public Support

Andrus, Susan Elizabeth. *The Economic Impacts and Benefits of Whitewater Recreation in California*. Santa Barbara, CA: University of California thesis, 1984.

Boyle, Robert H. *The Hudson River: A Natural and Unnatural History*. New York: Norton, 1969.

Dolcino, Chiara, and Andersen, Stephen O. *River Valuation Bibliography: A Practitioner's Guide to River Valuation Literature.* Arlington, VA: Privately published, 1986.

Finnerty, Anthony A., Geologist. *Earthquake: Seismic Safety at Auburn Dam—An Evaluation of Geotechnical Studies.* Sacramento: Friends of the River, 1990.

Johnson, Kenny, Shauna Whidden, and Lindy Walsh. *River Wise.* Portland: River Network, 1992. Case histories of successful activities to promote public education and involvement in river conservation.

Kirkman, Larry, and Menichelli, Karen, eds. *Strategic Communications for Nonprofits.* Benton Foundation and Center for Strategic Communications, 1992. A series of media guides covering talk radio, voice programs, op-eds, using videos, media advocacy, cable access, electronic networking, and strategic media. For more information: Benton Foundation, 1710 Rhode Island Avenue, NW, 4th Floor, Washington, DC 20036, (202) 857-7829.

Martinez, Barbara Fultz, and Weiner, Roberta. *Guide to Public Relations for Nonprofit Organizations and Public Agencies, Or How To Avoid The Potential Perils of Public Relations.* Los Angeles: The Grantsmanship Center, 1979.

Ober, Richard. "Muddying the Waters," *Forest Notes,* November/December, 1992. Concord: Society for the Protection of New Hampshire Forests, 1992. Article about Wise Use movement defeat of the Pemigewasset River Wild and Scenic plan.

Olsen, Ken. "Natural Rivers and the Public Trust." Washington, D.C.: American Rivers, 1988.

Promoting Issues and Ideas: A Guide to Public Relations For Nonprofit Organizations by Public Interest Public Relations, A Division of M Booth and Associates. New York: The Foundation Center, 1987.

River Voices. "Unlikely Allies as Partners in River Protection." Portland: River Network, Winter 1992.

Talbot, Allan R. *Power Along the Hudson: The Storm King Case and the Birth of Environmentalism.* New York: E. O. Dutton, 1972.

U.S. Department of the Interior, National Park Service. *Economic Impacts of Protecting Rivers, Trails and Greenway Corridors: A Resource Book.* Washington, D.C.: National Park Service, 1992.

Welych, Maria T. "The Merrimack: A River's Odyssey." Nashua, NH: *The Telegraph,* June 1989. Seven-part newspaper series.

Wilson, Wendy. "Payette Campaign Offers Strategy Lessons," *Currents,* Fall 1991. Colorado Springs: National Organization for River Sports, 1991.

Chapter 4   Getting It Done

Boland, Joseph, and Smiley, Marc. *The Coalition for the Deschutes and the Upper Deschutes River: A Case Study.* Portland: River Network, 1989.

Clean Water Action. *Basic Questions and Answers on Two Forks.* Denver: Clean Water Action and Clean Water Fund, Colorado Office, 1990. Good simple analysis of a dam project and alternatives to it.

Close, E. Burt. *How To Create Super Slide Shows.* Cincinnati: Writer's Digest Books, 1984.

Fisher, Roger, and Ury, William. *Getting to Yes.* New York: Penguin Books, 1983.

Lord, James Gregory. *Marketing Nonprofits.* Los Angeles: The Grantsmanship Center, 1981.

Magsig, Justine. *No Cost Stream Restoration on an Agricultural Watershed in Northwest Ohio.* Bowling Green: Center for Environmental Programs, Bowling Green State University, 1988. Report on the restoration of Sugar Creek.

Meral, Gerald. "Questions to Ask About Water Projects: A Guide for Those Who Wish More Information about Proposed Water Resources Development Projects." Sacramento: Planning and Conservation League Foundation, 1986.

Palmer, Tim. *Endangered Rivers and the Conservation Movement.* Berkeley and Los Angeles: University of California Press, 1986.

River Network. *River Activists Directory.* Portland: River Network, 1993. Periodically updated listing of more than 2000 river conservation organizations and individuals.

River Voices. "The Resource Abuse Movement and River Conservation Efforts." Portland: River Network, Summer 1992.

U.S. Department of the Interior, National Park Service. Rivers Trails and Conservation Assistance Program, and American Rivers. *1992 River Conservation Directory*. Washington, D.C.: U.S. Department of the Interior, National Park Service, RTCAP, and American Rivers, 1992. A directory of both public agencies and private, nonprofit groups involved in river conservation.

The Volunteer Monitor. The National Newsletter of Volunteer Water Quality Monitoring. Editor, 1318 Masonic Avenue, San Francisco, CA 94117.

Williams, Philip. "Alternatives for Providing 200-Year Flood Protection for the Lower American River". San Francisco: Philip Williams & Associates, Ltd., 1990. Memo to Environmental Defense Fund. Good example of use of expert opinion to provide credible alternative to a dam project.

Chapter 5   River Saving Tools

Adler, Robert, Jessica Landman, and Diane Cameron. *The Clean Water Act Twenty Years Later*. Natural Resources Defense Council. Covelo, CA: Island Press, 1993.

Association of State Wetland Managers, Association of State Floodplain Managers, National Park Service. *A Casebook in Managing Rivers for Multiple Uses*. Washington, D.C., 1992.

Audubon. "America's Wild Rivers" special river issue November/December 1993. National Audubon Society, 700 Broadway, New York, NY 10003

Babcock, Richard. *The Zoning Game*. Madison: University of Wisconsin Press, 1969; and *The Zoning Game Revisited* by Babcock and Charles L. Siemon, Boston: O, G & H Publishers, 1985. Humorous, fascinating, and stimulating analyses of the problems and promise of zoning regulations and land use control in the United States.

Bowers, Richard J. *A Nuts & Bolts Approach to Whitewater Recreation Studies*. Conservation Program, American Whitewater Affiliation, 8630 Fenton Street, Suite 910, Silver Spring, MD 20910. (301) 589-9453.

Brooks, Richard O., and Lavigne, Peter. "Aesthetic Theory and Landscape Protection: The Many Meanings of Beauty and Their Implications for the Design, Control, and Protection of Vermont's

Landscape." *UCLA Journal of Environmental Law and Policy* Vol. 4, p. 128, 1985. Comprehensive and interesting article on the development and application of aesthetic protection law in the United States.

Cairns, John Jr. et al. *Restoration of Aquatic Ecosystems.* Washington, D.C.: National Academy Press, 1992.

California Resources Agency. *Upper Sacramento River, Fisheries and Riparian Habitat Management Plan.* Sacramento: California Resources Agency, 1989.

Coyle, Kevin. *The American Rivers Guide to Wild and Scenic River Designation.* Washington, D.C.: American Rivers, 1988.

Coyle, Kevin J., and Brown, Christopher N. *Conserving Rivers: A Handbook for State Action.* Washington, D.C.: U.S. Department of the Interior, National Park Service, Rivers, Trails and Conservation Assistance Program, and American Rivers, 1992.

Curtis, Christopher. *Grassroots River Protection: Saving Rivers Under the National Wild and Scenic Rivers Act Through Community-Based River Protection Strategies and State Action.* Washington, D.C.: American Rivers, 1992.

Dealing with Change in the Connecticut River Valley: A Design Manual for Conservation and Development. Yaro, Arendt, Dodson, and Brabec. The Center for Rural Massachusetts, Lincoln Institute of Land Policy, 26 Trowbridge St., Cambridge, MA 02138. 1988. An eye-opening book which uses 48 color plates to illustrate the differences between creative and conventional methods of residential and commercial development in rural areas.

Diehl, Janet, and Barrett, Thomas. *The Conservation Easement Handbook: Managing Land Conservation and Historic Preservation Easement Programs.* Alexandria, VA: The Land Trust Alliance and Trust for Public Land, 1988.

Doppelt, Bob, Mary Scurlock, Chris Frissell, and James Karr. *Entering the Watershed: A New Approach to Save America's River Ecosystems.* The Pacific Rivers Council. Covelo, CA: Island Press, 1993.

E: The Environmental Magazine, October 1993, Westport, Connecticut. "Troubled Waters: America's Endangered Rivers."

Echeverria, John D., Pope Barrow, and Richard Roos-Collins. *Rivers at Risk: The Concerned Citizen's Guide to Hydropower.* Washington, D.C.: Island Press, 1989.

Economic Impacts of Protecting Rivers, Trails and Greenway Corridors: A Resource Book. Washington, D.C.: National Park Service, 1991.

Endangered Rivers of America: A Report on the Nation's Ten Most Endangered Rivers and Fifteen Most Threatened Rivers of 1993. Washington, D.C.: American Rivers, 1993

EPA Nonpoint Source News Notes. U.S. EPA, NPS News Notes (WH-553), Assessment and Wastersheds Protection Division, Washington, D.C. A periodical covering polluted runoff issues, management, and restoration techniques.

Firestone, David. *Environmental Law For Non-Lawyers,* 2nd Edition, revised and expanded. South Royalton, VT: SoRo Press, 1993. This book is used to teach courses at many colleges and universities and is also widely read by lawyers, nonlawyer professionals, and those in the general public who want an easily understandable introduction to environmental law.

Flink, Charles A., and Searns, Robert. *Greenways: A Guide to Planning, Design, and Development.* The Conservation Fund. Covelo, CA: Island Press, 1993.

Giffen, R. Alec, and Parkin, Drew O. *Using Systematic Field Evaluations to Determine Instream Flow Needs for Recreation.* Land and Water Associates. 9 Union Street, Hallowell, Maine 04347, or National Park Service, 15 State Street, Boston, MA 02109.

Guide to Federal Water Quality Programs and Information. Environmental Protection Agency, Washington, D.C. (EPA-230-B-93-001). February 1993.

Guide to Riverland Stewardship: A Selected Bibliography. Portland: River Network, 1993.

Hansen, Nancy Richardson, Hope M. Babcock, and Edwin H. Clark II. *Controlling Nonpoint-Source Water Pollution: A Citizen's Handbook.* The Conservation Foundation and National Audubon Society. Lancaster, PA: Wickersham Printing Company, 1988.

Herbkersaman, Neil C. *A Guide to the George Palmiter River Restoration Techniques.* Oxford, OH: Institute of Environmental Sciences, Miami University.

Hoban, Thomas More, and Brooks, Richard Oliver. *Green Justice, The Environment and the Courts.* Boulder, CO and London: Westview Press, 1987. An unusually clear and accessible text on the principles and process of environmental law.

Hunter, Christopher. *Better Trout Habitat: A Guide to Stream Restoration and Management.* Montana Land Reliance. Covelo, CA: Island Press, 1990.

Huntington, Matthew H., and Echeverria, John D. *The American Rivers Outstanding Rivers List.* Washington, D.C.: American Rivers, 1991.

Jorgensen, Eric. *The Poisoned Well: New Strategies for Groundwater Protection.* Sierra Club Legal Defense Fund. Covelo, CA: Island Press, 1989.

Klein, Richard D. *Everyone Wins! A Citizen's Guide to Development.* American Planning Association. Chicago and Washington, D.C.: Planners Press, 1990.

Labaree, Jonathan. *How Greenways Work: A handbook on ecology.* Ipswich, MA: National Park Service and Atlantic Center for the Environment, 1992.

Lackawanna River Corridor Association. *Lackawanna River Citizens Master Plan.* Scranton, PA: Lackawanna River Corridor Association, 1990.

Lamb, Berton L. "The Public Trust Doctrine: A Tool to Protect Instream Flows," *River Voices,* Summer 1993. Portland: River Network, 1993.

Little, Charles. *Greenways for America.* Baltimore: John Hopkins University Press, 1990.

Maine Department of Conservation. *Maine Rivers Study.* Augusta: Maine Department of Conservation, 1982.

Marston, Ed. *Western Water Made Simple.* High Country News. Covelo, CA: Island Press, 1987.

National Geographic Special Edition, Water: The Power, Promise, and Turmoil of North America's Fresh Water. Fall 1993. Includes special double map of United States water resources.

National Wildlife Federation, *Waters at Risk: Keeping Clean Waters Clean.* Washington, D.C.: National Wildlife Federation, May 1992. A report stressing the need for strategies to prevent water pollution of outstanding national resource waters.

New Hampshire Office of State Planning. *Upper Merrimack River Corridor Plan.* Concord: New Hampshire Office of State Planning, 1991.

No Water To Spare: A Challenge for New England's Future. Conservation Law Foundation, 62 Summer Street, Boston, MA 02110, (617) 350-0990.

Palmer, Tim. *The Wild and Scenic Rivers of America.* Washington, D.C.: Island Press, 1993.

Reisner, Marc, and Bates, Sarah. *Overtapped Oasis: Reform or Revolution for Western Water.* Covelo, CA: Island Press, 1990.

Riparian Management: Common Threads and Shared Interests. USDA Forest Service General Technical Report RM-226, 1993. Proceedings of a Western Regional Conference on River Management Strategies.

River Voices. "The Public Trust Doctrine as a River Protection Tool." Portland: River Network, Summer 1992.

River Voices. "Water Efficiency as a River Protection Tool." Portland: River Network, Spring 1993.

"Rocky Mountain Institute's Water Efficiency Resources." Snowmass, CO: Rocky Mountain Institute.

San Joaquin River Parkway and Conservation Trust. *The San Joaquin River Parkway and Environs Conceptual Plan.* Fresno: The San Joaquin River Parkway and Conservation Trust, 1991.

Schulman, Neil. *Protecting Instream Flows: A Resource File for River Activists.* Portland: River Network, 1993.

Slade, David C. "The Public Trust Doctrine: A Primer for Friends of America's Rivers," *River Voices,* Summer 1993. Portland: River Network, 1993.

Slade, David. *Putting the Public Trust Doctrine to Work: The Application of the Public Trust Doctrine to the Management of Lands, Waters and Living Resources of the Coastal States.* Washington, D.C.: Coastal States Center, 1992.

Smith, Daniel S., and Hellmund, Paul C. *Ecology of Greenways: Design and Function of Linear Conservation Areas.* Minneapolis: University of Minnesota Press, 1993.

Steinhart, Peter. *California's Wild Heritage: Threatened and Endangered Animals in the Golden State.* Sacramento: Sierra Club Books,

The California Department of Fish and Game and the California Academy of Sciences, 1990.

Stokes, Samuel N., A. Elizabeth Watson, Genevieve P. Keller, and Timothy J. Keller. *Saving America's Countryside: A Guide to Rural Conservation.* Baltimore: Johns Hopkins University Press, 1989.

Tarlock, Dan. "Using the Public Trust Doctrine Effectively," *River Voices,* Summer 1993. Portland: River Network, 1993.

U.S. Department of the Interior, National Park Service. *A Casebook in Managing Rivers for Multiple Uses.* Washington, D.C.: U.S. Department of the Interior, National Park Service, 1991.

U.S. Environmental Protection Agency. *Merrimack River Watershed Protection Initiative: Past, Present, Future.* Boston: U.S. Environmental Protection Agency, 1987.

Water Quality 2000 Final Report: A National Agenda for the 21st Century. Alexandria, VA: Water Environment Federation, 1992.

Whittaker, Doug, Bo Shelby, William Jackson, and Robert Beschta. *Instream Flow for Recreation: A Handbook on Concepts and Research Methods.* National Park Service and the state of Oregon. Available from Alaska Region of National Park Service, 2525 Gambell Street, Anchorage, AK 99503-2892.

Chapter 6   Values of Free-Flowing Rivers

Abbey, Edward. *Down The River.* New York: E. P. Dutton, 1982. Incomparable book by an incomparable writer. An American original.

Abbey, Edward. *The Hidden Canyon: A River Journey.* New York: The Viking Press, 1977.

Bickford, Walter E., and Dymon, Ute Janik, eds. *An Atlas of Massachusetts River Systems: Environmental Designs for the Future.* Amherst: University of Massachusetts Press, 1990.

Brown, Bruce. *Mountain in the Clouds, A Search for the Wild Salmon.* New York: Simon and Schuster, 1982.

The Elwha Report: Restoration of the Elwha River Ecosystem & Native Anadromous Fisheries. A report submitted pursuant to Public Law 102-495. Public Review Draft, September 1993. U.S. Department of the Interior, National Park Service, (L7425(Olym-s)).

Leopold, Aldo. *The River of the Mother of God and Other Essays,* edited by Susan L. Flader and J. Baird Callicott. Madison: University of Wisconsin Press, 1991.

Lufkin, Alan, ed. *California's Salmon and Steelhead: The Struggle to Restore an Imperiled Resource.* Berkeley and Los Angeles: University of California Press, 1991.

Nash, Roderick. *Wilderness and the American Mind.* New Haven: Yale University Press, 1967.

Palmer, Tim. *Endangered Rivers and the Conservation Movement.* Covelo, CA: Island Press, 1988.

Palmer, Tim. *Lifelines: The Case for River Conservation.* Covelo, CA: Island Press, 1994.

Prunuske, Liza, *Groundwork: A Handbook for Erosion Control in North Coastal California.* Point Reyes, CA: Marin County Conservation District, 1988.

Chapter 7   Problems

Benke, Arthur C. "A Perspective on America's Vanishing Streams," *Journal of the North American Benthological Society,* Vol. 9, No. 1, March 1990.

Brody, Jane E. "Water Based Animals Are Becoming Extinct Faster Than Others," *The New York Times,* p. C4, April 21, 1991.

Cairns, John Jr., et al. *Restoration of Aquatic Ecosystems.* Washington, D.C.: National Academy Press, 1992.

California Advisory Committee on Salmon and Steelhead Trout. *Restoring the Balance: 1988 Annual Report.* Sacramento: California Advisory Committee on Salmon and Steelhead Trout, 1988.

Collins, Brian, and Dunne, Thomas. *Fluvial Geomorphology and River-Gravel Mining: A Guide for Planners, Case Studies Included.* Sacramento: California Department of Conservation, Division of Mines and Geology, 1990.

Coyle, Kevin, and Brown, Christopher. *Conserving Rivers: A Handbook for State Action.* Washington, D.C.: National Park Service and American Rivers, July 1992 Draft.

Doppelt, Bob, Mary Scurlock, Chris Frissell, and James Karr. *Entering the Watershed: A New Approach to Save America's River Ecosystems.* The Pacific Rivers Council. Covelo, CA: Island Press, 1993.

Dunnette, David A. "Assessing Global River Water Quality: Overview and Data Collection," pp. 241–259 in *The Science of Global Change: The Impact of Human Activities on the Environment,* David A. Dunnette and Robert J. O'Brien, eds. Washington, D.C.: American Chemical Society, 1992.

Duvall, Bill, and Sessions, George. *Deep Ecology: Living as if Nature Mattered.* Salt Lake City: Peregrine Smith Books, 1985.

Echeverria, John, Pope Barrow, and Richard Roos-Collins. *Rivers at Risk: The Concerned Citizen's Guide to Hydropower.* Covelo, CA: Island Press, 1989.

Ehrlich, Paul R., and Ehrlich, Anne H. *The Population Explosion.* New York: Simon and Shuster, 1990.

Endangered Rivers of America: A Report on The Nation's Ten Most Endangered Rivers and Fifteen Most Threatened Rivers of 1993 Washington, D.C.: American Rivers, 1993.

Engelman, Robert, and Leroy, Pamela. *Sustaining Water: Population and the Future of Renewable Water Supplies.* Washington, D.C.: Population Action International, 1993.

EPA Nonpoint Source News Notes. U.S. EPA, NPS News Notes (WH-553), Assessment and Wastersheds Protection Division, Washington, D.C. A periodical covering polluted runoff issues, management, and restoration techniques.

Firestone, David. *Environmental Law For Non-Lawyers,* 2nd Edition, revised and expanded. South Royalton, VT: SoRo Press, 1993.

Focus: Carrying Capacity Selections "500 MILLION AMERICANS by 2050?" Vol. 3, No. 1, 1993 Carrying Capacity Network, 1325 G Street NW, Washington, DC 20005-3104.

Gottlieb, Robert. *A Life of Its Own: The Politics and Power of Water.* San Diego: Harcourt Brace Jovanovich, 1988.

Goldsmith, Edward, and Hildyard, Nicholas. *The Social & Environmental Effects of Large Dams.* San Francisco: Sierra Club Books, 1984.

Heuvelmans, Martin. *The River Killers.* Harrisburg: Stackpole Books, 1974.

Hoban, Thomas More, and Brooks, Richard Oliver. *Green Justice, The Environment and the Courts.* Boulder, CO and London: Westview Press, 1987.

Huntington, Matthew, and Echeverria, John. *American Rivers Outstanding Rivers List*. Washington, D.C.: American Rivers, 1992.

Jorgensen, Eric. *The Poisoned Well: New Strategies for Groundwater Protection*. Sierra Club Legal Defense Fund. Covelo, CA: Island Press, 1989.

Kahrl, William L. *Water and Power*. Berkeley: University of California Press, 1982.

Karr, James R., Testimony to the Subcommittee on Energy and the Environment, House Interior and Insular Affairs Committee, U. S. Congress, April 29, 1992.

Karr, James R. "Biological Integrity: A Long-neglected Aspect of Water Resource Management," *Ecological Applications* Vol. 1, No. 1, pp. 66–84, 1991.

Lavigne, Peter M. "The 1990's: A Watershed Decade?" *Proceedings of the Merrimack Initiative Watershed Management Conference U.S.E.P.A.*, June 1993 (U.S.E.P.A. release date April, 1994).

Marston, Ed. *Western Water Made Simple*. High Country News. Covelo, CA: Island Press, 1987.

Master, Larry. "The Imperiled Status of North American Aquatic Animals," *Biodiversity Network News* (Arlington, VA) Vol. 3, No. 3, 1990.

Miller, R. R., J. D. Williams, and J. E. Williams. "Extinctions of North American fishes during the past century." *Fisheries (Bethesda)* Vol. 14, pp. 22–38, 1989.

"National body fears wide damage to aquatic ecosystems," Associated Press, *The Boston Globe*, p. 10, December 12, 1991.

Nehlsen, Willa, Jack E. Williams, and James A. Lichatowich. "Pacific Salmon at the Crossroads: Stocks at Risk from California, Oregon, Idaho, and Washington," *Fisheries (Bethesda)* Vol. 16, No. 2, March–April 1991.

Norcross, Elizabeth, and Calvo, Gabriel. "Private Lands River Protection—Balancing Private and Public Concerns," Washington, D.C.: American Rivers, February 1993.

No Water To Spare: A Challenge for New England's Future. Conservation Law Foundation, 62 Summer Street, Boston, MA 02110, (617) 350-0990.

Palmer, Tim. *The Wild and Scenic Rivers of America.* Covelo, CA: Island Press, 1993

Reisner, Marc. *Cadillac Desert: The American West and Its Disappearing Water.* New York: Penguin Books, 1986.

Reisner, Marc, and Bates, Sarah. *Overtapped Oasis: Reform or Revolution for Western Water.* Washington, D.C.: Island Press, 1990.

Rifkin, Jeremy. *Beyond Beef: The Rise and Fall of the Cattle Culture.* New York: Dutton, 1992.

Steinberg, Theodore. *Nature Incorporated: Industrialization and the Waters of New England.* New York: Cambridge University Press, 1991.

Stevens, William K. "River Life Through U.S. Broadly Degraded," *The New York Times,* p. C1, January 26, 1993

Udall, Stewart R. *The Quiet Crisis and the Next Generation.* Salt Lake City: Cross-Smith, 1988.

U.S. EPA Region I, "Merrimack River Watershed Protection Initiative: Past, Present, and Future," Boston, MA: U.S. EPA, 1987.

Water Quality 2000: A National Water Agenda for the 21st Century. Alexandria, VA: Water Environment Federation, 1992

Worster, Donald. *Rivers of Empire: Water, Aridity & The Growth of The American West.* New York: Pantheon Books, 1985.

Yoffe, Emily. "Silence Of The Frogs" *New York Times Magazine,* December 13, 1992. pp. 36–39, 64–66, 76.

General

Ackerman, Bruce et al. *The Uncertain Search For Environmental Quality.* New York: The Free Press, MacMillan, 1974. Outstanding analysis of failure in protection and restoration efforts in the Delaware River Basin.

Horton, Tom, and Eichbaum, William M. *Turning the Tide: Saving the Chesapeake Bay.* The Chesapeake Bay Foundation. Covelo, CA: Island Press, 1991.

Hunt, Constance Elizabeth, with Huser, Verne. *Down By the River: The Impact of Federal Water Projects and Policies on Biological Diver-*

sity. Covelo, CA: Island Press, 1988. Valuable history with numerous case studies on major river systems across the United States.

Huser, Verne, ed. *River Reflections: A Collection of River Writings.* Old Saybrook, CT: Globe Pequot Press, 1988.

Morgan, Arthur. *Dams and Other Disasters: a century of the Army Corps of Engineers in civil works.* Boston: Porter Sargent, 1971. Still the definitive history and analysis of the policies and attitudes of the Army Corps of Engineers written by one of the great engineers and historians of philosophy of the 20th century.

New York State Department of Environmental Conservation. *Stream Corridor Management: A Basic Reference Manual.* Albany, NY: New York DEC, 1986. A good basic reference covering stream problems, assessment and planning techniques, conservation options, and best management practices.

Palmer, Tim. *Endangered Rivers and the Conservation Movement.* Berkeley: University of California Press, 1986. *The Wild and Scenic Rivers of America.* Covelo, CA: Island Press, 1993. *Lifelines: The Case For River Conservation.* Covelo, CA: Island Press, 1994. A trilogy on the river conservation and protection movement by one of the country's best writers on river issues. A must read for anyone interested in rivers and their protection.

Ridgeway, James. *The Politics of Ecology.* Dutton, 1971. A well-written, and well-researched account of the development of water pollution control legislation in the United States. Valuable history to the Clean Water Act.

U.S. Water News. U.S. Water News, Inc. and the Freshwater Foundation, 230 Main Steet, Halstead, KS, 67056. Valuable monthly newspaper on water resource and development issues.

Wallin, Philip, and Haberman, Rita. *People Protecting Rivers: A Collection of Lessons from Grassroots Activists.* Portland: River Network, 1992.

Yates, Steve. *Adopting A Stream: A Northwest Handbook.* Seattle: Adopt-A-Stream Foundation, University of Washington Press, 1988. An excellent basic reference about the life of a stream and how to organize community stream protection and restoration projects.

Organizations

American Rivers
801 Pennsylvania Avenue, SE, Suite 400, Washington, DC 20003. E-mail: amrivers@igc.apc.org; Fax: (202) 543–6142; Phone: (202) 547-6900.

American Whitewater Affiliation, Conservation Program
8630 Fenton Street, Suite 910, Silver Spring, MD 20910. Phone: (301) 589-9453; Fax: (301) 589-6121.

Citizens Clearinghouse for Hazardous Wastes
P.O. Box 6806, Falls Church, VA 22040, (703) 237-2249. CCHW has numerous helpful publications about grassroots organizing and fighting polluters.

Clean Water Network
1350 New York Avenue, NW, Washington, DC 20005. E-mail: cleanwaternet@igc.apc.org; Fax: (202) 783-5917; Phone: (202) 624-9357.

Floodplain Management Resource Center
Natural Hazards Center, University of Colorado, IBS #6, Campus Box 482, Boulder, CO 80309-0482, (303) 492-6818. A service of the Association of State Floodplain Managers offering a computerized database, library, and referral service for floodplain management publications.

Friends of the River
128 J Street, Second Floor, Sacramento, CA 95814. Phone: (916) 442-3155; Fax: (916) 442-3396.

International Rivers Network
301 Broadway, Suite B, San Francisco, CA 94133. E-mail: irn@igc.apc.org; Fax: (415) 398-2732; Phone: (415) 986-4694.

Izaak Walton League of America
Save Our Streams Program, 1401 Wilson Blvd., Level B, Arlington, VA 22209, (703) 528-1818.

Lincoln Institute of Land Policy
113 Brattle Street, Cambridge, MA 02138. A school organized to study and teach about land policy, including land economics and land taxation. The institute prints an impressive collection of references.

National Smallflows Clearinghouse
West Virginia University, P.O. Box 6064, Morgantown, WV 26506, (800) 624-8301. An excellent source of information to help small communities reach practical, affordable solutions to their wastewater treatment issues.

Northwest Environmental Advocates
133 SW 2nd Avenue, Portland, OR 97204, (503) 295-0490. Two of their publications, *Portland/Vancouver Toxic Waters* and *Columbia River, Troubled Waters,* are beautifully illustrated, documented, and produced maps (available folded for pocket use or flat) detailing pollution problems along the Willamette and Columbia rivers, respectively.

River Network
P.O. Box 8787, Portland, OR 97207. E-mail: rivernet@igc.apc.org; Fax: (503) 241-9256; Phone: (503) 241-3506 or (800) 423-6747.

RiverWatch Network
153 State Street, Montpelier, VT 05602, (802) 223-3840.

The Society for Non-Profit Organizations
6314 Odana Road, Suite One, Madison, WI 53719. The Society distributes numerous references about nonprofit management issues.

Trout Unlimited
800 Follin Lane, SE, Suite 250, Vienna, VA 22180-4959. E-mail: salmonid@igc.apc.org; or Compuserve: 70534,3234; Fax: (703) 281-1825; Phone: (703) 281-1100.

Index

About the Author

David M. Bolling has twenty-five years of experience as a newspaper editor, journalist, and radio reporter. His work has won more than twenty local, state, and national awards, and he has been writing about rivers and water issues for twenty years. He is the former executive director of Friends of the River, a California river conservation organization, and is cofounder and president of Friends of the Russian River, a grassroots river coalition in Sonoma County, California.
